Self Experiences in Group

The International Library of Group Analysis

Edited by Malcolm Pines, Institute of Group Analysis, London

The aim of this series is to represent innovative work in group psychotherapy, particularly but not exclusively group analysis. Group analysis, taught and practised widely in Europe, has developed from the work of S.H. Foulkes.

Other titles in the series

Active Analytic Group Therapy for Adolescents
John Evans
International Library of Group Analysis 6
ISBN 1 85302 617 4 hardback
ISBN 1 85302 616 6 paperback

Taking the Group Seriously
Towards a Post-Foulkesian Group Analytic Theory
Farhad Dalal
International Library of Group Analysis 5
ISBN 1 85302 642 5 paperback

Attachment and Interaction
Mario Marrone with a contribution by Nicola Diamond
International Library of Group Analysis 3
ISBN 1 85302 587 9 hardback
ISBN 1 85302 586 0 paperback

Circular Reflections
Selected Papers on Group Analysis and Psychoanalysis
Malcolm Pines
International Library of Group Analysis 1
ISBN 1 85302 493 7 hardback
ISBN 1 85302 492 9 paperback

Self Experiences in Group

Intersubjective and Self Psychological Pathways to Human Understanding

Edited by Irene N.H. Harwood and Malcolm Pines

Foreword by Robert D. Stolorow

Introduction by Ernest Wolf

Jessica Kingsley Publishers
London and Philadelphia

First published in the United Kingdom in 1998 by
Jessica Kingsley Publishers Ltd
116 Pentonville Road
London N1 9JB, England
and
1900 Frost Road, Suite 101
Bristol, PA 19007, U S A

Copyright © 1998 Irene N.H. Harwood and Malcolm Pines

Library of Congress Cataloging in Publication Data
A CIP catalogue record for this book is available from the Library of Congress

British Library Cataloguing in Publication Data
A CIP catalogue record for this book is available from the British Library

ISBN 1 85302 596 8 hb
ISBN 1 85302 597 6 pb

Printed and Bound in Great Britain by
Athenaeum Press, Gateshead, Tyne and Wear

Contents

Foreword

Robert D. Stolorow

This is a book about embeddedness – the embeddedness of experience in constitutive relational contexts – and the implications of this embeddedness for the understanding of group process and the conduct of group psychotherapy. The essays contained herein move therapeutic practice far beyond the isolated-mind thinking of traditional psychoanalysis. Kohut's self psychology made great strides toward loosening the grip of what Atwood and I (Stolorow and Atwood 1992) called 'the myth of the isolated mind' (p.7) on contemporary psychoanalytic thought. The concept of 'selfobject function' (Kohut 1971; 1977; 1984), in emphasizing that the organization of self-experience is co-determined by the felt responsiveness of others, is a prime example. In what might be considered a prologue to a self psychology of group life, Kohut (1984) wrote:

> Self psychology holds that self–selfobject relationships form the essence of psychological life from birth to death, that a move from dependence…to independence…in the psychological sphere is no more possible…than a corresponding move from a life dependent on oxygen to a life independent of it in the biological sphere. (p.47)

Despite such powerful challenges to the myth of the isolated mind, remnants of this myth persist in self-psychological writings, in the form, for example, of a reified self with its poles, its tension arc, and its inherent nuclear design. As Bacal and Newman (1990) pointed out, Kohut seemed reluctant to consider his framework a relational theory, probably because he wanted to preserve its link to the intrapsychic tradition of Freudian psychoanalysis. Such reluctance has not been a characteristic of the intersubjective perspective, which, since first introduced two decades ago (Stolorow, Atwood and Ross 1978), has been avowedly and thoroughgoingly relational. The concept of an intersubjective system brings to focus both the individual's world of inner experience and its embeddedness with other such worlds in a continual flow of reciprocal mutual influence. In this vision, the gap between the intrapsychic and interpersonal realms is closed, and, indeed, the old dichotomy between them is rendered obsolete (Stolorow and Atwood 1992).

In our first book devoted to the theory of intersubjectivity, Atwood and I (Atwood and Stolorow 1984) wrote in our concluding remarks:

We found the concept of an intersubjective field – a system of differently organized, interacting subjective worlds – to be an invaluable one in illuminating both the vicissitudes of psychoanalytic therapy and the process of human psychological development. This concept can readily be extended to shed light on a wide range of human interactions, including intimate love relationships, family patterns, group processes, and even intergroup relations. The concept of intersubjectivity thus provides a broad basis for a psychoanalytic understanding of human social life, bridging the gap between the analysis of individual subjective worlds and the study of complex social systems. While expanding the scope of psychoanalytic inquiry, the intersubjective viewpoint also enriches the field of social systems analysis. (p.119)

The chapters of this present, groundbreaking volume – the first book to apply the principles of self psychology and intersubjectivity theory to groups – go a long way toward bringing this enriching potential to fruition.

References

Atwood, G. and Stolorow, R. (1984) *Structures of Subjectivity: Explorations in Psychoanalytic Phenomenlogy*. Hillsdale, NJ: The Analytic Press.

Bacal, H. and Newman, K. (1990) *Theories of Object Relations: Bridges to Self Psychology*. New York: Columbia University Press.

Kohut, H. (1971) *The Analysis of the Self*. Madison, CT: International Universities Press.

Kohut, H. (1977) *The Restoration of the Self*. Madison, CT: International Universities Press.

Kohut, H. (1984) *How Does Analysis Cure?* A. Goldberg and P. Stepansky (eds). Chicago: University of Chicago Press.

Stolorow, R. and Atwood, G. (1992) *Contexts of Being: The Intersubjective Foundations of Psychological Life*. Hillsdale, NJ: The Analytic Press.

Stolorow, R., Atwood, G. and Ross, J. (1978) 'The representational world in psychoanalytic theory.' *Int. Rev. Psycho-Anal., 5*, 247–256.

Preface

Irene N.H. Harwood

It has been over twenty-five years since the theory of self psychology was given birth by Heinz Kohut's publication of *The Analysis of the Self* in 1971. Since that time, though there have been many individually published papers applying self psychology and intersubjectivity theory to group, it is probably not a coincidence that there has never been a book published on this subject, barring a doctoral dissertation (Harwood 1983a). The chapters by Frederic Arensberg (Chapter 1) and Howard Bacal (Chapter 13) will enlighten the reader about some of the reasons for this delay, since both of them knew Kohut, experienced his ambivalence, observed the narcissistic injuries delivered by group dynamics, and heard his explanations. The reasons for the delay may be further explained both by the existing group dynamics within psychoanalysis and Kohut's ambivalence towards groups. In identification with Kohut many psychoanalysts stopped doing group altogether.

Some psychoanalysts, like Kohut, have been wounded by the narcissistic wars of psychoanalytic theoretical groups and retreated to the more comfortable couch of empathic introspection within to the warm, safe bosom of individual psychoanalysis. Because of Kohut's negative intersubjective experience within the psychoanalytic group community as he emerged with his own theories, and because of the negative experiences of some of his patients who were in groups with classical analysts, and because he had no training as a group analytic therapist, Kohut shied away from therapeutic groups.

Though Kohut did not conduct groups, the importance of group dynamics was not lost on him and actually concerned him profoundly. He was touched deeply and personally by how a charismatic, messianic group leader led Nazi Germany into self-destruction while systematically destroying millions of other human beings. The lucky ones, both Freud and Kohut among them, were able to escape, warning against the potential and actual dangers of destructiveness in a regressed, ragefully fragmenting group. Kohut correctly feared the power of destructive group dynamics and was aware of the group self, as Sigmund Karterud so articulately notes in Chapter 7.

I would cheat the reader and not do justice to Kohut by paraphrasing him. Thus, in fairness to both, I will quote him. This will enable you to directly familiarize yourself with Kohut's concerns about group dynamics, as well as to note and understand the legacy he left us, with the hope that group therapists/analysts will not give up in bringing about both new theoretical knowledge and additional pathways to human understanding. In 1976, when he first published 'Creativeness, Charisma, Group Psychology', he wrote:

> There are, of course, many obstacles standing in the way of an objective assessment of the psychoanalytic community by psychoanalysts. Such a self-study is a difficult but by no means impossible task.
>
> .... Group pressure diminishes individuality; it leads to a primitivization of the mental processes, in particular to a partial paralysis of the ego and to a lowering of resistances. The diminution of the influence of the ego is then followed by the cathartic expression of archaic (or at any rate undisguised) impulses, emotions, and ideation, i.e., by the revelation of material not accessible in normal circumstances. The insights I have in mind cannot be obtained in a regressive atmosphere. The valid self-analysis of the psychoanalytic group – or of any group – must not only rest on the clear, nonregressive perception of archaic psychological experiences that arise within the group; it also requires the intellectual and emotional mastery of this material. The validity of the insights obtained will be demonstrated by the fact that the pressure to act out (especially to act out angrily, the principal symptom of group psychopathology) will be diminished within the group. The individual who wishes to make decisive steps toward new depth-psychological insights concerning the group must therefore be able to remain deeply and directly involved in the group processes – but instead of acting them out, he must be able to tolerate the tension of seeming passivity: all his energies must be withdrawn from participating action and concentrated on participating thought. Only if he can maintain full emotional participation with the group processes of his own group, yet channel all his energies toward his cognitive functions (specifically the gathering of data through empathic observation and the subsequent explanation of the observed data) – only then will he be able to make those decisive discoveries and obtain those crucial new insights which will deepen our understanding of the behavior of the group and its members. (Kohut 1978, pp.839–841)

Kohut was not ready due to personal reasons to engage in 'the creative act of the group's [*psychoanalytic community*] self-analysis to make a valid contribution to psychoanalytic group psychology and to the psychology of the historical process.' But, in 1976 he did believe that 'the time is not far off when psychoanalysts will indeed be able to undertake such studies with the hope of reaching objectively valid conclusions.' (Kohut 1978, pp.839–841).

In this book, self psychologically informed group therapists who look at interactions intersubjectively are beginning to undertake the study that Kohut hoped for.

Kohut's interest in group dynamics did not wane. While struggling with his terminal illness, on September 28, 1980, a year before his death, Kohut wrote to me, first apologizing for not having responded to my manuscript and then thanking me for sharing with him an application of his theory to group psychotherapy. Two days later, on September 30, he wrote to me again saying that he had shared my manuscript (subsequently published as Harwood 1983b) with a friend, Dr Howard Bacal.

Thus, in his last year of life Kohut maintained an interest in group dynamics and supported and connected clinicians who practiced in that modality. Though Heinz Kohut may not have led clinical groups, he behaved as a 'good-enough' group conductor laying the foundation for an international group of therapists and psychoanalysts to come together, building intersubjective pathways from Toronto to Los Angeles, from Rome to New York, from Washington DC to Oslo, and from London, the birthplace of group analysis, to every major city around the world.

The contributions in this book speak to the umbrella of protection, care, inspiration, and validation which Kohut widely spread over the group conductors who contributed so richly and diversely to this book. Fred Arensberg shares the richness of his supervision with Heinz Kohut and enlightens us about Kohut's fears regarding certain kinds of clinical groups (Chapter 1). Malcolm Pines welcomes self psychology to the established European world of group analysis (Chapter 2). My earlier 1992 paper integrates the advances in group by applying both self psychology and intersubjectivity (Chapter 3). Emanuel Shapiro (Chapter 4) and Martin Livingston (Chapter 5) update Kohut's concept of twinship within the theory of intersubjectivity, illustrating it with both clinical and life examples.

Franco Paparo and Gianni Nebbiosi (Chapter 6) reconceptualize group process growing from the beginning roots of self psychology to intersubjectivity theory integrating the European group analytic tradition. Sigmund Karterud places intersubjectivity into a historical philosophical world context, challenging all not to forget Kohut's agreement with the powerful dynamics of the group self (Chapter 7).

Joan Schain-West in Chapter 8 focuses on the interweaving and application of infant research to group psychotherapy, crystallizing the application of self psychology/intersubjectivity not only to psychopathology, but to biological and psychological growth as well.

My chapter (Chapter 9), which also cites infant research, pleads not to forget all environmental influences affecting the growing child, and points out the benefits of adding group treatment to individual, in order to both understand and work through the early impingements and traumatizations. Damon Silvers' chapter (Chapter 10) enlarges on my chapter, by illustrating how to address multiple selfobject and traumatizing experiences through a co-therapy model, including a rich clinical vignette illustrating numerous simultaneous transferences at work.

Rosemary Segalla enriches this book by demonstrating everyone's inborn need for a groupobject, which she illustrates through the use of Joseph Lichtenberg's model scene which is embedded in his reformulation of human motivational systems (Chapter 11).

My last chapter (Chapter 12) challenges psychoanalysis to include Kohut's call to observe, study and formulate new approaches in observing its own group dynamics, as well as not to forget to examine all of the environmental and cultural group dynamics each patient brings with them. Group therapists/analysts have always learned from all the varied theories that psychoanalysis gave birth to. Individual psychoanalysts would do well to follow Kohut's invitation to future social scientists to learn about the effects of the dynamics of the group self on both the individual and the smaller or larger holding or fragmenting environments around that human being.

Howard Bacal closes the book by suggesting that Kohut's fears that group pressure always diminishes individuality were unfounded, since an attuned group conductor knows how to orchestrate optimum responsiveness in a well composed group, while utilizing reactiveness for the working through of previous impingements and traumatizations (Chapter 13).

Heinz Kohut proposed that optimum frustration was needed for transmuting internalizations to occur and for new psychic structure to develop for the individual. The group therapists and group analysts who contributed to this book beautifully and unequivocally demonstrate through clinical examples the 'good-enough' healing power of optimally composed and orchestrated groups conducted by those who continue to apply both Kohut's self psychological concepts and the evolving ones from intersubjectivity, not only in the USA, but worldwide.

Kohut may be assured that a community of social scientists and psychoanalysts have heeded his call and have undertaken such a study with successful clinical applications and will continue to do so for the benefit of all.

References

Harwood, I.H. (1983a) The evolution of the self in group psychotherapy. Doctoral Dissertation. CA: California Institute for Clinical Social Work, Berkeley.

Harwood, I.H. (1983b) 'The application of self psychology concepts to group psychotherapy.' *International Journal of Group Psychotherapy 33*, 469–487.

Kohut, H. (1978) 'Creativeness, charisma, group psychology.' In P. Ornstein (ed) *The Search for the Self,* Vol. 2. New York: International Universities Press.

Acknowledgements

I cannot write the acknowledgements for this book without mentioning all the wonderful people who in some very significant way supported its creation many years ago – from the beginning of my professional career and at the beginning of my life. In other words, those who backed my professional development are inseparable from those who are also responsible for the creation of this book. I was born into a group, my immediate and extended family, family friends and neighbours from different cultures. My holding environment included group diversity. There were individual and groupobject functions. Traumatizations were balanced with attunement to individual needs. Deficits and reactiveness were mitigated by sensitive human beings who could project their own humanity into another.

When I first read Heinz Kohut's work, I understood what he meant by optimum development and I felt it was translatable to clinical groups, as well as to our understanding of couple, family and historical/political dynamics.

Over lunch, Hindy Nobler mirrored my ideas with interest and encouraged me to present them to a group therapy conference and later to a group journal.

It was Ann Younger, my dear friend and colleague, who warmly insisted I send my papers to Kohut. It was Ann who forwarded my name for my very first professional presentation and who for over 20 years has listened to my ideas, responding both supportively and critically, while always encouraging my professional writing.

It was a struggle to put my ideas in my third language and Will Harriss came to the rescue with his expertise as editor, finding time away from his work as head editor at the Rand Corporation and from his Edgar award-winning mystery novel. I thank him for being there at the beginning and for believing in my growing potential with the English language.

I want to acknowledge Heinz Kohut for encouraging me to continue applying his theory to other modalities and for forwarding my application of self psychology to group to Howard Bacal. I am grateful to Howard for optimally encouraging its publication.

A big thank you to Malcolm Pines, my co-editor, who from 1983 has invited me to share my integration of Winnicott's and Kohut's work with my European brothers and sisters. Malcolm has been an invaluable mentor, colleague, friend, and fellow workshop and panel participant in group meetings around the world.

A warm hug of appreciation to three of the four musketeers (Miriam Harriss, Phyllis Deutch Owensmith, June Steg) and to our supervisor Ruth Steiner from the L. A. Center for Group Psychotherapy where I received my group training.

The Director, Andrew Ollstein, also allotted me the function of Intake Director, which allowed me an invaluable opportunity to observe all the groups through a one-way mirror, to learn about patient selection, group composition, styles of different group leaders, and most importantly to learn not only what to do, but also what not to do as a group conductor – an attunement to interventions beyond optimum frustration.

A special thank you to Bernice Augenbraun for her invaluable consultation at the beginning of my career and for sending me my first private practice patient who needed treatment in Spanish. I honor her memory, her understanding of the value of group diversity, and her humane wisdom: 'Whenever in doubt, be human.'

Thank you to Verneice Thompson who facilitated my PhD training with her keen understanding of groups and organizational dynamics and allowed me to learn research from one of the masters – Jay Cohen. Jay headed both my master's thesis and PhD dissertation and encouraged me to publish the latter, 'The evolution of the self in group psychotherapy: an integration of Winnicott's and Kohut's theories.' Through the years Jay has been a mentor, a colleague and a dear friend.

Althea Horner has been a one-of-a-kind colleague, mentor and friend. She is both an inspiration and a pioneer in her own creative way and has continually encouraged me to be my own true professional self.

Marshall Friedman, a dear friend and colleague, has co-led one of my groups since 1989. His intuition and balance have been invaluable, both in our group and in our couples work together.

Ernie Wolf long ago told me that I should write a book applying self psychology to group. Ernie, thank you for your trust, and now for your Introduction.

To Robert Stolorow I owe both the idea and the backing for this edited book. Throughout the years, he has been an invaluable consultant on my publications integrating self psychology and intersubjectivity theory to group psychotherapy. Thank you, Bob!

Many, many thanks to my dear friend and colleague David Meltzer who in 1984 co-founded the Society for the Study of the Self with me and has continued to participate in co-leading it monthly to the present time.

I am indebted to the hundreds of presenters and participants in the group discussions at the Society for the Study of the Self for their continual inspiration and developing of new ideas for integration within a most congenial and collegial Saturday morning coffee group atmosphere.

To all of my group, individual and conjoint patients I give my never-ending appreciation. It is their struggles for self and mutual understanding which have helped me in parallel process to learn and grow with them while developing clinically, theoretically, and personally.

This book would not be possible without the contributions of my wonderful group therapy colleagues and contributors: Frederic Arensberg, Howard Bacal, Sigmund Karterud, Martin Livingston, Gianni Nebbiosi, Franco Paparo, Malcolm Pines, Joan Schain-West, Rosemary Segalla, Emanuel Shapiro, and Damon Silvers. Each and every one has been a pleasure to work with. It has been a wonderful group process to put this book together and it has provided an important groupobject function for me – joyous work filled with play.

Many thanks to my son, Stephen Daniel Harwood, for his technical competence as well as his artistic contribution.

Last but not least, and actually most, I would like to thank Roxana Andrews, personal assistant, who has contributed in immeasurable ways. She has been involved in the creation of this book from the very start as a sounding board, proof-reader, word-processor, but most importantly as a colleague and a friend.

Irene N.H. Harwood

Introduction

Ernest Wolf

Persons as individuals or as members of families or even as components of larger social aggregates have always been vitally interested in elucidating who they are and have wondered how they fit into their surround. Traditionally, the questions arising from a dawning awareness of the human condition have been responded to by the conventional authorities who have supplied answers in the form of myth, philosophy and religion. Related questions about the non-human world, its origin, purpose and aims, were similarly formed in integration with the ideas about humanity. They formed seamless and satisfying conceptual images of the kind for which the German word *Weltanschauung* seems the perfect label. However, during the last few hundred years of human history there has also emerged a different trend that is having a significant impact on this awareness of the human condition. This more recent trend – it is not new but has become significant only lately – is not based on handed-down authority but on fallible convictions gained by human experience filtered through human logic. We have constructed methods for testing the truth value of our convictions and those that elicit our strong beliefs we call science. Among these, during the past century, we have witnessed one of the most fundamental developments in the study of how human beings experience themselves and act upon each other. This book, so aptly titled *Self Experiences in Group: Intersubjective and Self Psychological Pathways to Human Understanding*, brings us thirteen essays by authoritative scientists in human psychology that illuminate the age-old questions for us via enlightened contemporary answers.

Psychology emerged out of the sciences that study the non-human world. Initially, therefore, the concepts of the older natural sciences formed much of the frame in which psychology approached the human condition. Both individuals as well as groups were studied intensively. Even a relatively enlightened field of inquiry, Freudian psychoanalysis, borrowed from physics the concepts of a mental apparatus, a unit, i.e. the individual psyche, and the concept of force, i.e. instinctual drives, as well as the concepts of these basic constituents both being constituted of more elemental parts and acting on each other, i.e. intrapsychic and interpersonal dynamics. A careful reading of this present volume reveals how far we have come from those roots in the physical sciences. The key words here that point to the contemporary and truly psychological sensibility represented by these essays are *experience, organization* and *self.* The self is constructed as an organization of experiences within a field of inquiry that is defined as the inner life of humankind. With the focus on experiencing, it no longer is so important to talk about individuals or about groups – they all experience without a clear boundary separating individual from group. When we experience these experiences we do so with a motivation of making order out of the chaos of perceptions: we are moved to organize and the most important insights we gain are about the type and comprehensiveness of these organizations of experience. Different theoreticians will be selectively interested in different aspects of experience and give them labels in their own language by making up more or less useful neologisms. Thus classical psychoanalysts talk about drives being regulated via id, ego and superego. Kleinian object relations analysts discuss internal objects and their manifestations in projective identifications. Winnicott's followers are especially interested in issues of development and good-enough mothering. Kohutian self psychologists focus on selfobject experiences while intersubjectivists led by Stolorow have expanded self psychology to include the phenomena occurring in the area of interaction between self and other. This book is testimony to our being gradually successful in integrating our diversities.

CHAPTER I

A Consideration of Kohut's Views on Group Psychotherapy

Frederic Arensberg

While I was in supervision with Heinz Kohut, several years prior to his death, his attitudes and feelings toward group therapy emerged. He was somewhat negative toward group therapy for specific historical and possibly personal reasons. First, he talked about the tremendous power of the group leader, which could possibly be quite negative and dangerous. Specifically, he was very worried about the charismatic leader who could use empathy to control throngs of people for his own purposes. This would not only serve the narcissistic needs of the leader, but would give him enormous power as well. Kohut talked of Hitler's enormous power and attraction to the German people in the 1930s. He intuited selfobject needs, both mirroring and idealization, within the German people, reflecting their feelings, exploiting their deprivations, both sociologically and economically. The Nazis were joined together through general hatred and a wish to be élite, superior and omnipotent. The grandiosity which generally had been so inadequately mirrored previously could now be made manifest through the shared power of the group. An archaic need for the twinship selfobject would also have been called into powerful play as well. Thus, a mass fragmentation resulting from failures around idealization was exploited by a skilful, maniacal, heroic figure, Hitler, who was going to provide for the economically and sociologically defeated Germany the missing idealization – that is the 'Master Race' gaining omnipotent power in its destruction of all perceived obstacles.

Kohut had a second problem with group therapy – the concern about patients engaged in an 'individual self analysis' and then adding group therapy (which to most practitioners would take place between two and four years following the beginning of the analysis). He felt that such a patient would be used to interaction in which the analyst responded from a stance of empathic introspection and might be counting on and expecting responses from an empathic introspective perspective from the group as well. However, Kohut felt that since the patients in group are striving for maximum honest self-expression, responses in group at times would be anything but from trying to understand the patient's point of view. This would be especially true, he felt, if some of the patients in the group were engaged in a drive-oriented individual analysis.

Furthermore, if patients were encouraged to express their own feelings, thoughts and needs to advance their own 'voice', serious injuries could occur to those patients coming from a 'self analysis'. This could occur, he thought, even when the group leader models an empathic approach in the group. What we are talking about here is a resulting feeling of assault and breakage, of the selfobject matrix, when the expectation of the empathic understanding received in the individual analysis sharply contrasts with the responses to that patient in the group.

Kohut did not live long enough to become familiar with the work of many self psychologically informed group therapists. There is special attention paid in self-analytical intersubjective groups, where each patient's views are understood and validated just because his/her experiences are valid. Intersubjective self-delineation is allowed and encouraged for each group member.

Many self psychological psychoanalysts today are no longer engaged in doing group therapy. Since many self psychologists are identified with Kohut as an idealized selfobject, it is natural that they would adopt his negative concerns towards group therapy.

I would like to turn to how some of Kohut's thinking is a very positive contribution to our work in doing group therapy. I would like also to examine some techniques and different perspectives that might mitigate against Kohut's worries.

The power of the idealizing selfobject transference emerges as a central factor within the group. This occurs in relation to the leader, the group as a whole, and various other constellations in the group (such as how serious conflict between one's own ambitions/views or those of other group members can be brought out and then resolved in the group). To this end, the idealization pole can lead to a plethora of early affective memories which can be activated. In addition, as in any significant interpersonal experiences, there are opportunities for different types of twinship to emerge and work through. The depth and power of the experience in group will lead toward significant merger longings and early memories of the needs for mirroring. Obviously, these same selfobject transferences exist within the dyad as well, but the group expands significantly the various arrays of their manifestation. Group also can more easily bring out early experiences with siblings, peers and significant others. The dimension of safety is also seen as a particular important parameter in group since, in the dyad, safety is usually achieved more quickly and easily, and with less difficulty. In the group, the empathic expectation is far less in place, so the dangers of non-safety are more apparent and experienced more. Obviously, for the group to work, a good-enough and safe-enough environment and group composition must exist as described by Harwood (1995).

On the other hand, multiplicities of dyads in group allows for a more complex and thorough working through of conflict where all subjectivities are brought out, valued and understood, and self-delineation is held as a group value.

The safeguards against the 'over-charismatic' group leader using the group for his own selfish and sometimes negative purposes are fairly obvious. The leader should be well analyzed, and should have had considerable time as a patient in a group informed by self psychology. He/she should have had considerable supervision of group by a self-psychologically informed group leader. It is assumed here that a prerequisite of any group work for the analyst is solid knowledge, cognitively and emotionally, of dyadic and multiple experiences. Moreover, the group leader should be well aware of the dangers of the misuse of empathy, the 'bandwagon effect' that herds people into constrictive systems, and, as much as possible, his own narcissistic and grandiose needs. He/she should be able to tolerate these, understand them, and not feel self-contempt or over-evaluation toward them. There should be a consistent monitoring of countertransference, one's own character traits and selfobject experiences to be able to tolerate and empathically accept them. The group therapist needs to be able to place external boundaries on the gratification of these understandable propensities, and to be able to fully feel the type of transferences elicited when gratification is denied.

Furthermore, the group leader should be experientially knowledgeable of the particular emotional dimensions that are provoked within the group. Historically, the group leader should be well informed of the dangers considered by Kohut. I have found that the grandiosity stimulated by leading a group is qualitatively different from that of the dyad, and should be understood in the context of the revival of familial and communal/tribal affects and experiences.

If there is an atmosphere of safety, ability to self-reflect and accept each other's right to a different point of view, and non-defensiveness within the group, most members do have an emotional, intuitive awareness of the inappropriate use of empathy – empathy used to one's own ends to hurt another. One dimension particularly important to me is the constant attention paid to each individual's history and current experience in the group, with an attitude of guarding each person's autonomy, voice and rights. I almost never make any 'group interpretations' or comments that herd people into an undifferentiated pack or system. It is clear that the group atmosphere supports individual positions above the overall welfare or system of the group (Stolorow's self-delineation). Stereotypic and automated (over-regulated) assumptions in group are generally explored, so that there is always a return to the emphasis on the individual and his/her experiences.

An example of this is when a group develops a stereotype of each week when one of the patients brings in a problem, and the rest of the group behaves as helpers to that person. As a group therapist, I will not do anything to manifestly interrupt that process, but will later investigate what it means and feels like to each person engaged in that process. The group process is always used for the purpose of investigating each individual's dynamics and experience.

Another example would be when one group member is ill, and the whole group seems to want to send that person a 'get-well' card and sign it. I always wonder what it is like for the person who really doesn't want to sign the card, and might particularly address that to those individuals who show some subtle signs of that position, utilizing my knowledge of their histories and dynamics. Thus, for me, group is another analytic dimension for exploring the intersubjective field. I always try to be aware of what selfobject and traumatic transferences are elicited by my experience as group leader as well as by the other group members.

Finally, I want to address the issue of the 'shock' of entering a less safe environment, one with greater incidence of empathic failures, for the patient that has possibly been in a highly empathic dyad. But all individuals come from families and need to rework and heal their old injuries. I am much more careful of group composition than I was prior to my knowledge of self psychology, similar to Harwood's (1995) views. I will not place someone in the group who is likely to be wounded in a manner that is not easily subject to repair through interpretation. I am more careful about the timing of putting someone in group – that is, I will not place someone in a group that is non-receptive to a newcomer or place an individual who is in a current state of fragmentation. Furthermore, all the group members are aware of the intersubjective position of the newcomer – that is how each group member may transferentially be affected by the newcomer's issues. I also am more prone to rule out certain patients for group, thus affecting the composition of the group. Primarily, I rule out anyone who is not capable of an empathic position, at least from an intellectual frame. I also rule out people who are manifestly hurtful to others as a syntonic character trait, even if their position can be readily seen as a fragmentation by-product. With these considerations in mind, and in fully heeding Kohut's dangers, I have found doing group therapy an exceedingly useful and safe therapeutic medium.

Kohut never did group, nor was he trained in doing group. He just heard about its failures. During the time Kohut voiced his concerns, he was personally also being subjected to hurtful, rejecting psychoanalytic group dynamics. There were psychoanalytic circles/groups which would not recognize Kohut's self-delineation – developing and contributing to the development of a new theory, Self Psychology. Conversely, to his credit, he did encourage those who had successes with group analytic self psychological informed therapy to continue applying and developing the theory to which he gave birth.

References

Harwood, I. (1995) 'Towards optimum group placement from the perspective of the self or self-experience.' *Group 19*, 3, 140–162.

Stolorow, R.D., Atwood, G.E. and Brandchaft, B. (1992) 'Three realms of the unconscious and their therapeutic transformation.' *Psychoanalytic Review 79*, 25–30.

Stolorow, R.D. and Brandchaft, B. (1987) 'Developmental failure and psychic conflict.' *Psychoanalytic Psychotherapy 4*, 241–253.

CHAPTER 2

The Self as a Group
The Group as a Self[1]

Malcolm Pines

The notion of 'the group as a self' is challenging. Is there any point in linking an individualistic notion such as the self with the plurality of a group? The rationale for doing so becomes more evident when we consider in the first place 'the self as a group'. For if there is an essential element of 'group' in the constitution of the individual, as indeed group analysis affirms, then it becomes more possible to consider that there is value in regarding 'the group as a self'.

Indeed, group analysis gives primacy to the social. The individual is conceived of as being born into and constituted out of a network of other persons, who gains a sense of personal identity from the possibilities offered by the nature of their network: the horizontal or lateral dimension of social organizations, therefore – notions of culture, politics, religion, economical and historical circumstances – have to be considered as constituents of the individual self. Norbert Elias uses the term 'figuration' to indicate our fundamental connectedness. This is in contradiction to the notion of the individual as a monad, standing alone amidst a multitude of others, connected through instinctual needs or for self-preservation: the vertical dimension. The notion of a plurality of selves, rather than a single unitary self constituting the person, is closer to psychological reality and is gaining recognition. Thus the idea 'of multiple selves' does not relate only to pathology, as in the concept of 'multiple personality disorder' but is representative of the multi-faceted complex structure of each one of us.

Modern western society released individuals from the grip of compelling religious ideologies but has left us with the problems of constructing our own individual identities. One of the pioneers of western psychology in facing the question of personal identity was the great American psychologist and

1   Published in *Group Analysis 29*, 2, 183–190 (1996).

philosopher William James who distinguished between the 'I' and the 'me', between the physical, material and spiritual aspects of self, and who tried to deal with the question of how a sense of personal identity is created and maintained against the background of the constantly changing flowing level of consciousness. It was an associate of his, Mary Calkins, who elegantly epitomized this problem in the following poem:

> Within my earthly temple there's a crowd
> There's one of us that's humble, one that's proud.
> There's one in eager search of earthly pelf
> And one who loves his neighbour as himself.
> There's one who's broken hearted for his sins
> And one who, unrepentant, sits and grins.
> For much corroding care I should be free
> If once I could determine which is me.

The individual identity of each one of us is constituted by intrapsychic, interpersonal and transpersonal processes; the boundaries of the individual extend far beyond those of the corporeal self. Along the dimensions of selflessness to selfishness there is a wide range of human behaviour. All of us contain and manifest traits of selfishness and selflessness. Sometimes our self interests dominate, related to our personal concerns which, as William James pointed out, can extend to those persons and things that represent parts of ourselves, our family, children, prized possessions. Selflessness at its extreme leads to acts in which persons willingly give up their lives in the service of others, as when a father or mother will risk death in order to save their children, or comrades will endanger themselves to aid others, to situations where people give up their lives for symbolic causes, for nation, religion or politics.

If we grasp the complexity of the individual both constituted from and functioning as a group, it becomes less problematic to look at the contrasting notion of 'the group as a self'.

This is the definition of a person by the cultural anthropologist Clifford Geertz: 'A bounded, unique, more or less integrated centre of awareness, emotions, judgement and action organised into a distinctive whole and set contrastingly both against other such wholes and against its social and natural background'. It is a holistic concept that brings together consciousness, affect and conation, within a bounded entity, set as figure on ground, against its social and natural background and contrasting with other such bounded entities, other persons. Would this description not also apply to certain types of groups? It could apply to a family, to a group held together by a common history and by powerful bonds of attachment, a group which allows differentiation but still retains a distinctive wholeness. This is also the nature of a group analytic group.

The theory of group analysis derives from social psychology, Gestalt psychology individual psychology, primarily psychoanalysis, from a sociohistorical viewpoint on the nature of human personality. This makes it imperative to set the notion of 'the individual' against the sociohistorical background of family, society and culture. Norbert Elias coined the term 'figuration' to illustrate how an individual can only be understood as part of a connected set of relationships, a figuration. In group analytic theory and the practice of face-to-face therapy in the group circle, we rely upon Foulkes' concept of the *matrix* which develops from the web of interrelationships occurring in the group situation, the *dynamic matrix*, set against the *foundation matrix*, based on the biological and on the sociohistorical cultural setting from which the individuals derive fundamental aspects of their personality (Roberts 1982). Amongst these one of the strongest factors is the sharing of a common language, as language is the filter through which we perceive and apprehend both external and internal realities. I want now to consider the notion of 'the group as a self' in relation to our concept of the matrix.

The matrix is the shared common history of the group, the conscious and unconscious repository of all events. The group analyst's faith, belief in the matrix concept, enables him or her to offer this to the group members from the moment of conception of the group in the mind of the therapist. By offering a group analytic situation there already is in mind a field of interaction, a social space, somewhat, though not completely, empty to be filled by the evolving history of the group; through conversations, through evolving understandings, each group member brings their own personal matrix, based essentially upon their own family experiences, to this new potential space. The resultant matrix is derived from the intermeshing of all these personal matrices within the setting offered by the group analyst. The therapist offers and maintains the boundaries of time, space and search for meaning, which shapes the dynamics of interaction of the individual members and by maintaining a belief that it is possible to understand 'the group as a whole' attempts to see the dynamic interactions within the group matrix, as figure against ground of the evolving group history. Thus the group offers both a 'culture of embeddedness' and a 'culture of enquiry'. The 'culture of embeddedness' enables each person to develop a strong attachment to the group situation, to the other group members and to the group conductor.

The '*culture of enquiry*' offers group members the opportunity to investigate the nature of one's own self and those of their group neighbours. This culture of enquiry both enables and requires persons to look at and listen to others, to themselves, and consider, perhaps accept, the viewpoint of others. This is an opportunity to see ourselves 'in the round', to see those invisible and hidden dimensions which constitute our individual selves, for just as we cannot see our physical selves without reflections from mirrors, so we cannot perceive ourselves as social persons without the seeing and hearing of the responses of others to us and considering, if not always accepting, the ways in which we are experienced by others.

The Russian philosopher/psychologist Michael Bakhtin described the human situation as one of 'alterity'. By this he means that we gain ourselves only through our dialectical relationships with others. We need the others to aid in the creation and completion of ourselves, through the vision the other bestows upon us. Each one of us has a 'surplus of vision', as compared with any other person, for each one of us lives in a unique space–time dimension (the chronotope). What we see can be seen by no other person; thereby others can give to us aspects of the world that cannot be ours. Ultimately the other person is my friend, he or she through whom I gain myself; therefore the other can be a cause for celebration rather than for frustration and conflict.

Healthy human beings grow within a *culture of embeddedness* where others provide reciprocity, gratification and impetus for continued growth. Within the culture of embeddedness provided by good-enough caregivers to infants the vital developmental processes of attachment and relatedness develop. From attachment and relatedness develop both autonomy and connectedness, the psychological double helix of human life. The thrust of research into early human development exemplified in the work of Daniel Stern, Robert Emde (1992), Beebe and Lachmann (1992), Alan Fogel, Trevarthen and the Papouseks, amongst others, points to the central reciprocity of human relationships. *Reciprocity* is an 'inborn organized capacity for initiating, maintaining and terminating social interactions'. 'Turn taking' – action, pause, response, interaction – is the basic rhythm of human life as pointed out many years ago by Rita Leal in her papers on group analysis and early infant development. Through this turn taking of gesture, and later on of language, between infants and caregivers, the basis is formed for fundamental procedures of communication through language, whereby the person enters not only into the cultural system but also into the moral systems of society. Reciprocity implies a sense of fairness, of good-enough exchanges between persons that leave both partners satisfied. From this fundamental biologically rooted sense of reciprocity leading to a sense of fairness develops the drive to 'get it right' and to get satisfaction from doing so. Getting things right means also putting things right when they have gone wrong; that is, the drive for reparation and the origins of the sense of 'getting things wrong' from which comes the sense of human guilt without which human relationships become impossibly destructive. Thus the human infant and its caregivers are 'prosocial' beings, biologically programmed to turn towards and to care for others. The very early smile of the newborn infant, appearing at only two weeks, is a prosocial gesture that increases the bonding between itself and its caregivers.

The school of self psychology (Kohut 1971) has added to the psychoanalytic vision of object relationships the concept of the 'selfobject'. This fundamentally refers to the functional relationships that caregivers provide so that the developing sense of self of the infant is affirmed, strengthened and repaired through the vicissitudes of the early years. The well known functions of mirroring, idealization and twinship, to which now can be added the idea of friendly opposition, are essential nutrients to the infant's developing sense of self. What needs, however, to be added to the self psychological vision is that of the active interaction between selves, the self of the infant and the selves of the caregivers. The infant seeks out and secures the active responses of the caregivers, particularly seeking a sense of completion of its own actions. By the response of the other the infant begins to derive a sense of efficacy, of closure, of contingency, of acting in the world in such a way that the world begins to take on a satisfying sense of shape and meaning. The infant's cries obtain appropriate responses, physical gestures elicit reciprocal gestures, cries and gestures are interwoven into narratives and plays and the infant begins to enter into human culture. What is important is the acquisition of 'mentality', the sense of possessing a mind of one's own in a world where meaningful contact can be made with other minds. This is the world of intersubjectivity, not simply of object relations.

To elaborate upon this, object relation theory is grounded in a system of categorization, that of subject and object, inner and outer, and which centres primarily upon the psychic life of the subject. There is much reliance on projection, on drives, fantasies and a belief that the psychological precedes the social. The group analytic viewpoint is complementary to this. Here the social precedes the psychological, internalization precedes projection, the categories of subject and object, inner and outer, are not taken as constituents to the early sense of reality. Foulkes stressed that the social is so deeply within the individual that how can one begin to say where the social ends and the personal begins? Where is the boundary between inner and outer? Is reality not more like the Moebius strip where the same surface endlessly turns both inwards and outwards.

Another contribution from early development to 'the self as a group' comes from recognition of the essential 'we-ness' of human beings. No one of us survives and develops outside a nexus of relationships: as many years ago George Klein (1976) put it, psychoanalysis lacks the concept of the 'we-go' to complement that of the single ego. Now Robert Emde (1992) offers the concept of the 'executive we', the sense that the infant discovers, enjoys and utilizes the capacities of the caregivers to act in concert, to achieve a sense of power and effectiveness in the world. We help the child to grasp, to walk, to talk, and in this we freely share our executive powers. Freud (1923) wrote of the ego as being the rider on the horse of the id; how can we fail to think of the child riding on the back of the parent or the older sibling secure in sharing in the power of that greater entity of which it feels itself to be a part? Emde describes the 'executive we' as creating a sense of togetherness, bestowing a sense of power and control for guiding behaviour and for resisting temptation! This approach combines well with the approach of Vigotsky who through his 'law of proximal development' showed that the potentiality of any individual, particularly a child, can only be estimated properly when it is in the proximity of and in relationship to a more developed other (see Wertsch 1991). The child will succeed whatever task it is set much better when aided by or in the company of another person who will help it to get it right. This is the basic nature of the human condition and one which we draw on freely in the group analytic orbit, that of human beings who are trying to understand and to help themselves and each other.

Bibliography

Benjamin, J. (1992) 'Recognition and destruction: an outline of intersubjectivity.' In N.J. Skolnick and S.C. Warshaw (eds) *Relational Perspectives in Psychoanalysis*. Hillsdale, NJ: Analytic Press.

Beebe, B. and Lachmann, F. (1992) 'The contributions of mother–infant mutual influence to the origins of self- and object representations.' In N.J. Skolnick and S.C. Warshaw (eds) *Relational Perspectives in Psychoanalysis*. Hillsdale, NJ: Analytic Press.

Emde, R.N. (1992) 'Positive emotions for psychoanalytic theory: surprises from infancy research and new directions.' *Journal of the American Psychoanalytic Association 39*, 1991 Supplement. In T. Shapiro and R.N. Emde (eds) *Affect: Psychoanalytic Perspectives*. Conn: International Universities Press.

Freud, S. (1923) *The Ego and the Id*. Standard Edition 19. London: The Hogarth Press.

Harris, A. (1992) 'Dialogues as transitional space: a rapprochement of psychoanalysis and developmental psycholinguistics. In N.J. Skolnick and S.C. Warshaw (eds) *Relational Perspectives in Psychoanalysis*. Hillsdale, NJ: Analytic Press.

Horowitz, M., Fridhandler,B. and Stinson, C. (1992) 'Person schema and emotions.' *Journal of the American Psychoanalytic Association 39*, 1991 Supplement. In T. Shapiro and R.N. Emde (eds) *Affect: Psychoanalytic Perspectives*. Conn: International Universities Press.

Kohut, H. (1971) *The Analysis of the Self*. Conn: International Universities Press.

Person, E.S. (1992) 'Romantic love: at the intersection of the psyche and the cultural unconscious.' *Journal of the American Psychoanalytic Association 39*, 1991 Supplement. In T. Shapiro and R.N. Emde (eds) *Affect: Psychoanalytic Perspectives*. Conn: International Universities Press.

Wertsch, J.V. (1991) *Voices of the Mind: A Sociocultural Approach to Mediated Action*. London: Harvester Wheatsheaf.

CHAPTER 3

Advances in Group Psychotherapy and Self Psychology
An Intersubjective Approach[1]

Irene N.H. Harwood

The theory of the self as applied to group psychotherapy has had particular meaning in this age and culture wherein people strive for independence, autonomy and self-sufficiency, but all too often at the cost of alienation from others. The much-talked-about phenomenon of the 'me' culture can be viewed as a product of the times we live in, but a closer look also reveals it to be a common compensatory response to psychological factors going back to an early period of life when a child's developmental needs were misunderstood, ignored, mocked, overvalued or overwhelmed by caretakers who could not relate to the child phase-appropriately. In such a case, a foundation for good-enough object relations never emerged. Children who experienced little or no enthusiastic responsiveness from such caretakers, except perhaps by taking on a submissive, compliant false self, can hardly be expected to relate spontaneously and with mature reciprocation.

This chapter discusses clinical issues in group psychotherapy with narcissistic and borderline patients; but first a brief review of the principal concepts of self psychology will be useful, especially more recent developments. For a deeper immersion into the earlier concepts, Kohut and Wolf (1978) and Kohut (1977; 1984) are recommended.

1   This chapter was presented at the Patients with Narcissistic and Personality Disorders in Group Psychotherapy Conference in Basel, Switzerland at the Kantonsspital Basel Psychiatrische Universitatspoliklinik, 5 September 1989, and first published in *GROUP 16*, 4, 220–232 (1992).

Theoretical constructs

Self psychology views development as a continuum. The infant and child require special attunement and responsiveness to their psychobiological states – by their caretakers if psychological growth and development are to continue without major injury or derailment. Winnicott (1947; 1960a; 1960b; 1962) regarded as adequate the natural, good-enough responsiveness of a caretaker. Kohut (1966; 1971; 1972; 1977; 1984), however, perceived that adequacy was not enough – that empathic responsivity was necessary for development to proceed. In therapy, on the other hand, the *empathic introspective approach* consists of a mode of listening, sensing, and a temporary immersion into the feeling state of the other, only for the purpose of understanding that state, without losing one's own boundaries. He emphasized that empathy is not the same as sympathy or just being kind.

The infant's development needs arise very early, but not at birth, for it seems safe to assume that, strictly speaking, the neonate has not yet acquired a self (Kohut and Wolf 1978). The baby has certain needs for physical survival, and its psychological survival hinges on the presence of responsive-empathic selfobjects (persons whom we experience as part of ourself). The earlier and/or the more traumatic the insults to the developing self, the more the potential for a greater severity in the disturbance of the self exists.

At first Kohut identified two types of selfobjects: *mirroring* selfobjects, 'who respond to and confirm the child's innate sense of vigor, greatness, and perfection'; and the *idealized parent imago,* selfobjects 'to whom the child can look up and with whom he can merge as in image of calmness, infallibility and omnipotence.'

In 1984, Kohut reconceptualized *twinship* from a phase under the developmental line of the grandiose self, to another distinct developmental line. In twinship, Kohut recognized the need to experience sameness with someone seen as similar to oneself. An example of this would be appreciating with another the same cultural experiences or going through feelings of mourning. These definitions in turn imply the salutary functions of the selfobject caretaker. In the matrix of the selfobject environment, the nuclear self of the child will crystallize through a specific process of psychological structure formation that Kohut and Wolf (1978, p.416) call *transmuting internalization* and specify:

> (1.) that it not occur without a previous stage in which the child's mirroring and idealizing needs had been sufficiently responded to; (2.) that it takes place in consequence of the minor, non-traumatic failures in the responses of the...selfobjects; and (3.) that these failures lead to the gradual replacement of the selfobjects and their functions by a self and its functions. [That is,] the autonomous self is not a replica of the selfobject.

The good (not necessarily faultless) caretaker, then, exults with the child, encourages the child, and serves as a mature imago for the child, but helps lead the child to understand that reality imposes bounds on the urge toward omnipotence. It is inevitable that the caretakers themselves will sometimes frustrate the child's wishes – but hopefully this will fall within the range of *optimal frustration*.

Kohut's (1971; 1972) and Kohut and Wolf's (1978) use of the term *selfobject* at times appears ambiguous, giving the impression that it can also be an external agent. They describe *archaic selfobjects* as objects that the infant experiences as part of the self and expects to control, much as the grown-up expects to have control over his or her mind or body. With normal unfolding and growth and phase-appropriate responsiveness, along the developmental poles of the grandiose self and idealized parent imago, the archaic selfobject becomes a *mature selfobject*.

The mature selfobject, on the other hand, is perceived as a separate center of initiative, with needs and wishes of his or her own, with whom one can establish an empathic, reciprocal relationship, based not on demands, but on mutuality, caring, and understanding. The achievement of mature relating takes place in what Wolf (1980) calls the *empathic selfobject ambience*. Shapiro (1991) reviewed how feeling safe in group is a result of experiencing empathy first.

Advances in self psychology

More recently, Stolorow and Brandchaft (1987) have redefined the concept of selfobject to mean not an entity or an agent, but a class of psychological functions pertaining to the maintenance, restoration, or consolidation of self-experience. In addition, a specific tie (determined by the particular nuclear self in question) is required with the subjectively experienced object in order to maintain, restore, or consolidate the organization of self-experience. Another way of putting it is that since selfobject by definition refers to the presence of a function, there is no selfobject experience without a selfobject function.

M. Tolpin (1982), Stolorow (1985) and Harwood (1986) disputed the existence of and human need for *many different selfobject functions*. Consequently, Harwood (1986) identified the *extended selfobject function*; Wolf (1988) identified the need for the *adversarial* and *efficacy experiences*; and Stolorow, Atwood and Brandchaft (1992) designated the *self-delineating selfobject function* to be basic to the emergence of a separate sense of self.

In the above-mentioned article (Harwood 1986), I integrated and pointed out the relevance of current developmental research to group literature and to group therapy. I especially focused on the importance of *cross-modal integration* (Spelke 1976). I also introduced the importance of multiple selfobject functions, or what I termed the 'extended selfobject function'. This function is in place in the social milieu of most babies in almost all cultures, except when there is only one caretaker without family or friends. Otherwise, from the very beginning the baby benefits from group membership in a larger group, the extended family.

I also emphasized the child's ability to internalize into his or her self-structure a multiplicity of selfobject functions from *various consistently available caretakers*, an ability that then enables the child to develop a less rigid, more flexible functioning and interrelating repertoire, which is the *basic foundation for all human relating and understanding*. Thus, the early internalizations of extended selfobject functions are crucial precursors for the development of empathy – the ability to understand the many subjective experiences of people different psychologically and culturally from oneself – a mandatory tool for the therapist.

In the group psychotherapy literature, Schwartzman (1984) has stressed how the entity of the group can be used as an archaic selfobject, while I (Harwood 1983b) have pointed out how a member's obtainment of selfobject functions from any individual in group can be shifted among different group members or to the therapist when a misunderstanding or a subjectively experienced empathic failure occurs. In contrast to individual treatment, Bacal (1985) states that patients in group therapy will have less difficulty establishing the selfobject relations they require, simply because of the multiplicity of candidate selfobjects.

Many authors agree that the entity of the group, which is often referred to as the *group self* is often experienced as a provider of selfobject functions (Bacal 1985; Harwood 1983a; 1983b; 1990; Lonergan 1982; Meyers 1978; Paparo 1983; Schwartzman 1984; Stone and Whitman 1977; Weinstein 1991; Wilson 1982). As with any individual, the group as an entity can also lose its idealizing (Weinstein 1987) and mirroring function for a member. For example, the entry of a new member may set off a regression in a less than cohesive group (Kohut 1978). The resulting sense of fragmentation may be similar to an ill or demanding child's experience with a marginally functioning parent who cannot provide soothing (Harwood 1983b; 1990). (See also the turmoil provoked by the group member described below.)

Restoration of the selfobject tie and structure building

Socarides and Stolorow (1984–1985) hold that psychological structure building occurs when the *ruptured bond* between the person and the one (caretaker or therapist) providing psychological functions is restored. Restoration of the tie is facilitated by the caretaker's or therapist's differentiating, synthesizing, modulating, and cognitively articulating the emergent emotional states, thus, helping integrate the fragmenting affect into new psychic structure. Kohut (1971, 1977) believed that psychic structure is built primarily through *transmuting internalization*, whereby the child eventually takes over and internalizes some selfobject functions that the caretakers had been performing. Stolorow (1985), though not disagreeing with the clinical manifestations of this phenomenon, believes – as described in his paper with Lachmann (1984–1985) – that it is the restoration and maintenance of the selfobject bond that enables and contributes to the building blocks of new psychic structure.

Intersubjectivity

The notion of *intersubjectivity* (Atwood and Stolorow 1984; Stolorow, Brandchaft and Atwood 1987) has emerged as a significant revision in the theoretical thinking of self psychology. It holds that all interactions occur in an intersubjective field with each participant experiencing a given situation from his or her own point of view, the latter being a product of a multiplicity of causes including genetic history and present psychic organization. In the treatment situation, both patient and psychotherapist bring their own subjective point of view, creating an intersubjective field.

The notion of intersubjectivity is not totally foreign to group therapists. On the surface, intersubjectivity may appear to be no more than Lewin's (1947) concept of paratactic distortions in different dress. In that concept, a group member's perceptions are viewed solely as transference manifestations based on old genetic, historical distortions, which are contraposed against an *actual, correct* group reality with the therapist usually acting as judge and jury. That however, differs greatly from the concept of intersubjectivity, which would accord validity to each participant's subjective point of view. Thus, every member's contribution (regardless of what it is) is accepted as important and valid because it brings out a particular subjective point of view which is organized around previous experience. This subjective organization of experience calls for understanding and analysis from the group therapist, not judgement. Therefore, there is no need for the therapist to intervene with pronouncements on objective reality. The group members, of course, present a collection of individual subjective realities – not objective realities. Objective reality may only exist in mathematics.

Within the group therapeutic process, one of the most important elements is the member' efforts to understand the basis of each individual's subjective experience. Such understanding is quite crucial after a narcissistic injury or a disconnection has occurred with another member, the therapist, or the entire group either through misunderstanding or through lack of response to a patient's subjectively felt need. In these instances, the injured member may perceive the group as a repetition of earlier caretakers who disappointed or traumatized the young, vulnerable self. Thus, when a person's subjective experience is not understood and held as valid, group members may become compliant, disorganized, enraged, or may flee treatment altogether. Stone, Blaze and Bozzuto (1980) cite examples of fleeing treatment.

On the other hand, when everyone's subjective experience is understood, validated, and worked through, it allows for restoration of selfobject bonds and for the building of new psychological structure. Depending where the initial rupture occurred, the bond needs to be restored either between individual members, the group-as-a-whole, or wherever it was ruptured.

Conflict

More recently, Stolorow and Brandchaft (1987) separated out the notion of *conflict* from its origin in drive theory. They believe that conflict becomes structuralized only when the child's authentic nuclear strivings are pitted against the compliance that is required if the child is to maintain the selfobject bond with the caretakers. Though such compliance is definitely adaptive in terms of the environment, it begins a process of perverting and contorting the natural evolution of the authentic self (Harwood 1987). Conflict is seen by Stolorow and Brandchaft (1987) as becoming destructive only when caretakers (parents or therapists) are not able to adapt themselves and provide the specific functions needed by the developing child. Though not disagreeing with this notion, I (Harwood 1986) have pointed out that unusually stressful environmental circumstances also can prevent developmentally mature and good-enough responsive caretakers from reacting optimally. If the caretakers impose too great a demand for compliance, the child may surrender and give up his or her own goals. If the child has not received the affect attunement that he or she subjectively requires, the unintegrated affect states become sources of lifelong inner conflict and can manifest themselves in unresolved anger, rage, and different degrees of self-destructiveness (Stolorow and Brandchaft 1987).

In group, when there is compliance to the group's or another member's point of view, without recognition of understanding of a member's wishes or subjective experience, conflict re-emerges for the individual in question. Conflict can be structuralized into inner conflict, as Stolorow and Brandchaft (1987) suggest. The less-than-cohesive individual can also take on a 'false self based on identification' (Harwood 1987), thus also giving up whatever nuclear strivings were beginning to emerge. Noncompliance in a group that demands agreement, on the other hand, may result in ostracism or the need to leave the group altogether.

Thus, it is a particularly important task of the group leader to safeguard and protect the individual members' emergent goals and expressions of the authentic self from pressures to comply to suggestions from individual members or the group-as-a-whole. Only when it is a group ideal that every member has a right to his or her own direction, can the individual not only hope to attain his or her own way, but find and define his or her own self.

Transference

As previously alluded to, transference in contemporary self psychology is *not* viewed solely as a distortion of an objective present reality prevailing with the therapist or another group member, with the patient seen as viewing the present situation only through old historical, genetic glasses.

Kohut's significant contribution in the evolution of his reconceptualizing narcissistic disorders was his recognition of patients' pathognomonic evolution of specific selfobject transferences with the analyst. The specificity of the transference was related to a developmental phase when early selfobject functions had been deficient. These transferences might remain silent until there was an empathic failure, at which time the patient would respond with an effort to re-establish the disturbed inner equilibrium. Stolorow and Lachmann (1984–1985) expand upon and modify these original formulations focusing on specific transferences – mirroring, idealizing, or alterego (twinship) transferences – to include the contributions of both patient and analyst, or what Atwood and Stolorow (1984) and Stolorow *et al.* (1987) termed the *intersubjective field*.

Transference as defined by Stolorow and Lachman (1984–1985) is an *organizing activity*, which can be viewed as deriving from a microcosm of the person's total psychological world, including the person's very early conscious and unconscious configurations of self and other. Seen from this angle, transference is not merely an unconscious tendency to repeat the past, but rather *the only* way the person can organize experience and construct meanings about his or her internal and external world.

The patient's view of the analyst's contributions are not negated, debated or validated. Instead, the patient's view of the analyst's contributions are used to further explore the meanings and organizing principles that form the patient's psychological world. Therefore, transference can exist only in the intersubjective context, with the therapist/analyst contributing to it simply by being who he or she is and by the patient's attributing meaning to who the therapist/analyst is and what he or she does, whether these be self-expressions or countertransference manifestations. In addition, Atwood and Stolorow (1984) warn against the specific impasses that occur when therapists/analysts are not aware of the contributions of their subjective points of view, and either agree or disagree with the patient's view (actions that the authors refer to as intersubjective *conjunction* and *disjunction*).

Bipolar conception of transference

Stolorow (1988) reformulated the ebb and flow of treatment through a *bipolar concept of transference* (which is different from Kohut's initial bipolar formulation of the tension arc). For Stolorow, one pole is the *selfobject dimension of transference*. This is when the patient looks to get from the therapist the functions that were missing during earlier development. Like Kohut, Stolorow believes that the therapist needs to understand consistently, not through sympathy or by just being nice, but through empathy (the putting oneself in the state of the patient while maintaining one's own regulated state). This type of understanding and emotional resonance, not agreement, is then experienced by the patient as the very nutrition necessary for arrested development to resume. Further, Socarides and Stolorow (1984–1985) believe that it is the therapist's acceptance of the patient's affects and needs (inherently woven into the selfobject bond) that promotes self-articulation and self-demarcation, modulation and synthesis of affective discrepant experiences, affect tolerance and the use of affects as signals, desomatization and cognitive articulation of affect, as well as other structuralizations of self-experience.

The other pole, for Stolorow (1988), is the *conflictual, repetitive, and resistive dimension of transference*. Ornstein (1974) has elucidated the patient's dread of repeating earlier childhood traumas in treatment. At this pole of the transference, the patient fears – perhaps expects – repeating earlier selfobject failures.

When the transference shifts from the first pole to the second, the therapist needs to be aware that the patient has shifted into the conflictual, repetitive and resistive dimension of the transference and therefore should try to identify the patient's perception of the therapist's selfobject failure without blaming the patient. Such attunement to the patient's change in feelings and reaction, Stolorow believes, mends the ruptured bond. Restoration of the bond brings back the selfobject pole of the transference, while the conflictual, resistive, repetitive dimension fades into the background.

In a group conducted from a self psychological perspective, within an inter-subjective context, selfobject and conflictual, repetitive, resistive transferences are at play as group members intertwine past and present, both inside and outside of group experiences. Within the group process, spontaneous growth proceeds during the selfobject pole of the transference and, when needed, during the conflictual pole of the transference. The group therapist clarifies experiences and constructs intelligible meanings, thus helping to reinstate selfobject bonds between individual members and the entire group.

Group example

A group member, whom I will call Ron, announced that he had enrolled in an actualization type of group on his friend's strong recommendation. This other group – a 'don't worry, be happy' type – was supposed to be more 'upbeat', to talk more about 'doing' and how to become a 'winner', and to help people who were afraid of physical closeness learn how to hug. In our therapy group, he complained, people were not responsive physically.

As the therapist, I perceived Ron to be protesting, though provocatively and not very directly, against the lack of touching and holding he missed early in life. He seemed to require not only the mirroring selfobject function, but also the touching, holding, soothing function of Kohut's early idealized parent imago pole. I speculated to myself whether Ron had experienced rejection and narcissistic injury toward the end of a recent group session. In that session, Nan told Ron that when he tried to hug her, she felt as if he was trying to get something from her by force, since she gave no sign that she wanted to hug him. She experienced Ron as wanting to be in total control of her reactions, treating her not as an individual but only as an object to be used. She declined to be used in such a way.

As Ron continued to praise the virtues of the 'touch-action' group, the members began vigorously defending the virtues of their own group. Almost all of them joined in to defend the idealized virtues of the present group against the imagined shortcomings of the other group. As the therapist, I did not feel that this group-as-a-whole reaction against one member should be considered as majority confirmation of objective reality.

I sensed that the group's banding together against one member indicated strong feelings of potential rejection, injury and threat to the integrity of the group which the members were experiencing both individually and as a group. In the intersubjective group field, each member was reacting, in different degrees and configurations, to both prior and present fears of being rendered powerless or found deficient. With this, the group-as-a-whole was also losing its potential to function as a selfobject for Ron. While I, as the group therapist, remained quiet, sorting out the individual and group dynamics as well as my own reactions, I was not yet providing any tension-regulating functions. My silence was not subjectively experienced as containment, since it was my group that Ron was finding wanting, and it appeared that I abandoned the members to defend the group's worth. My lack of protective intervention frightened the group further and intensified the angry standoff.

During that time, I was considering whether I agreed with Nan and disagreed with Ron, and remembered how I, like Nan, had also experienced Ron as physically demanding. I remembered how, at the beginning of treatment, he would routinely put his hand on my shoulder and tell me how he liked what I was wearing. I remembered how uncomfortable that made me, but even then, I sensed that to comment on or even ask about the meaning of this ritualistic behaviour would be an outgrowth merely of my discomfort. I feared Ron would have experienced my inquiry as a painful rejection or even condemnation of his attempt to be pleasing – or perhaps, in self psychological terms, to merge with an idealized parent imago.

I began to understand his behavior as deriving from his desperate desire for someone to notice him, to approve of him, and to touch him, as a confirmation of his goodness and desirability, thus, to mirror his authentic self. As a child, he had felt that in his parents' eyes he could do no right, while his brother could do no wrong. Though he remembered no touching or other physical comforting from his nuclear family, he recalled his paternal grandmother once standing up for him to his father, and how much it meant to him. I concluded that he indeed required the selfobject functions provided through tactile contact, which this very verbal group did not hand out automatically and had not established as a group value (under the idealized parent imago pole). Though Kohut's paradigm does not specifically include tactile functions as mirroring functions, it could be loosely adopted here. On the other hand, both Stolorow (1985) and I (Harwood 1986) believe that there are many more possible selfobject functions than those Kohut mentions.

Turning to the group, I first decided to address the group process, keeping with the notion of responding first to the shared tension of the here-and-now atmosphere. I pointed out that Ron and the group had ended up being locked in opposite positions – Ron contending that the other group was superior, and this group, feeling devalued, stoutly defending its own virtues. As the therapist, I added my opinion that both groups had something to offer Ron, though what they had to offer was different. I recalled for them Ron's words about his early deficits, owing to being cared for physically while often being severely punished corporally. Perforce, Ron would feel a left-over yearning for unfulfilled needs. Although his needs may have been reawakened in this group and an attempt was being made to gain understanding of them, I added that maybe the other group had something different, but also of value, to offer Ron.

Thus, the therapist's empathic understanding of Ron's selfobject needs allowed him to call a cease-fire. He relaxed, became misty-eyed, and thanked me. Drawing an analogy with his paternal grandmother, he said he experienced the therapist as protecting him from his tyrannical, overbearing, know-it-all father, in this case the group. In turn, the rest of the group seemed to experience relief from the overheated emotional situation, with the verbal interaction it valued no longer being under threat of de-idealization. With this therapeutic intervention, I was able to diffuse the escalating intensity of unregulated affects as well as identify and integrate the fragmenting components. The restoration of the selfobject bond between the therapist and the group members, including Ron, re-established a sense of cohesion (Kohut 1978) and coherence (Pines 1986) for the group. Earlier, while I was silently reflecting, the group seemed to have experienced me as abandoning them, or possibly as being overwhelmed by Ron's attack. Thus, the therapist during this period was not experienced as the much needed powerful container of unregulated affects. But once the selfobject bond was re-established and members no longer felt abandoned and without a conductor, they were able, little by little, to show some understanding of Ron's needs. The process concluded with the members recalling what Ron's attack had touched off in each of them from their own past. Ron and each member's organization of subjective experience was brought out and understood. This accomplished, the group was able to leave the resistive, conflictual aspects of transference behind, re-established its cohesion, and resumed its work without needing the therapist's further intervention.

Ron also was able to express his own present feelings and past associations, re-establish the ruptured bond with the group, and remain with the therapy group. In addition, he continued to participate in the actualizing group, including its advanced course, in which later he became a teacher. He did appear to gain from each group. He received the physical touching he so much needed from the actualizing group and was better able to internalize both emotional and cognitive components in the therapy group. As a result, he was able to integrate multiple or 'extended selfobject functions' from very different caretaking agents – in this case, two groups. He is no longer a member of either group. After getting the most out of both groups, he left his employment of 16 years to form his own company and to design and produce his own products. During the holiday season, some members of this old group (including Nan) and I receive cards with updated news.

Though Ron may be considered as borderline and with a proclivity for splitting by therapists from other theoretical points of view, I did not see him as untreatable in a psychoanalytic psychodynamically oriented group. As group therapists, it is essential to understand the subjectively needed selfobject functions of individuals who have been severely deprived early in life and not to repeat the traumas by responding rigidly.

In my experience of conducting groups from an intersubjective perspective, it is rare that a whole group will turn on one member without someone being able to empathically understand that member's point of view, unless the whole group becomes threatened. In such a situation, it is up to the therapist to understand and bring out the intersubjective elements among the members, as well as take into account his or her own subjective contributions.

Schlachet (1985), summarizing and building on previous group psychotherapy literature, enumerated 10 criterion behaviors that are present in group process and can be used to validate the therapist's interventions: depth of response, group participation, accessibility of feelings, anxiety reduction, decrease in acting out, greater directness of expression, development of a common language, increased acceptance of self and others, greater group cohesion, and greater autonomy and self-reliance. The above example of a group conducted from a self psychological perspective appears to meet most, and perhaps all, of Schlachet's criteria.

Disorders of the self and borderline conditions

In his first book, Kohut (1971) viewed the narcissistic and borderline conditions as separate pathological entities. He modified that view in his second book (Kohut 1977, p.192), in which the differences in the derailments of the self in the narcissistic and borderline disorders were characterized primarily by the *degree* of the experienced injury or trauma in response to the experienced narcissistic blow, as well as by the *duration* of the fragmentation and enfeeblement of the self.

P. Tolpin (1980), while stating that '"borderlineness" of patients is not to be judged from the standpoint of an observer outside the field but from the standpoint of an observer participating in a system – the self–selfobject system of the patient and therapist' (p.312), appears to set the stage for Atwood and Stolorow's (1984) notion of intersubjectivity. On the other hand, when Tolpin further suggests that 'a highly vulnerable narcissistic personality disorder might be considered (incorrectly) to be a true borderline condition because of the limitations of even a competent analyst's empathic understanding of certain constellations of severe disorders' (p.312), he also plants the seed for Brandchaft and Stolorow's (1984) significant paper on the iatrogenic myth.

In a groundbreaking contribution, Brandchaft and Stolorow (1984) affirm that the conception of the borderline condition as a discrete character structure is an *iatrogenic myth*, meaning that a borderline condition can be brought about by an unempathic therapist who does not or cannot immerse herself or himself into the subjective experience of a patient, and understand and acknowledge it as real or valid. These authors state that the borderline configuration only remains unchanged when the analyst continues to ignore the intersubjective field, through lack of attunement and understanding of the patient's subjective experience. When the therapist/analyst further insists on interpreting reactive narcissistic rage to be a split-up projective identification of drive derivatives, the fragmenting situation only becomes further intensified and perpetuated. Supporting their premise with clinical examples, Brandchaft and Stolorow see the borderline disorders positively, as both treatable and analyzable, a view that they say Kohut also came to share in the last part of his life.

Self psychologists now generally view persons with borderline disorders as having experienced less attunement to their nuclear strivings; indeed, as having experienced traumatic blows to the basic fabric of the self at the very time when beginning strivings would start to emerge. Persons who suffer from borderline disorders experience more lengthy or permanent derailments in their self-states, while persons with narcissistic disorders seem to experience more temporary enfeeblements or fragmentations of the self. Upon the reinstatement of a selfobject bond and needed selfobject functions, the latter can more quickly restore their sense of equilibrium.

Treatability of self disorders

Others have cited the treatability of severe self disorders, or those with psychotic configurations, with a self psychological approach. Trop (1984) illustrates, through a case study, a clinical application of self psychology to the psychotherapy of a psychotic patient. Similarly, Stolorow *et al.* (1987) describe the analyzability and treatment of psychotic states. More recently, I (Harwood 1992) have underscored that what is labelled primary aggression in borderlines (or even psychotics) is nothing more than ongoing reactive rage to continually being misunderstood or experiencing lack of containment or retaliation from a vulnerable therapist with permeable self boundaries. When the therapist or group is subjectively experienced as forcing the self to contort, reactive rage prevails. On the other hand, when the reasons for reactive rage of those who are labelled borderline or psychotic are accurately understood, what appears to be primary aggression dissipates.

In a significant contribution to the group psychotherapy literature, Lonergan (1982), in great detail and primarily using a self psychological approach, discusses how to begin and maintain inpatient and outpatient groups with medical patients and schizophrenics. I (Harwood 1983a) have given a verbatim example describing the type of enabling group atmosphere in an outpatient setting, which is needed for persons with little or no sense of self to begin discovering their nuclear strivings.

Group psychotherapy and self psychology

Kohut did not practise group psychotherapy. Like Freud (1921) before him, Kohut was also interested in the dynamics of group phenomena and in the role of the group leader. In his paper 'Creativeness, Charisma, Group Psychology', Kohut (1978) warned that group pressure can diminish individuality, leading to primitivization of mental processes and to a lowering of resistance. The warnings take on special meaning when working in group psychotherapy with vulnerable individuals who suffer from self disorders that are considered to fall into the narcissistic and borderline diagnostic category. These individuals can be easily led from their emerging nuclear strivings by a charismatic and/or authoritarian group leader, by individual members, or by any given direction a group may take. Kohut's theories (1971; 1977; 1984) found quick applicability to group psychotherapy, (Arensberg 1990; Bacal 1985; Harwood 1983a; 1983b; 1986; 1990; 1992; Kriegman and Solomon 1985; Lonergan 1982; Meyers 1978; Paparo 1983; Schwartzman 1984; Shapiro 1991; Stone and Gustafson 1982; Stone and Whitman 1977; 1980; Weinstein 1987; 1991; Wilson 1982; Wong 1979).

Group psychotherapy from a self psychological perspective accords with such group pioneers as Slavson (1950), Wolf and Schwartz (1962) and Yalom (1985), who championed the concept of the individual as the focus in the group process. In addition, a group conducted from a self psychological perspective would envision, as its primary goal and purpose, the development of each person toward freedom of his or her own convictions, toward cohesion, coherence (Pines 1985; 1986), and self structure, along with the capacity for reciprocity and mutuality in personal relationships.

I have elsewhere (Harwood 1986) spelled out the importance, for a developing individual, of extended or multiple selfobject functions and experiences in the family and larger community, and how these add toward the building-up and flexibility of individual psychic structure. Multiple consistent selfobject functions are of equal importance to persons who are regressed, arrested, or at a critical point in their individual development. The self psychological group atmosphere, by its variety of potential selfobject functions and selfobject ties, offers a multitude of possibilities for Kohut's transmuting internalizations and for the creation, restoration, and maintenance of selfobject bonds (Socarides and Stolorow 1984–1985) through which individuals can resume the building of psychic structure along with a new or renewed sense of life.

References

Arensberg, F. (1990) 'Self psychology groups.' In I.L. Kutash and A. Wolf (eds) *Group Psychotherapist's Handbook: Contemporary Theory and Technique.* New York: Columbia University Press.

Atwood, G.E. and Stolorow, R.D. (1984) *Structures of Subjectivity: Explorations in Phenomenology.* Hillsdale, NJ: Analytic Press.

Bacal, H. (1985) 'Object relations in the group from the perspective of self psychology.' *International of Group Psychotherapy 35*, 483–501.

Brandchaft, B. and Stolorow, R.D. (1984) 'The borderline concept: Pathological character or iatrogenic?' In J. Lichtenberg, M. Bornstein, and D. Silver (eds) *Empathy II.* Hillsdale, NJ: Analytic Press.

Freud, S. (1921) 'Group psychology and the analysis of the ego.' *Standard Edition 18*, 67–143.

Harwood, I. (1983a) The evolution of the self in group psychotherapy. Paper presented at the 40th Annual Conference of the American Group Psychotherapy Association, Toronto.

Harwood, I. (1983b) 'The application of self psychology concepts to group psychotherapy.' *International Journal of Group Psychotherapy 33*, 469–487.

Harwood, I. (1986) 'The need for optimal, available selfobject caretakers: Moving toward extended selfobject experiences.' *Group Analysis 19*, 291–302.

Harwood, I. (1987) 'The evolution of the self: An integration of Winnicott's and Kohut's concepts.' In T. Honess and K. Yardley (eds) *Self and Identity: Individual Change and Development.* London: Routledge & Kegan Paul.

Harwood, I. (1990) 'The application of self psychology concepts to group psychotherapy.' *Official Journal of the Japan Association of Group Psychotherapy 6*, 190–192.

Harwood, I. (1992) 'Group psychotherapy and disorders of the self.' *Group Analysis 25*, 19–26.

Kohut, H. (1966) 'Forms and transformations of narcissism.' *Journal of the American Psychoanalytic Association 14*, 243–272.

Kohut, H. (1971) *The Analysis of the Self.* New York: International Universities Press.

Kohut, H. (1972) 'Thoughts on narcissism and narcissistic rage.' *Psychoanalytic Study of the Child 27*, 360–400.

Kohut, H. (1977) *The Restoration of the Self.* New York: International Universities Press.

Kohut, H. (1978) 'Creativeness, charisma, group psychology.' In P. Ornstein (ed) *The Search for the self* (Vol.2). New York: International Universities Press.

Kohut, H. (1984) *How Does Analysis Cure?* Chicago: University of Chicago Press.

Kohut, H. and Wolf, E.S. (1978) 'The disorders of the self and their treatment.' *International Journal of Psychoanalysis 59*, 413–425.

Kriegman, D. and Solomon, L. (1985) 'Cult groups and the narcissistic personality: The offer to heal defects in the self.' *International Journal of Group Psychotherapy 35*, 239–361.

Lewin, K. (1947) 'Group decision and social change.' In T. Newcomb and E. Hartley (eds) *Readings in Social Psychology.* New York: Holt.

Lonergan, E.C. (1982) *Group Intervention: How to Begin and Maintain Groups in Medical and Psychiatric Settings.* New York: Jason Aronson.

Meyers, S.J. (1978) 'The disorders of the self: Developmental and clinical considerations.' *Group 2*, 131–140.

Orstein, A. (1974) 'The dread to repeat and the new beginning.' *Annual of Psychoanalysis 12/13*, 195–119.

Paparo, F. (1983) Self psychology and the group process. Paper presented at the 6th Annual Self Psychology Conference, Los Angeles.

Pines, M. (1985) 'Psychic development and the group analytic situation.' *Group 9*, 1, 24–37.

Pines, M. (1986) 'Coherency and its disruption in the development of the self.' *British Journal of Psychotherapy 2*, 3, 180–185.

Schlachet, P.J. (1985) 'The clinical validation of therapist interventions in group therapy.' *International Journal of Group Psychotherapy 35*, 225–238.

Schwartzman, G. (1984) 'The use of group as selfobject.' *International Journal of Group Psychotherapy 34*, 229–241.

Shapiro, E. (1991) 'Empathy and safety in group: A self psychology perspective.' *Group 15*, 219–224.

Slavson, S.R. (1950) *Analytic Group Psychotherapy.* New York: Columbia University Press.

Socarides, D.D. and Stolorow, R.D. (1984–1985) 'Affects and selfobjects.' *Annual of Psychoanalysis 12*, 105–119.

Spelke, E. (1976) 'Infants' intermodal perception of events.' *Cognitive Psychology 8*, 553–560.

Stolorow, R.D. (1985) Personal communication.

Stolorow, R.D. (1988) 'Transference and the therapeutic process.' *Psychoanalytic Review 75*, 245–254.

Stolorow, R.D., Atwood, G.E. and Brandchaft, B. (1992) 'Three realms of the unconscious and their therapeutic transformation.' *Psychoanalytic Review 79*, 25–30.

Stolorow, R.D. and Brandchaft, B. (1987) 'Developmental failure and psychic conflict.' *Psychoanalytic Psychotherapy 4*, 241–253.

Stolorow, R.D., Brandchaft, B. and Atwood, G. (1987) *Psychoanalytic Treatment: An Intersubjective Approach.* Hillsdale, NJ: Analytic Press.

Stolorow, R.D. and Lachmann, F.M. (1984–1985) 'Transference: The future of an illusion.' *Annual of Psychoanalysis 12*, 19–37.

Stone, W.N., Blaze, M. and Bozzuto, B. (1980) 'Late dropouts from group psychotherapy.' *American Journal of Psychotherapy 34*, 401–413.

Stone, W.N. and Gustafson, J.P. (1982) 'Technique in group psychotherapy of narcissistic and borderline patients.' *International Journal of Group Psychotherapy 32*, 29–47.

Stone, W.N. and Whitman, R.M. (1977) 'Contributions of the psychology of the self to group process and group therapy.' *International Journal of Group Psychotherapy 27*, 343–359.

Stone, W.N. and Whitman, R.M. (1980) 'Observations on empathy in group psychotherapy.' In L.R. Wolberg and M.L. Aronson (eds) *Group and Family Therapy.* New York: Brunner/Mazel.

Tolpin, M. (1982) Injured self-cohesion: Development, clinical and theoretical perspectives. A contribution to understanding narcissistic and borderline disorders. Paper presented at the UCLA Symposium on Narcissistic and Borderline Disorders: Current Perspectives.

Tolpin, P. (1980) 'The borderline personality: Its makeup and analyzability.' In A. Goldberg (ed) *Advances in Self Psychology.* New York: International Universities Press.

Trop, J. (1984) 'Self psychology and the psychotherapy of psychotic patients: A case study.' *Clinical Social Work Journal 12*, 292–302.

Weinstein, D. (1987) 'Self psychology and group psychotherapy.' *Group 11*, 144–154.

Weinstein, D. (1991) 'Exhibitionism in group psychotherapy.' In Goldberg (ed) *The Evolution of Self Psychology: Progress in Self Psychology* (Vol.7). Hillsdale, NJ: Analytic Press.

Wilson, A. (1982) 'Treatment of the narcissistic character disorder in group psychotherapy in the light of self psychology.' *Group 6*, 6–10.

Winnicott, D.W. (1947) 'Further thoughts on babies as persons.' In *The Child, the Family and the Outside World.* Harmondsworth, UK: Penguin, 1964.

Winnicott, D.W. (1960a) 'Ego distortion in terms of the true and false self.' In *Maturational Processes and the Facilitating Environment.* New York: International Universities Press, 1965.

Winnicott, D.W. (1960b) 'The theory of the parent–infant relationship.' In *Maturational Processes and the Facilitating Environment.* New York: International Universities Press, 1965.

Winnicott, D.W. (1962) 'Ego integration in child development.' In *Maturational Processes and the Facilitating Environment.* New York: International Universities Press, 1965.

Wolf, A. and Schwartz, E.K. (1962) *Psychoanalysis in Groups.* New York: Grune & Stratton.

Wolf, E.S. (1980) 'On the developmental line of selfobject relations.' In A. Goldberg (ed) *Advances in Self Psychology.* New York: International Universities Press.

Wolf, E.S. (1988) *Treating the Self: Elements of Clinical Psychology.* New York: Guilford Press.

Wong, N. (1979) 'Clinical considerations in group treatment of narcissistic disorders.' *International Journal of Group Psychotherapy 29*, 325–345.

Yalom, I. (1985) *The Theory and Practice of Group Psychotherapy*. New York: Basic Books.

CHAPTER 4

Intersubjectivity in Archaic and Mature Twinship in Group Therapy

Emanuel Shapiro

The relationship between intersubjectivity, twinship, and group therapy is the connection between a theoretical perspective, a basic need, and a mode of treatment respectively. An analytic therapy group provides more opportunities for twinship and a broader matrix of intersubjective moments than does the therapeutic dyad. It is these increased possibilities for intersubjective interpretations and the bonding for twinship gratification that make group therapy a particularly effective method of treatment.

Stolorow (1994a; 1994b) argues that it is not the isolated, individual mind, but the larger system created by the mutual interplay between the worlds of patient and analyst or of child and caregiver that constitutes the proper domain of psychoanalytic inquiry. The organization of a patient's experiential world is the result of the '...recurring patterns of intersubjective transaction originating in the child–caregiver system of mutual regulation' (Stolorow and Atwood 1992, p.23). These unconscious, intersubjectively derived, organizing principles form the foundation of personality development. Stolorow, Atwood and Brandchaft (1994) use the term 'subjective world' to describe the contents of experience and 'structures of subjectivity' to denote the consistent principles unconsciously and recurrently organizing those contents according to specific themes and meanings. 'Subjective world' is a more inclusive concept than 'self'. Therefore, an '... intersubjective field – the field constituted by the reciprocal interplay between two (or more) subjective worlds – is broader and more inclusive than the self–selfobject relationship; it exists at a higher level of generality' (Stolorow 1994, p.37). It should be noted that the 'or more' referred to by Stolorow in parenthesis provides a basis for viewing group therapy as an intersubjective field.

In an earlier paper, I (Shapiro 1990, p.182) stated that the concept of intersubjectivity can be extended to include the interplay of each patient's subjective world with those of the other group members: 'The group situation, colored as it is by the patient's previous experiences and perceptions of groups and families is experienced through the patient's organization of his or her unique experiential world.' This intersubjective field includes the therapist's subjectivity as well: 'The therapist should be aware that his or her perception of the patient, in particular the patient's transference, is viewed through the…lens of the therapist's own organization of his or her experience' (Shapiro 1990, p.181). The organization of experience is co-determined by pre-existing principles and by an ongoing situation that favors one over the others. Stolorow and Atwood (1992) differentiate between the 'selfobject' and 'repetitive' dimensions of the transference. In the former, the patient desires the provision of selfobject experiences that were missing during the formative years. In the latter, the patient expects and fears the repetition of early experiences of empathic failure. These two situations continually seesaw in foreground and background in response to perceptions of another's attunement to the patient's needs.

The group therapist sees transference as all the ways in which the patient organizes his or her experience of the other group members, subgroups, the group itself, and the therapist. Intersubjectivity in group therapy is the meeting of the various subjectivities, in varying combinations, of all the group members and the therapist.

Trop (1994) differentiates the cure process in self psychology from the cure process in intersubjectivity. Self psychology views cure as a process in which selfobject needs are replaced by an 'empathic resonance' with the therapist. Thus, cure is manifested when the patient develops the capacity to experience selfobject functions from more appropriate objects than previously. In contrast, intersubjectivity pictures the curative process as derived from '… the elucidation and understanding of the unique, unconscious, organizing principles of the patient that *shape* disruptions of the bond with the therapist' (Trop 1994, p.80). Trop emphasizes that cure involves not only the restoration of the tie to the analyst, but '… understanding the principles that organize the disruption of the tie' (Trop 1994, p.80).

This clarification and understanding may be viewed as new learning on the part of the patient. Learning – the application of cognitive tools and skills – is inherent in the twinship selfobject function. According to Kohut (1984), it is in twinship that the patient acquires tools, skills and the learning required to achieve his ambitions and ideals. Becoming aware of one's organizing principles in an intersubjective context may be one of the most important functions of the twinship experience.

Kohut (1984) elevated twinship from an aspect of mirroring to its own selfobject status. According to Basch (1989), this indicated an awareness on Kohut's part that twinship, the alterego experience, was a basic human need: '… the need to have one's humanness, one's kinship or sameness with others of the species quietly acknowledged' (Basch 1989, p.15). Gedo (1989) perceives that the need for an alterego or twinship is much broader and more fundamental than the other 'narcissistic transferences'. He believes twinship needs are more basic to human development because learning and the acquisition of skills will not take place without having these needs met. Gorney supports this view when he states: 'The twinship experience is a necessary precondition for the activation and vitalization of an individual's unique, core-capabilities and talents' (Gorney 1995).

Detrick (1985) develops the concept of the primary role of twinship and/or alterego selfobject functions when he addresses the issue of human sameness as having an intrinsic role in the acquisition of tools and skills and the use of one's talents. He stresses that tools and skills include cognitive tools such as thinking, ideas, concepts and problem solving strategies. For Detrick, it is only in this feeling of sameness that the individual can learn.

In developing his twinship theory, Kohut (1984) describes scenes in which a little boy works with tools alongside his father and a little girl bakes cookies in the kitchen next to her mother. At such moments, the children's feelings of similarity to the adult figures permit them to begin to develop their skills. The experience of sameness allows for the transmission of information. Learning occurs easily when it is experienced by the child as coming from a benign, empathic, parent figure. Kohut (1984) describes how this experience is revealed in analysis: 'Within the context of the transference, an outline will gradually come to light of a person for whom the patient's early existence and actions were a source of genuine joy; the significance of this person as a silent presence, as an alterego or twin next to whom the child felt alive ...' (p.204).

Lee and Martin (1991) note that by adding twinship to the idealizing and mirroring transferences, Kohut was in effect expanding his theory of motivation. Kohut's 'self' is motivated to act because of ideals, ambitions, and the need to develop competence in talents and skills. Basch (1988) addresses the importance of the experience of competence and describes it as basic to self-esteem and the therapy experience: 'The search for competence is the basic motivation for behavior...' (Basch 1988, p.25). He further states that competence is experienced as self-esteem and that 'true self-esteem' is a genuine sense of one's self as worthy of nurture and protection, capable of growth and development.

In our current society, many of these traditional sources of identity and continuity have significantly decreased. The older mainstays of community and identity such as the extended and even nuclear family, the neighborhood, the church and in some instances the ethnic group, have all diminished in stability and dependability. Modern society offers many choices, with few sources of permanence and identity. The diminishing importance of religion, family, neighbourhood and social stratum has led to a greater ambiguity in values (Rutan and Stone 1984). Thus, there is a loss of twinship, the powerful bond that comes from participating in a community of shared values. The basic human need for twinship becomes further exacerbated in a society such as ours that stresses autonomy and individualism.

Changes have occurred even in eastern cultures where family ties and strong paternal leadership were the rule. Gehrie (1980) uses current Japanese social, political and religious organizations as an example of a shift from familial organizations to a kind of group consciousness that is based upon unity of action and sense of community. He notes that access to influence and power seems to be increasingly sought through membership in non-familial groups. He also notes a corresponding decline of the relevance of the family in an increasingly broad range of political, economic, religious and social activities. He asserts that there is a group cohesiveness – a consciousness – that is based more on a sense of community than previous cultural values. This sense of community may be perceived as an experience of twinship.

In response to western society's increasing absence of opportunities for twinship, recent social phenomena have developed. Value-based homogenous groups such as the women's movement, the student movement and ethnic pride have arisen to fill the gap previously provided for by family, community and religion. Gehrie believes that these movements provide a sense of belonging and '... it is the "belonging" itself which is celebrated and which creates a sense of power for both the individual and for the group' (1980, p.369).

In support of this point is Lee and Martin's (1991) theory that much of the effectiveness of religious healing rested on the powerful bond that comes from participating in a community of shared values. They believe that the breakdown of such totemic systems in an urban industrialized society leads to a loss of common values as a major source of cohesiveness. Thus, the loss of common values leaves unfulfilled the need for twinship affirmation that had formerly been taken care of through sibling relationships and affiliation with an extended family or tribal structure.

Kohut described the earliest and most basic manifestations of alterego experiences, which are found as the human infant discovers itself surrounded by the human environment, human sounds, human smells and human responsiveness. He theorized that the alterego selfobject developmental line begins very early in life. According to infant research (Stern 1985) the infant, at birth, has a sense of self and other. This awareness includes a sense of belonging arising from experiences of attuned engagements and attuned disengagements of the caretaker. The emerging sense of belonging (Stern 1985) is the early representation of the twinship experience. Wolf (1988) agrees with Stern that the need to experience the essential likeness of the selfobject and to be strengthened by its quietly sustaining presence is already present during infancy.

Lee and Martin (1991) elaborate upon this idea by utilizing the concept of mutual regulation of mother and infant described by Beebe and Lachmann (1988) to suggest a primitive twinship experience. They further support the notion of a primitive twinship experience by a re-interpretation of Conrad Lorenz' classic observations of the dance of the Greylag goose. Lorenz (1996) interpreted the female's joining of her mate's dance of triumph as ritualized behavior to curb the male goose's aggression toward her. Lee and Martin (1991) offer another interpretation: they view the dance as an expression of a twinship bond in which the female goose imitates the male's behavior in an operation similar to the infant's deciphering the mother's feelings from her facial muscles. In other words, when the infant imitates the mother's facial expression its own facial muscles stimulate its autonomic nervous system leaving the infant to feel what she is feeling. They conclude: 'Without the "dance" that takes place between mother and child, growth and development are constricted. Such a mutual influence experience, especially involving synchronicity, suggests that some form of primitive twinship is necessary from day one of an infant's life' (p.154).

Gorney (1995) refers to Stern's infant studies mentioned above to support his view that twinship leads to vitality which leads to pleasure. For Gorney, twinship involves mutual affirmation and mutual pleasure; it is the vitalizing effect of successful twinship which enhances pleasure in learning and mastery of tasks and ideas. Lichtenberg, Lachmann and Fosshage (1992) emphasized the vitalizing function of selfobject experiences in the affiliation–attachment motivational system. For Gorney, twinship is the basis for vitality, and to that degree is the basis for affiliation and attachment. He perceives the full impact of twinship as an experience of shared humanity, of likeness and similarity. Through this experience, the human community is vitally connected in kinship. This context of shared experiences provides for the awareness of one's abilities as well as the pleasure derived from their use in mastering situations.

While gratified twinship needs facilitate the use of one's innate skills and potentials, unmet twinship needs lead to emotional states which hamper learning – feelings of alienation, emptiness and being different from others. These emotional states occur in depression and addiction, devitalizing experiences that derive from a lack of twinship according to Gorney (1995).

Detrick (1986) suggests that addictions related to alterego needs are those that reinforce a sense of oneness or communality with others. He theorizes that energizing drugs are related to ambitions and mirroring while depressants are related to the soothing of the idealized selfobject. Whether mirroring or idealizing related drugs are the addictive substance, a sense of community develops in the world of addiction. It is not surprising then that groups, which build on a sense of community, are used in the treatment of these addictions.

The sense of community and belonging can be related to empathy itself. Detrick (1985) states that the empathic process is the finding and experiencing of a sameness in another's experience. This sameness that is used as a basis of understanding in empathy is also involved in a feeling of belonging or community. The prevalence of the sameness experience may be why Detrick and Gedo believe that alterego experiences are in some sense more basic to human experience than either being mirrored or idealizing. Thus, it appears that the twinship experience is a requirement of the therapy or analytic process itself. 'Nothing that is called therapeutic will happen if there is no sense of kinship' (Basch 1995, p.30). Basch states that without the bonding of twinship a patient cannot connect well enough to the analyst to 'take for granted' that he or she will be understood.

If, as Gorney (1995) states, facilitating the vitalizing twinship experience is the fundamental goal of therapeutic technique, then group would be a natural component of a treatment plan. The experience of twinship is the cohesive force that bonds group members together in an analytic therapy group. Once these bonds are created, interventions can be made that recognize and elucidate intersubjective conjunctions and disjunctions. Interactions between group members, where their subjectivities intersect, are explained to the interacting members. Yalom (1975) noted that when a group member walks a mile in another member's shoes he/she can lose his/her hostility to a former adversary. That the alterego or twinship relationship is basic to group process is confirmed by statements which reveal similarity of experience and have become clichés: 'I can relate to that' or 'I've had a similar experience.' In fact, part of the group leader's role is to elicit similarities of experience in the group setting. As Detrick puts it: 'Alterego phenomena are those experiences of sameness or likeness that anchor the individual in a group process' (1986, p.300). Groups such as interest groups, recovery groups, and homogeneous, focused issue groups manifestly provide increased opportunities for experiences of similarity or universality. Psychoanalytic groups generate these opportunities in a more subtle, perhaps more meaningful, fashion. These group configurations provide opportunities for the individual to make use of the group for twinship selfobject experiences. To the degree that one experiences oneself as similar to others, one feels less inferior, less inadequate. Further, as one's life experience is perceived as similar to others, one is less prone to humiliation and shame. The selfobject experience of twinship reduces the feelings of shame with regard to the perception of one's 'unique' negative thoughts, feelings or actions as atypical and isolated. This may be why Yalom (1975) considers universality a 'curative' factor in group therapy. Let me illustrate with an example from my group:

In the early 1970s I worked with Jeff, a 32 year old, homosexual male who worked as a counselor. His presenting problems included anxiety, depression, and narcissistic vulnerability. He was the younger of two siblings in a middle class Italian family residing in a suburb of New York. Of primary concern to Jeff was that he be able to maintain a heterosexual facade in the workplace and with his friends and family. He had a secret life wherein he met lovers in gay bars, baths and subway bathrooms. Although his goal in treatment was to remain homosexual, he suffered great shame for his intense interest in men. His heterosexual facade was so developed that Jeff found himself engaged to a woman for several months.

Jeff was seen for several years in individual treatment and for two additional years in combined individual and group therapy. He experienced me as empathic, yet felt our differences pointedly. He believed that he was fully accepted as himself, by the group and the therapist, but experienced a poignant sense of alienation. He experienced the other group members as sharing a bond to which he could not fully connect.

Little by little I began to appreciate that Jeff needed to be with others who shared the secret part of his life. This was before much was known about self psychology, much less twinship. The group explored Jeff's need for bonding with others similar to himself in his sexual life. The group, including Jeff, came to a consensus that a homosexual group led by a homosexual leader might give Jeff the sense of bonding that he missed. We all seemed to understand that Jeff needed to experience a greater sense of kinship in his therapy. This is not to say that Jeff did not have strong bonds with various members of the group and to the group as whole. It was some basic sense of sameness, something about the shared, shameful secret, and society's potential ostracism that was lacking in this group setting. I did not think in terms of twinship selfobject functions, but I realized that he needed to experience a sense of kinship in his therapy. It may very well be that Jeff's low self esteem derived from his 'shameful habits' and a lack of competence in the heterosexual sphere.

Jeff shared his search for the 'proper group' and 'proper group therapist' with the group. When he finally found the group for which he was searching, he slowly worked toward termination in my group. Years later, Jeff contacted me and gratefully acknowledged the importance of my understanding and support for his 'bonding needs'. He stated that he was no longer in treatment, but should he seek treatment at this point in his life he would prefer a group like his first group. If I had to do this over again, I would have placed Jeff first in a sexual-orientation homogeneous group and later in a heterogeneous analytic group.

Harwood (1995) states that homogenous groups of 'same issue' members should not substitute for a heterogeneous analytic group. However, she believes that if the patient is in need of an archaic twinship experience then a same issue group may be in order. In Harwood's view an archaic twinship experience may require sameness in demographic or similar experience aspects. Harwood notes that while feeling understood by people like oneself is structure enhancing, a heterogeneous group is a necessary step for readying oneself to deal with differences in the world: 'Learning that those different from ourselves, but who possess the important capacity for empathy, can understand us and reach out to us simply as one ordinary human being to another can be a profound human experience' (p.146). Utilizing Harwood's system for evaluating group members, one might have placed Jeff first in a gay group and later in a heterogeneous analytic group. The assumption would be that after an initial experience of twinship based on similarities the patient would be ready for a more mature experience of twinship in a group where expectations of empathy from people of varied backgrounds and different experiences form the bond.

Archaic twinship has been perceived as more akin to a merger phenomenon (Kohut 1984): 'The more archaic the twinship transference, the more it approaches the merger transference' (Lee and Martin 1991, p.156). It may be that we are not only dealing with archaic versus mature twinship, but also with superficial and more developed expectancies. Therefore, the more developed, mature individual will have expectancies of empathy and connectedness from other human beings, whatever their physical or experiential dissimilarities. It is the development of a capacity for empathy that may more readily determine readiness for a heterogeneous group. Kleinberg (1991) developed an empathy scale for use in determining a patient's readiness for analytic group therapy. Should one desire to use instruments to evaluate appropriate group placement, a combination of Kleinberg's and Harwood's scales may be valuable.

Detrick (1985) believes that Kohut's ideas regarding alterego phenomena will gain their greatest significance when related to group dynamics and the process of group therapy. He proposes that the motivational core of the group is the experience of similarity among the group members. It is a function of the group process as it is directed by the ambitions or ideals of the therapist. Thus, the alterego experience is essential to group cohesion and the boundary of the group. The alterego experience is primary in the relationship among group members. Thus, for Detrick, the cure process in group therapy '... involves the acquisition of skills in the context of an interpretation that evokes an experience of twinship' (1986, p.302). He contrasts that with the cure process in individual treatment which involves working through the mirroring and/or idealizing developmental needs that were functionally impaired. It may be that twinship, as it is involved in empathy, forms the background in which individual therapy can succeed. With some patients it may be a central focus, as it was with the patient who led Kohut to elevate twinship to an independent selfobject function.

This awareness of twinship as basic to the group experience sheds a new light upon what has been traditionally perceived as resistance in group. At the beginning of a group session, group members may be making small talk that does not seem to have therapeutic value. It would traditionally have been viewed as resistance to the analytic work of the group. With an understanding of the importance of twinship, such 'small talk' may be viewed as an attempt to find the similarities needed for the therapeutic work.

Pairing and subgrouping have also been considered as common group resistances. Such phenomena are supposed to be the patients' attempts to avoid exposure to the group's analytic work. It was seen as: 'I'll help you avoid looking at yourself, if you help me avoid looking at myself.' The concept of twinship provides a different, growth-promoting view of these processes. Pairing and subgrouping may be attempts to find similarity and connectedness with particular individuals in the group. In fact, Morrison (1990) notes the similarity of Bion's (1959) description of pairing in group to the twinship selfobject experience. Let me offer another clinical vignette:

> Dan, a 34 year old, male, group member began giving advice to Roy, a 45-year-old group member. Dan was imploring Roy to forget the friends whom he was trying to convince of the rightness of his cause. Roy had been involved in a law suit with his ex-girlfriend over property they jointly owned. This woman had convinced their mutual friends that Roy was taking unfair advantage of her.
>
> At first glance, Dan's behavior seemed to be superficial and in resistance. Dan knew that advice giving was not the best means of working in group. However, I perceived him to be reacting out of an experience of archaic twinship. His efforts to communicate with Roy were attempts to demonstrate that they had endured experiences that were so similar they were all but identical. Thus, Dan was warning Roy to avoid the same pitfalls that he had experienced.
>
> Ten years ago Dan had been ostracized by his family and friends as a result of revelations that he and his sister were both abusing drugs. Dan's family and friends blamed him for involving his sister in their mutual drug activity. While Dan's sister had been a willing accomplice, the family chose to blame Dan for this situation. It seems that Dan's family needed to create a myth of the sister's victimization to protect her custody rights to her one-year-old child. Dan and his sister shared the same social group. This group accepted the family myth and shunned him.
>
> It seems that Dan's advice-giving behavior resulted from an archaic twinship identification with Roy's experience and an understanding of the pain that Roy was experiencing and was yet to experience. Once this interpretation was made to Dan, he understood and was able to share the feelings that Roy's material triggered. For the first time, Dan's attention was directed to the intensity of the loss of his friends rather than his previously held belief that it was isolation from family alone that troubled him so. This understanding helped Dan move from an archaic twinship experience whereby he viewed Roy's past experience and future outcome as exactly the same as his own. He was then able to maintain a twinship connection without the experience of identity he had previously felt. Roy's experience was now viewed by Dan as basically similar, but with differences. It is this awareness of differences that makes the twinship experience more mature.

From an intersubjective perspective, Roy's experience of Dan's advice giving also had to be explored. While Dan felt he was trying to be there for Roy, to save Roy's future as he wished someone had been there to save his, Roy believed he was being criticized for not 'putting this experience behind him'. While Roy and Dan were interacting, the other group members as well as the therapist were each reacting out of the organization of their own experience to the interaction itself as well as the content – isolation and rejection.

In the example above, twinship was demonstrated by Dan's attempt to find a basic human attachment based on a similarity of pain. However, the leader's involvement was necessary for the connection to be established. Gorney (1995) believes that the analyst's participation is crucial to the twinship process in individual treatment. He believes that all efforts at the outset of the therapeutic relationship are to forge elemental human connections. In this context, twinship is the experience of barriers breaking down and the formation of human attachments. This may be extended in group therapy to the breaking down of barriers between group members.

In summary, group therapy provides many opportunities for intersubjective exploration and to move patients from archaic to mature twinship experiences. Twinship provides for the bonds that exist in group. Intersubjectivity, on the other hand, provides the perspective from which to explore those bonds. The twinship or alterego experience is the foundation of cohesiveness in group therapy and may be more basic to the human condition than the other selfobject experiences. Cultural developments may have impeded the gratification of the twinship need, but group therapy may provide the solution to meeting this need. 'Despite our individual differences, we are born, we love, we work, and we die, amongst our kin, those fellow humans thrown in the world alongside us, accompanying us on our shared journey' (Gorney 1995).

References

Basch, M.F. (1988) *Understanding Psychotherapy: The Science Behind the Art.* New York: Basic Books Inc.

Basch, M.F. (1989) 'A comparison of Freud and Kohut: Apostasy or synergy?' In *Self Psychology Comparisons and Contrasts.* In D.W. Detrick and S.P. Detrick (eds). Hillsdale, NJ: Analytic Press.

Basch, M.F. (1995) *Doing Brief Psychotherapy.* New York: Basic Books.

Beebe, B. and Lachmann, F. (1988) 'Mother–infant mutual influence and precursors of psychic structure.' In A. Goldberg (ed) *Frontiers in Self Psychology: Progress in Self Psychology,* Vol.3. Hillsdale, NJ: Analytic Press.

Bion, W. (1959) *Experiences in Groups.* New York: Basic Books.

Detrick, D.W. (1985) 'Alterego phenomena and the alterego transferences.' In A. Goldberg (ed) *Progress in Self Psychology,* Vol.I. New York: Guilford Press.

Detrick, D.W. (1986) 'Alterego phenomena and the alterego transferences: some further considerations.' In A. Goldberg (ed) *Progress in Self Psychology*, Vol.2. New York: Guilford Press.

Gedo, J.E. (1989) 'Self psychology: A post-Kohution view.' In D. Detrick and S. Detrick (eds) *Self Psychology: Comparisons and Contrasts*. Hillsdale, NJ: Analytic Press.

Gehrie, M.J. (1980) 'The self and the group: A tentative exploration in applied psychology.' In G. Golderg (ed) *Advances In Self Psychology*. New York: International Universities Press.

Gorney, J. (1995) 'The origins of pleasure: The role of the twinship experience.' Audiotaped presentation at Association for Psychoanalytic Self Psychology. March 25, 1995.

Harwood, I. (1995) 'Towards optimum group placement from the perspective of the self or self-experience.' *Group 19*, 3, 140–162.

Kleinberg, J.L. (1991) 'Teaching beginning group therapist to incorporate a patient's empathic capacity in treatment planning.' *Group 15*, 3, 141–154.

Kohut, H. (1984) *How Does Analysis Cure?* In A. Goldberg (ed) with P. Stepansky. Chicago, London: University of Chicago Press.

Lee, R.R. and Martin, J.C. (1991) *Psychotherapy after Kohut: A Textbook of Self Psychology*. Hillsdale, NJ: Analytic Press.

Lichtenberg, J.D., Lachmann, F.M. and Fosshage, J.L. (1992) *Self and Motivational Systems*. Hillsdale, NJ: Analytic Press.

Lorenz, K. (1996) *On Aggression*. New York: Bantam.

Morrison, A.P. (1990) 'Secrets: A self psychological view of shame in group therapy.' In B.E. Roth, W.N. Stone and H.D. Kibel *The Difficult Patient in Group: Group Psychotherapy with Borderline and Narcissistic Disorders*. Madison, CT.: International Universities Press.

Rutan, J.S. and Stone, W.N. (1984) *Psychodynamic Group Therapy*. Lexington, MA: D.C. Heath and Company.

Shapiro, E. (1990) 'Self psychology, intersubjectivity and group psychotherapy.' *Group 14*, 3, 177–182.

Stern, D.N. (1985) *The Interpersonal World of the Infant*. New York: Basic Books, Inc.

Stolorow, R.D. (1994a) 'Subjectivity and self psychology.' In R.D. Stolorow, G.E. Atwood and B. Brandchaft (eds) *The Intersubjective Perspective*. Northvale, NJ: Analytic Press.

Stolorow, R.D. (1994b) 'Connecting psychotherapy to psychoanalysis.' In R.D. Stolorow, G.E. Atwood and B. Brandchaft (eds) *The Intersubjective Perspective*. Northvale, NJ: Analytic Press.

Stolorow, R.D. and Atwood, G.E. (1992) *Contexts of Being: The Intersubjective Foundations of Psychological Life*. Hillsdale, NJ: Analytic Press.

Stolorow, R.D., Atwood, G.E. and Brandchaft, B. (1994) *The Intersubjective Perspective*. Northvale, NJ: Jason Aronson Inc.

Trop, J.L. (1994) 'Self psychology and Intersubjectivity theory.' In R.D. Stolorow, G.E. Atwood and B. Brandschaft (eds) *The Intersubjective Perspective*. Northvale, NJ: Analytic Press.

Wolf, E.S. (1988) *Treating the Self*. New York: Guilford.

Yalom, I.D. (1975) *The Theory and Practice of Group Psychotherapy*. New York: Basic Books.

CHAPTER 5

Harvest of Fire

Archaic Twinship and Fundamental Conflict Within a Community and in Group Therapy

Martin S. Livingston

'Harvest of Fire', a Hallmark Hall of Fame production for television (21 April 1996), begins with a series of barn burnings in an Amish community. The barn is the 'heart of a farm' and the arson endangers human life as well as livestock. The outbreak of fire is a serious threat to the economic and emotional survival of the community. The symbolism of destructive rage out of control, a product of breakdown and fragmentation (Kohut 1971), is quite striking. The mystery to be investigated is who and what process is responsible.

The Amish refer to themselves as the 'plain' people. They dress and live simply and quietly in a manner that emphasizes sameness and eschews the expression of uniqueness. Their community is a very cohesive group that provides a sense of sameness of values and behavior. In his last book, Kohut (1984) elevated this need for a sense of sameness or humanness from an aspect of the need for mirroring to a distinct and equally essential selfobject need. Twinship, as he referred to the need for these experiences of basic alikeness, was now considered to have a developmental line of its own. He described it as ranging from the archaic selfobject needs that are the normal requirement early in life and are reactivated at times of severe stress or disturbance to the more mature forms that all of us need from birth to death. Examples of these experiences in childhood are abundant. Kohut describes a little girl kneading dough in the kitchen as her grandmother baked and a little boy working next to his father with his own set of play tools. Examples of twinship in later life are also easily found in two concert lovers sitting quietly together and listening or two writers sharing their thoughts in a mutually stimulating discussion. Kohut found the archaic precursors of these experiences harder to put in such clearly defined terms. He points to the 'mere presence of people in a child's surroundings – their voices and body odors, the emotions they express, the noises they produce as they engage in human activities, the specific aroma of the foods they prepare and eat – creates a security in the child, a sense of belonging and participating…these feelings derive from confirmation of the feeling that one is a human being among other human beings' (Kohut 1984, p.200). The specific features of these early experiences vary from one group to another. However, any threat to whatever features these early impressions have for a particular individual (or a group) becomes a threat to their core sense of self – to their basic sense of humanness.

Kohut felt that the task of examining this developmental line was still largely incomplete. However, twinship experiences were postulated as necessary for the vitalization and maintenance of a cohesive self. They are thus just as important as the much more familiar needs for mirroring responsiveness and the presence of an idealizable selfobject that is able to provide safety and comfort. One of the purposes of this chapter is to begin to examine the effect of twinship needs within a group process as they vary from more mature to archaic forms.

The primary intent of this chapter is to use 'Harvest of Fire' as a springboard to discuss the importance of twinship needs in group therapy. Particular emphasis will be placed on the usefulness of this concept in relationship to empathy and countertransference. Following that we will return to the story as an analogy depicting a pitfall of overemphasizing twinship needs, particularly when they are experienced in an archaic form. The understanding of twinship as a basic selfobject need and a source of cohesion, similar to Yalom's (1975) concept of universality, is only one aspect of a group process. This understanding must be balanced with an awareness of the frequent presence of conflict between inherent needs for self expression and delineation on the one hand, and an underlying conviction (based on childhood experience) that attachment requires the renunciation of these basic needs on the other hand. In other words, this conflict, which Stolorow, Brandchaft and Atwood (1987) refer to as a 'fundamental conflict', is 'the product of an unconscious organizing principle according to which self delineation and attachment preclude one another' (Stolorow, personal communication). As mentioned above, we will explore this danger more fully after the following discussion of how much the concept of twinship adds to an understanding of group process.

Intersubjective and self psychological concepts lend themselves very readily to psychoanalytic group psychotherapy. This is especially true of Kohut's examination of twinship needs. It is thus noteworthy that self psychologists have not been eager to work with groups or to write about group process. *Progress in Self Psychology* did not include a single article on this topic in its first ten volumes. Perhaps it is because self psychologists find it easier to provide an empathic ambience and a sense of safety without the intrusion of multiple subjectivities. The orderly working through of selfobject transferences is much clearer in the dyadic setting of individual analysis. Perhaps it is related to Kohut's never having worked with therapy groups. In the one paper he wrote that touches upon group psychology (Kohut 1978) he acknowledged that: 'a firm group self supports the productivity of the group just as a firm individual self supports the productivity of the individual' (p.799). He also expressed a concern that: 'group pressure diminishes individuality; it leads to a primitivation of the mental process' (p.834). Arensberg (1994) relates that Kohut also expressed caution about the possibility that the charisma of the leader might interfere with self development in group patients. However, a number of self psychology articles have appeared in the group therapy literature and several of these stress the importance of twinship.

Shapiro (1996) proposes that twinship is 'the foundation of group cohesiveness in group therapy.' He asserts that this phenomenon is more important to human development than the need for either mirroring or idealizing and that it is basic to any group process. He illustrates the importance of twinship in reducing feelings of shame related to a person's perception that their negative and needy feelings are atypical and isolating. He also demonstrates how an understanding of twinship needs can in some situations provide a growth-promoting view of a patient's behavior as an alternative to considering it resistance.

I would like to draw out the usefulness of an understanding of twinship transferences in relationship to empathy and countertransference. Kohut (1984) was very clear that self psychology did not discover empathy. Also, self psychologists do not achieve a cure through a novel kind of empathy. A new concept (in this case twinship) simply allows the analyst to be empathic with deeper or different aspects of the patient's inner experience. Shapiro provides a good example of this process. He illustrates how what might have been seen as a 'resistance' can also be seen, in a more experience-near manner, as the expression of a need for twinship experience. Thus a change in our theory can allow the group leader to remain more empathic rather than responding from an experience-distant position that could lead to a countertransference-based confrontation.

The following is a further example of how a transference–countertransference disruption can sometimes be reduced through the use of this concept. Larry, an older member of a psychoanalytic group, had been judgmental and often contemptuous of the other group members. He resented their lack of appreciation of his more experienced understanding of the interactions in the group. After all, he argued, 'I am more grown up than anyone else in the group. Also, I have been a patient in several groups and I have acquired a great deal of experience with what goes on in a group.' In his previous group experiences he felt more valued and seemed to be trying to force an affirmation of his importance and his value upon an uncooperative group. I understood Larry's discomfort in the group as an expression of his need for mirroring of his specialness and value on a fairly archaic level. I tried to approach his demands on the group from an empathic position, reflecting gently that his judgements and anger at the group were understandable since they failed to appreciate his contribution to the group. Even though I saw myself as responding empathically, Larry felt repeatedly misunderstood and angry with me. He usually experienced me as siding with the other group members and failing to see his needs or their repeated rejection of him. He became angry at me for encouraging him to stay in this group. When we explored the experience he was having in the present group, what unfolded was that he felt different from all the other members. He was older and more experienced. They were not at all like him. Finally, I caught on and reflected on how awful it feels to be different and not to have people in the group who feel the way he does because (in his subjectivity) they have had such different experiences. He softened completely, talked about other times he had wished for friends who were like him, and went on to find his niche in the group. It is noteworthy that it was not necessary to provide a concrete twinship experience. What was essential was that I understand the needs that were not being met. He then began to relate to ways in which some of the members had similar human issues rather than focusing on the age difference and their lack of group experience. Many of them had also felt deprived by not having anyone in their family who felt enough like them to provide a sense of humanness and belonging. Working through proceeded.

Another countertransference experience was a feeling that I had of a young woman repeatedly competing with me. She frequently seemed to be avoiding the role of patient by giving advice or interpretations to the other patients. I misinterpreted her frequent discomfort with me as a defence against an idealizing transference. She described her father as repeatedly critical. This made it very tough to get close to him. Any attempt to relate her many achievements to him seemed to be received without excitement and often belittled. She saw me as never allowing her to be big and only feeling close to her when she was in need. I found myself irritated and often wanting to contradict her advice and interpretations to other group members. I contained these feelings as best as I could. Then I proceeded to suggest that she explore her need to avoid being more vulnerable in the group and her need to treat me as unimportant. She was upset that I did not know how important I was to her and how much she wanted to be closer. The impasse broke one day when I felt particularly put down by one of her subtle rejections and got angry. After a brief hot interchange I pulled back to regain my balance.

When she was upset by my silence I responded that I was trying to get a sense of the difficulty we were having together. I related that she seemed to be hitting some of my buttons and that I was having trouble understanding what it meant for me or what was happening between us. She was greatly relieved by my comment.

She was then able to express how scared she had been that we would never be able to get through the impasse. She expected that I would never consider that we were similar and both struggling. She anticipated that I would pull rank and insist that she was the crazy one; that I would insist on being idealized if she wanted to be closer to me; that, like her father, I would not accept her need to be like me in responding to the other group members; that I would never see her as a colleague, a fellow adult, who could be very much like me. In essence, what I understood as a defence against an idealizing transference, or an attempt to resist being a patient in the group, was actually her attempt to engage me in a twinship transference. Once I was able to reframe that for myself, I was much more able to understand her view of the last few months and to re-establish an empathic stance.

This is an example of conceptualization helping the analyst to self-right and to understand the patient and the intersubjective situation better. It also fits very well with Shapiro's use of Gorney's (1995) point that the analyst's participation is crucial to the twinship process in treatment. Twinship is the experience of barriers breaking down and the formation of human attachments. Shapiro points out that Gorney's concept may be extended in group therapy to the breaking down of barriers between group members. I would consider taking it a step further. As in this example, twinship may often also be an attempt at breaking down barriers between patient and therapist (barriers to the sharing of vulnerability and vulnerable moments; see Livingston 1975).

At this point, having established my agreement that Kohut's concept of twinship adds a great deal to the understanding of group process and its application to group psychotherapy, I would like to return to the story with which we began our discussion. Sally, an FBI agent working in the 'hate crimes division', is dispatched to investigate the barn burnings. Her department has been involved because of the likelihood that the fires have been set by someone whose intent is to persecute a group of people who seem quite different. She enters the Amish community as a therapist might enter an ongoing group. She is well intentioned and perceptive, but she is an 'English,' an outsider, and thus not readily trusted. She has a lot to learn; not only about the crimes, but about the group and its organizing principles. She starts out asking questions about who the Amish think might be their enemies and finds that they do not organize their subjective world with such concepts. They grieve for their loss, forgive whoever is responsible, and begin to rebuild. Sally shifts from direct questioning to immersing herself in the community and learning their ways. Apparently, their plain and simple ways are a strong bond among them. They are a very cohesive group and all rally to help the victims of the fires as they have always supported each other. They are very sensitive to their children who in turn express intense loyalty. Their sense of alikeness and community clearly fulfills a need for twinship and belonging. They seem very secure in their identity and in their beliefs. Surely no one among them could have set the fires. They are not a violent or aggressive people.

Sally's first suspects are a group of adolescent boys from a neighboring town. They hang around a local pool hall making hostile remarks about the farm people and are quite nasty and disrespectful to Sally when she questions them. It turns out that they are angry at some of the attention that one of their girl friends has been paying to an Amish boy. They end up in jail on a minor charge and, while they are locked up, yet another barn is burned.

Another suspect is a real estate salesman who seems very eager to take advantage of the situation by offering to 'help' the victims of the arson by buying some of their land at distress prices. Sally proceeds with her empathic immersion by spending more and more time in the Amish community and joining them in some of their toils. She begins to earn their trust. She saves the deacon's granddaughter from a burning barn and is increasingly in tune, especially with one mother, whose name is Sarah. She and Sarah learn from each other, go through a few empathic rupture and repair sequences, and become close friends. She observes Sarah's daughter meeting briefly and secretly with a boy and is told that Sarah has prohibited her from seeing him although he seems like a fine young man. She also learns that Sarah is afraid that the elders may disapprove of the friendship that has developed between the two women. It seems that if the elders disapprove and Sarah defies them she will be 'shunned' by the whole community. If anyone's behaviour is different from the code set out by the elders everyone will refuse to have anything to do with them. Even their children must refuse to eat at their table.

Suddenly the twinship experiences that seem to lead to such stability and cohesion are completely withdrawn. What is happening is that the group as a whole has twinship demands that, under threat, have become archaic. Any individual's need for self delineation threatens the group's need for basic alikeness. The demand for sameness is an attempt to maintain a precarious sense of safety and belonging. When these archaic demands are not met the whole community organization is threatened. The 'shunning' in response to such a threat is subjectively quite reasonable to the group as a whole. Clearly, though, if we empathize with the object of these measures they seem quite drastic. To the individual being shunned it must feel like a horrible selfobject failure and abandonment. Sally inquires further: 'Is there anyone being shunned right now?' 'Yes,' Sarah replies matter of factly, 'there is a man being shunned at present.' Sally senses that she is not to inquire any further but, of course, investigates on her own. She gets the man to talk to her after much difficulty. He seems quite pious and thoughtful. It is hard to imagine him doing anything to warrant the shunning or setting the fires. He is also clearly resentful and sullen as a result of his experiences. He explains that he built his barn with a curved roof to 'let in more of the Lord's light for the creatures in his care.' Everyone builds their barn with a straight roof and the elders disapproved of his defiance of their way. It eventually becomes clear that the young man whom Sarah forbid her daughter to see is the son of this man. When Sally asks Sarah if that is why she would not allow her daughter to be involved with him Sarah replies, again matter of factly, that the boy had 'refused to observe the shunning. Matthew had defied the elders and continued to eat at his father's table.' It is not too hard to imagine the conflict in which young Matthew found himself. His inner core, everything that made him feel whole and himself, clung loyally to his bond with his father. Even in the face of the archaic demands of the elders he could not betray this inner imperative. He wanted desperately to be connected to them and to be part of the community. He wanted to be like them and to be accepted, but the price of betraying the bond with his father was intolerable. In addition, the one person who might empathize with his plight, the girl who had been so responsive to his feelings, was torn away from him by the same code.

It is no longer a mystery who set the fires and what process led to his fragmentation and subsequent rage. Matthew's conflict centers around a severe threat to his sense of self-cohesion. His dilemma is that he is torn between conflicting attachments, each of which serves to organize his sense of identity. Lang (1984) describes an internalized and automatic judgment that is triggered when an individual is tempted to act in opposition to deeply ingrained ways of being. This judgement is a 'loud "that's NOT ME!" and [represents] an absolute, unchallengeable signal to desist and submit.' Matthew is besieged by not one, but two opposing imperatives. The result is fragmentation and raging fires. The analogy provides a clear warning to group leaders that conflicting twinship and self-delineation needs must be understood and interpreted in order to avoid such a harvest.

It is interesting to note that once Matthew confesses, with Sally's help, he is forgiven and the whole community rallies to support him in his ordeal of now facing criminal charges. In some way, again with Sally's empathic responsiveness, the community has begun to heal. Their solidarity and support, in the end, for one of their own were quite touching. However, I could not help wishing that the elders had been able to balance their archaic need for alikeness and twinship with an awareness of the fundamental conflict it set in motion. I could not help wishing that a 'harvest of fire' could have been avoided.

Perhaps it is grandiose to think of effecting any change in a whole subculture. However, when it comes to a psychotherapy group we have a much better opportunity. Stolorow et al. (1987) suggest a concept that, if kept in mind, can serve as a balance to the quite valuable stress on twinship needs in a group. Within a setting of individual treatment they point out that a fundamental conflict is often re-experienced within the intersubjective situation of transference and countertransference. They 'contend that derailment of the self-delineation process occurs in an intersubjective situation in which central affect states associated with the development of individualized selfhood are consistently not responded to or are actively rejected. A fundamental psychic conflict thereby becomes enduringly established between the requirement that one's developmental course must conform to the emotional needs of caregivers and the inner imperative that its evolution be firmly rooted in a vitalizing affective core of one's own' (p.52). In other words, some patients have a history of submerging their own affective strivings and individuality in order to maintain indispensable ties. This leads to submission and depression on the one hand or to fragmentation and rage on the other.

This balance is even more important in a group than it is in individual treatment because of several possibilities that can magnify the danger. First, there is the possibility that the therapist's valuing of mature twinship bonds can be experienced (by patients) as a demand. Group members might then strive to suppress their own needs to express self-delineation in order to please the leader. Members can experience a leader's attempt to provide safety for a patient to mean that they too must keep the selfobject surround safe by maintaining an empathic stance. They may not feel free to express any different affect or thought of their own.

A good example of this often occurs when a new member is introduced. Older members may be upset by the intrusion of an unwanted sibling or unhappy that the new arrival is a girl or is not as attractive as they had fantasized. On the one hand they may feel that they are expected to help the newcomer to feel welcome. At the same time their negative, previously disowned, affect needs to be expressed and legitimatized. Their need for a mirroring responsiveness is in danger of being suppressed once again in order to feel (or to be seen as) like the leader and other group members. In other words, there may be a conflict between their need for self-delineation and their need to maintain a twinship experience through sharing the group's value of welcoming new members. This may be experienced as an internal conflict between their own momentarily opposed selfobject needs (mirroring and twinship for example). It also may be experienced as a more fundamental conflict between their need to follow an inner imperative and their fear of disturbing the other members and the leader by not fulfilling their twinship needs.

Even more potentially troublesome is the possibility of a group process where not just individual members but the group as a whole demands alikeness and threatens to punish expressions of difference. The danger here is that group process tends towards regression if the group acts as a whole without individual responsibility. The result is that when a group, as in our analogy, establishes values and mores, twinship needs may take on a more archaic form. This is particularly true when the cohesiveness of the group is insecure and easily threatened. The greater the experienced danger of fragmentation is, the more archaic the need for selfobject support becomes. A danger exists in a leaderless group or in a group in which the leader fails to validate an individual's need for self-delineation. If the group does not value self-delineation then, as it does in the story, archaic demands for twinship can take the form of scapegoating or 'shunning' to enforce alikeness and thus to reassure the group of its continuance.

An even further complication the group situation adds to the conflict involved is the possibility that some individuals may develop a repetitive transference to the group as a whole. In other words, while the selfobject dimension of a patient's transferential experience stirs longings for a new experience that will enable him to resume and complete an arrested developmental process, there is a second dimension. In what Stolorow *et al.* (1987) refer to as the repetitive dimension of the transference the patient expects and fears a repetition of the original experiences of selfobject failure. At times even a mild expression of the group's need for alikeness can bring this repetitive dimension of the transference into the foreground of a patient's subjective experience. The mild demand for alikeness can then trigger a whole pattern of feelings and attitudes related to the patient's experience in his or her original family. If, as a young child, the patient experienced his or her parent's demands as archaic and overwhelming, then an early infantile terror may be reactivated.

For example, Tammy, an attractive young woman who saw herself as overweight, was afraid to talk about her struggles with food in the group. She experienced the other women in the group as all having serious eating disorders that were never mentioned. She believed that they were all accepting of their bodies as they were and had no need to explore issues around eating. She tried to express her dislike of her own body. However, each time she timidly broached the subject, she experienced one of the other women as scowling disapprovingly. For weeks she brought this into individual sessions where we explored the repetitive aspect of her beliefs. Her mother was severely depressed and had totally neglected her body. Any time Tammy showed any interest in the outside world, especially a sexual interest, mother felt abandoned and responded abusively, assaulting her both physically and verbally. The verbal abuse essentially communicated that Tammy was not at all like her and was no longer welcome in the house. The message was essentially: 'be depressed like me and don't make any attempt to be attractive because that will make you different and disgusting.' Tammy was understandably afraid to express her struggle to lose weight and to be attractive. She experienced the group as full of potentially abusive mothers who demanded that she remain unconcerned about her body in order to maintain an alikeness with them.

As often happens in situations like this, when Tammy eventually ventured to talk in the group about her fears she brought them up as accusations with a condescending tone. Her contempt was an attempt to protect herself from the abuse she anticipated. She spoke from a subtle position of superiority. She saw herself as younger and more attractive than the others and as more willing to face her eating problems without the massive denial she saw in her mother. These attitudes were picked up and reacted to by other group members. If left unanalyzed, intersubjective clashes like this one can produce a 'harvest of fire' of their own. In the present group, the subjective meaning that the experience had for each member was explored. The working through of the intersubjective relationships involved led to an understanding of how early patterns of organization had been triggered for Tammy, as well as for each of the other members, and to a clarification of the fundamental conflicts involved. The therapist's awareness of both concepts (twinship and fundamental conflict) permitted a balanced working through process to proceed and helped to resolve an explosive situation.

Still another pitfall is the possibility that in becoming excited about providing an experience of much needed twinship, a leader might unknowingly relinquish some of his position as an idealizeable object and interpreter of transference and intersubjectivity. This parallels the manner in which some parents become pals when the child needs an authority figure.

Essentially, what a group leader needs to be alert to is that some patients have a history of submerging their own affective strivings and individuality to maintain indispensable ties. In a group, a danger exists if sameness is overvalued. Some members will sacrifice their needs for affirmation and self-delineation to maintain their ties to the group and the leader. The key to working with these dynamics in a group is no different at its core from the way it would be in an intensive psychoanalysis. It is simply more complicated because of the multiple subjectivities and intersubjective interactions involved.

The essence of psychoanalytic process in group therapy is the understanding and working through of all the multiple transferences as they unfold. Repeatedly, experience teaches us that our primary role in the curative process is the understanding through empathic immersion and eventually the explaining of the selfobject and the repetitive, resistive and conflictual dimensions of the transference. A certain amount of provision of selfobject experience, be it mirroring, idealizing or twinship, furthers the process and provides the foundation of trust that allows interpretation to progress from understanding to explaining and to structure-building. However, to get too caught up in the provision of any need may interfere with being alert to a balancing need. The collision of needs for both twinship and for self-delineation in a therapy group often recreates a fundamental conflict. The patient's experience is at times similar to the one described by an old talmudic quotation: 'If I am not for myself, who will be? If I am only for myself, what am I? If not now, when?'

Before I close I would like to raise some other questions in the hope that they will stimulate further clinical and theoretical investigation. If the group leader promotes safety and twinship, does he also homogenize the group to the detriment of some of the individual members? How do these dangers apply to the creation of homogeneous therapy groups or self help and other groups that are formed on the basis of common symptoms or other characteristics? Patients are sometimes encouraged to be empathic towards each other. Could this retraumatize individuals who were raised to satisfy the selfobject needs of the other members of their family and to submerge their own? In analysis, especially in groups, answers are never simple.

Summary

This chapter began by highlighting the importance of understanding and appreciating the patient's twinship demands. These demands are growth-promoting attempts to fulfill phase appropriate legitimate needs that have been thwarted in childhood. They represent a hope for a 'new beginning'. Using a story about barn burnings in an Amish community as an analogy, the chapter illustrated the role of twinship experiences in the development of cohesion and vitality in both individuals and in groups. It then went on to use the same story as an analogy of how these needs can take an archaic form. When they run out of control, especially in a group, the results may be a 'Harvest of Fire'. 'Fundamental conflict' (Stolorow et al. 1987) is suggested as a counterbalancing concept. An understanding of how these concepts complement each other raises new challenges as well as hopes. This is especially true in regard to such concepts as optimal frustration (Kohut 1971), optimal responsiveness (Bacal 1985), optimal restraint (Shane and Shane 1994), optimal group composition (Harwood 1995), and optimal provision (Lindon 1994), as well as my ideas about closeness and distance in psychotherapy (Livingston 1992).

References

Arensberg, F. (1994) 'A discussion of Kohut's Berkeley address.' Presented to the Association for Psychoanalytic Self Psychology. New York.

Bacal, H. (1985) 'Optimal responsiveness and the therapeutic process.' In A. Goldberg (ed) *Progress in Self Psychology*, Vol.1. New York: Guilford.

Gorney, J. (1995) The origins of pleasure: The role of the twinship experience. Presented to the Association for Psychoanalytic Self Psychology. New York.

Harwood, I. (1995) 'Toward optimum group placement from the perspective of the self or self experience.' *Group 19*, 3, fall, 140–162.

Kohut, H. (1971) *The Analysis of the Self.* New York: International Univ. Press.

Kohut, H. (1978) 'Creativeness, charisma, group psychology: Reflections on the self-analysis of Freud.' (1976) in P. Ornstein (ed) *The Search for the Self*, V.2. Madison Ct: International Univ. Press.

Kohut, H. (1984) *How Does Analysis Cure?* Chicago: University of Chicago Press.

Lang, J. (1984) 'Notes toward a psychology of the feminine self.' In P. Stepansky and A. Goldberg (eds) *Kohut's Legacy: Contributions to Self Psychology*. Hillsdale, N.J.: Analytic Press.

Lindon, J. (1994) 'Gratification and provision in psychoanalysis: Should we get rid of "the rule of abstinence?"' *Psychoanal. Dial.*, 4, 549–582.

Livingston, M. (1975) 'On barriers, contempt and the concept of the "vulnerable moment."' In L. Wolberg and M. Aronson (eds) *Group Psychotherapy*. New York: Stratton.

Livingston, M. (1992) *Near and Far: Closeness and Distance in Psychotherapy*. New York: Rivercross.

Shane, E. and Shane, M. (1994) In pursuit of the optimal in optimal frustration, optimal responsiveness, and optimal provision. Presented at the 17th Annual Conference on the Psychology of the Self, Chicago.

Shapiro, E. (1996) The twinship and /or alterego experience in group Presented to the Alumni. Association of the Group Dept. Postgraduate Center for Mental Health. New York.

Stolorow, R., Brandchaft, B. and Atwood, G. (1987) *Psychoanalytic Treatment: An Intersubjective Approach*. Hillsdale, N.J.: Analytic Press.

Yalom, I. (1975) *The Theory and Practice of Group Psychotherapy*. New York, Chicago: Basic Books.

CHAPTER 6

How Does Group Psychotherapy Cure?

A Reconceptualization of the Group Process: From Self Psychology to the Intersubjective Perspective

Franco Paparo and Gianni Nebbiosi

Kohut, like most of his followers, had no direct experience of group psychotherapy, and his seminal contribution to the field of group dynamics was mainly interspersed and devoted to his experience of unstructured and structured social groups (as a member of both the American Psychoanalytic Association and the International Psychoanalytic Association) and to his interest and study of the historical process (see his paper 'Power' on German history and his interview to Charles Strozier; Kohut 1985).

Kohut's contribution to group psychology can be summarized as follows:

1. Group processes are largely activated by narcissistic motives (Kohut 1977).

2. Group cohesion is brought about and maintained not only by an ego ideal held in common by the members of the group (Freud 1921), but also by the shared subject bound grandiosity, i.e. by a shared grandiose self (Kohut 1971).

3. He suggests that: 'We point out the existence of a certain psychological configuration – let us call it the *group self* – which is analogous to the self of individuals' (Kohut 1977).

In a 1981 London presentation at the Group Analytic Society, Paparo demonstrated the remarkable convergence between the psychoanalytic psychology of the self (as it emerged from Kohut's work) and group analysis (as developed by Foulkes). Later, in a workshop on group process at the annual Self

Psychology Conference in Los Angeles (1983), Paparo further outlined the analogies and points of convergence in Kohut's and Foulkes' theories. These were:

1. The explicit use of empathy. Kohut's (1984, published posthumously) idea that: 'the skillful use of empathy can, via instruction and experience, be gradually improved, thus allowing the analyst to make increasingly correct, accurate and relevant observations about the inner life of the analysands.' In group analysis this may happen to each member *vis-à-vis* any other member and thus: 'we could define the entire course of a small analytic group as a *successful training in empathy* of its individual members (conductor included).'

2. The respect for the person and her/his resources in the psychotherapeutic environment.

3. The concept of 'the self–selfobject unit' in self psychology that parallels Foulkes'(1975) concept of the individual as a nodal point in a network of relationships. Paparo stressed the fact that both concepts lead to a conceptualization in which the observer's position is within the whole experiential unit.

4. The analogy between Foulkes' (1975) broad conceptualization of 'ego training in action', which is consistent with the main therapeutic process in group analysis, and Kohut's therapeutic process in individual psychotherapy which Paparo (1984) called 'self restoration in action' (paraphrasing Foulkes).

In summary, Paparo (1984) theorized about the common occurrence of the selfobject transferences observed in individual psychotherapy and in successfully conducted group-analyses. The group conductor catalyzes and maintains an atmosphere that allows the mobilization and working through of the selfobject needs identified by Kohut. The different selfobject functions can be performed for each single member by the group-as-a-whole, by the conductor, or by any other member of the group. He supported Howard Bacal's (1985) idea:

> Patients in group therapy will have less difficulty in establishing the selfobject relation they require since, in the group, the opportunity for selfobject relations with various group members can modulate the effect of conflicting selfobject needs.

Paparo (1984) concluded that:

> The self object transferences thus mobilized could be followed by optimal – that is not traumatic – frustration, leading in turn, through transmuting internalization, to the gradual building of lacking or inadequate psychic structures in individual patients.

Paparo (1984) thus assumed that the same process outlined by Kohut (1977), Wolf (1988), and by Kohut's (1984) posthumous book *How Does Analysis Cure?* also occurred in a properly conducted psychoanalytic group.

Paparo (1987), in his further clinical experience in group psychotherapy, used the main tenets of self psychology as an orienting frame of reference with the conductor as a compass. While observing in the group both the mobilization of selfobject needs and the occurrence of selfobject transferences, he started to see the same repeated cycles of disruption–restoration in individual analysis. These cycles did not appear as relevant as in the dual setting. Thus, Paparo began to doubt the importance of optimal frustration and transmuting internalization as the main therapeutic factors in the group therapeutic process.

Paparo began to agree with Terman's (1988) and Stolorow's (1986) questioning of optimal frustration in individual analysis. Stolorow's and his collaborators' concepts of the two dimensions of transference ('selfobject' and 'repetitive'), 'organizing principles', 'intersubjective field', and 'sustained empathic inquiry' provided new tools for the study of the group psychotherapy process.

Reconceptualization of transference in the group

Above all, the new intersubjective reformulation of selfobject functions and transference seemed to provide a satisfactory answer to our clinical experience, as well as the theoretical riddle about empathy and empathy disruption. According to these reformulations:

1. *The selfobject functions* 'pertain fundamentally to the integration of affect into the organization of self-experience and…the need of selfobject ties pertains most centrally to the need for attuned responsiveness to affect states in all stages of the life cycle' (Stolorow, Brandchaft and Atwood 1987, p.66).

This definition applies well to the dynamic reality of the group. It is our conviction, in fact (Paparo 1987; Nebbiosi 1995a; 1995b), that one of the most powerful experiences is the intensity with which the group regulates (or fails to regulate) the affect states of its members. There are new conceptualizations about the meaning and functions of *affiliation*. Lichtenberg (1989), describing the affiliative motivational system, equated the power of affect regulations in group to those accomplished by the attachment ties:

> The experience of pleasure in intimacy that begins with mother, father, or both at some point has as its corollary a pleasure in intimacy with the family. Modes of communication with and about family, especially defined in the presence of nonfamily, provide for the prelatency child the basis of a positive sense of intimacy in the group as compared with the individual. The difference between attachment and affiliation is in the composition of the unit – not in the affective

experience sought. And the affective experience sought is the positive sense of sharing and gaining and growing. (p.118)

In this chapter we will use the concepts of selfobject and selfobject functions in the group in the specific sense mentioned above. More specifically, we will take into consideration the selfobject functions that can be accomplished by the group-as-a-whole, the group analyst, and by a group member (or by a subgroup). *Selfobject functions in the group deal specifically with the intense and consistent regulation of affect states and they must be clearly separated from simple positive, caring functions..*

2. *The transference* is not considered either as a regression, a displacement, a distortion, or a projection, but as an *organizing activity* of the patient's experience in the analytic situation (co-determined by both the patient *and the analyst*). Even more important is the reformulation of the transference experience not as a:

> manifestation of a biologically rooted compulsion to repeat the past…[but as an] organizing activity [that] focuses more narrowly on the specific patterning of the experience within the analytic relationship to which both patient and analyst contribute. (Stolorow *et al.* 1987, p.37)

This reformulation allows the group analyst to focus more clearly on the contribution of all the members (including himself) as to the emergence of the organizing principles that characterize the dimension of the group-as-a-whole (see Conclusions). The understanding and the analysis of these 'group organizing principles', promoted first by the analyst and then by all the group members, may be considered one of the main goals of the analytic work. According to Foulkes (1975), this work is done not *in* the group, but *by the group.*

The two dimensions of transference in the group

According to the intersubjective perspective, the transference dimension shifts between *selfobject* transference and *repetitive* transference in the following way:

> …when the analyst is experienced as malattuned, foreshadowing a traumatic repetition of early developmental failure, the conflictual and resistive dimension is brought into the foreground, and the patient's selfobject longings are driven into hiding. On the other hand when the analyst is able to analyze accurately the patient experience of rupture of the therapeutic bond and demonstrate his understanding of the patient reactive affect states and the principles that organize them, the selfobject dimension becomes restored and strengthened and the conflictual/resistive/repetitive dimension tends to recede into the background. (Stolorow and Atwood 1992, p.25).

This description seems to fit particularly well with the complex transference dimension of the group that, in our view, is characterized by the fact that *repetitive and selfobject transferences occur simultaneously.* By this we mean that while a member can experience a repetitive transference (to the analyst), he can experience a selfobject transference *at the same time* (to the group-as-a-whole or to another member). In this last case, the group analyst should be able to handle both the dimensions of transference that can occur at different levels.

A very interesting example of the two dimensions of transference which occur simultaneously in group is found in a clinical vignette offered by Lichtenberg (1989, pp.118–119). While describing his memories of the Passover Seder services in his youth, a patient remembers both the warm feeling of being part of that family and religious group and the difficult, ambivalent feeling toward his grandfather, who conducted that service:

> …the therapist wondered why the patient did not recognize the contradiction between his positive feelings about the Seder and his anger toward his grandfather …. The patient neither saw paradox nor denied conflict, and, in my opinion, none need be presumed from this vignette. From the standpoint of attachment as a motivation, the patient was ambivalent about his grandparents, but from the standpoint of affiliation as a motivation, the patient was equivocally and unconflictedly positive in his experience of the expansiveness and building of a cohesive self that he had experienced as part of the family and religious group.

The model of two simultaneous transference dimensions – of the intersubjective perspective – is compatible with Lichtenberg's model of two different motivational systems (attachment/affiliation and aversive) which operate at the same time.

We will now examine configurations that commonly occur in group analytic therapy, and which exemplify more clearly the value of focusing attention on the two different dimensions of the transference.

The selfobject transference to the group-as-a-whole and the repetitive transference to the analyst and the other members

In a particular moment of a group, the group itself can become extremely important for each member. The group may be felt as a major support (if not the main support) in a person's life; the opportunities of idealizing the group and of being appreciated by it become extremely significant for the individual. At the same time, a member may experience conflict with another member or with the analyst. We consider that in this particular configuration it is very important that the analyst deal with the conflictual dimension of the transference (while clearly keeping in mind the need to support the selfobject transference to the group-as-a-whole).

CLINICAL VIGNETTE

After about two years of analytical work in a group of eight members, there was, over a period of many sessions, a consistent number of interventions in which the experience of being part of that particular group was an extremely important fact in the life of all the members. This situation allowed (for the first time) an excellent patterning of interactions, as well as an opportunity for affect regulation. One day, Antonio expressed a sentimental interest toward Maria. The group talked about this event in an accepting and understanding atmosphere. One month later, though, Maria revealed that Guilio (another group member) had called her and suggested they go to a movie together, which Maria declined. Her communication to the group was shaped in a friendly attitude toward Guilio and was intended mainly to stress the importance of sharing the information. Antonio, at this point, got angry and attacked Guilio for behaving in a deceptive way, expressing an intense rivalry. In his intervention, the analyst (having in mind the necessity of supporting the selfobject dimension of the transference to the group-as-a-whole) said that openly expressing feelings of rivalry was very valuable and was possible because of the cohesion existing in the group. The importance of the group-as-a-whole interpretation created a much calmer atmosphere and eventually made a detailed analysis possible of the rivalry experienced by all the group members (not only Antonio and Guilio).

The selfobject transference to the analyst and the repetitive transference to the other members and/or to the group-as-a-whole

Often the members of the group develop strong and intense feelings of idealization for the analyst. The analyst becomes very central in the interventions for all the members; they feel that he is the main support in the group life and the person from which each member can expect help with his personal problems and/or group problems. In this situation we notice frequent fantasies of being in a dual analysis with him, a strong conflictual transference with the group-as-a-whole, and a certain competition (with different forms and styles) in conquering the analyst's interest and attention. Instead of interpreting this particular transference configuration as an inappropriate and defensive (passive–dependent) attitude of the group, the analyst can utilize the selfobject dimension of the transference for a thorough definition and differentiation of the various affects experienced in the group. The affective content of the members' interventions can be repeatedly empathically understood, striving to achieve a definition of the single affect experienced, as well as a differentiation of different affects, and to show how contradictory affect states can emerge from a unitary continuous experience of the group (Stolorow *et al.* 1987).

CLINICAL VIGNETTE

At the end of the ninth session of a therapeutic group, several members voiced their fantasies about the analyst: Was he married? In what area of town did he live? Exactly how old was he? The analyst answered, indicating to the members that they all had the experience of being part of a group (family, friends, colleagues and so on). Yet this was their first experience in a therapeutic group, and such a group is characterized – among other things – by the presence of an analyst. Thus, their questions seemed to voice feelings of interest and curiosity about the new experience of being in that particular group. The analyst added that those feelings appeared to show that the group experience was becoming more relevant and how he considered it very important that the group had found a way, through the questions about the analyst, to recognize and express those feelings.

In the next session, Stella told the group about a dream in which she sat in the driver's seat of a car and the analyst sat in the back. It was raining outside, and she had a hard time operating the windscreen-wipers. She felt nervous but realized that the analyst was not nervous at all – he was relaxed, reading an article in a sports magazine about his favourite soccer team to her. She felt happy because she understood that the soccer team was the same one that her beloved grandfather liked.[1] Suddenly it stopped raining and she noticed thousands of micro-drops on the windscreen through which it was now possible to see once again. The analyst interpreted the dream in connection to the preceding session: the position of Stella and the analyst seemed to allude to a situation of dual analysis that is felt to be a perfect setting against stormy emotions. This situation seemed to be considered very anxiety-ridden for Stella (the wiper didn't work) and she felt reassured by the calm and interested attitude of the analyst toward the group (the soccer team). Federico, who was usually a very silent member, commented that he was impressed by the thousands of micro-drops. He thought of the analyst's surname (Nebbiosi in Italian means 'foggy') and added that in the preceding session, he thought that the analyst would have 'wiped away' all those personal questions. When Marco stressed the fact that he had also expected some 'mean' interpretations from the analyst, it became clear to the group that Stella's dream expressed a transition in the affective state of the group. It progressed from the interest and curiosity about the analyst, to the fear of retaliation and of being punished by the analyst's interpretations, to the preoccupation for the 'lack' of 'mean' interpretations, to a calming experience. The acceptance and understanding of the interest and curiosity towards the analyst involved a basic feeling of all the group members – the analyst, and thus the group experience, was becoming more important in their lives.

1　　Here Stella experienced, we believe, a trans-generational aspect of the group-as-a-whole that originated in the family group.

THE SELFOBJECT TRANSFERENCE TO A MEMBER AND THE REPETITIVE
TRANSFERENCE TO THE OTHER MEMBERS, THE ANALYST, AND THE
GROUP-AS-A-WHOLE

Another occurrence that is quite frequent in a group is that of a member becoming important for the other members and for the group life in a very special way. This situation is easily noticeable when that particular member is late or absent; the members experience the feeling that the group is not really there and/or, more dramatically, experience intense feelings of discomfort and confusion. In this situation it is, once again, extremely important to sort out as clearly as possible (from a delusional and generally chaotic affect state) the single affects which are present at the moment and show them to the group. Another very important characteristic of this configuration may be the strong idealization of the 'selfobject member'. The analyst should comprehend empathically how valuable these idealizations are for the group. In our opinion, the emotional understanding (Orange 1995) of these idealizations fosters their gradual resolution so much better than an interpretation aimed to show their inadequacy or danger to the group. We must remember, once again, that what the group is really doing, idealizing a 'selfobject' member, is stressing *the importance of that member in integrating and organizing the affect state of the group.*

CLINICAL VIGNETTE

Luigi (the youngest member of the therapeutic group of seven) was a typical 'selfobject member' in his group. He sought analysis for an ongoing depressive state. However, since the very beginning of the group, he had shown a calm, reflexive, and yet vital attitude to the group. Pretty soon Luigi (whose interventions were not frequent but very intense) was felt by the group to be the member that, in the words of another member, could make 'sadness happier' and make 'happiness calmer'. As the group experience was becoming very important for Luigi, Luigi was becoming very important for the group. At the end of the first year of therapy, Luigi told the group, with some preoccupation, that his mother had heart problems. The next session he was absent (previously he had never missed a session). The group spent a very difficult hour and a half, but succeeded in acknowledging rather clearly the important functions that Luigi had in the group. Before the next session Luigi called the analyst and informed him that his mother had died and said he would miss another session due to his mother's funeral. When Luigi came back to the group the initial reaction was very intense. He was greeted with great affection but the atmosphere was extremely tense. Soon after the beginning, Eleonora left the room crying and remained in the hallway for a few minutes. Bruna and Massimo were on the verge of crying, Franca broke a very dramatic silence, saying to Luigi, 'We all love you, do you know?' At that point the analyst said, 'Perhaps it's impossible to understand all the emotions that we are sharing. I think, though, that the group – and Luigi – doesn't only need to share the pain, but also tolerate it. Perhaps the sharing will help us tolerate it.'

The analyst's intervention was aimed at three goals that were extremely important for the group at that moment. First, to communicate to the group that the (selfobject) functions – of affect regulation – usually accomplished by Luigi, would not be there for some time. This would make it rather difficult to differentiate and understand the emotions that the members were experiencing in the group. Second, to show that, even without understanding, the group could resort to sharing. Third, to communicate that to share pain didn't mean to tolerate it, but can help to tolerate it. After a few minutes of a somewhat calmer silence, Massimo said that he admired Luigi for his behavior very much; his pain seemed so dignified…! This last intervention pivoted the group towards a number of very appreciative interventions for Luigi – he was 'cured', 'protected', 'idealized' and 'nourished'. The analyst realized a very interesting inversion – the group members were performing the selfobject function with Luigi that they felt they would have needed from him.[2] In a second intervention, the analyst stressed the fact that in this dramatic situation the group was successfully trying to function towards Luigi in the same way in which Luigi was experienced to function for the group. This was done not only to support Luigi, but to support the group itself.

Having illustrated the use of the two dimensions of transference in our clinical group example, we will examine the relevance of the organizing principle to the therapeutic group process.

Organizing principles and groups

Before examining the relevance of organizing principles in the group, we will summarize this concept as formulated by Stolorow *et al.* (1987) and Stolorow and Atwood (1992) in the dyadic situation. Drawing from the data of infant research, these authors argue in favor of a *prereflective unconscious* as constituted by the ordering principles that are the crystallization of the interactions between child and caregiver, as well as all the interactions with significant others. In *Contexts of Being* they say:

> Each of these authors [Lichtenberg, Sander, Stern, Emde, Beebe and Lachmann], in different language, is describing how recurring patterns of intersubjective transaction, within the developmental system, result in the establishment of invariant principles that unconsciously organize the child's subsequent experiences (Atwood and Stolorow 1984; Stolorow *et al.* 1987), a realm of

---

2   This inversion of the selfobject functions recalls the desperate and yet very often successful attempts of an individual, whose selfobject is failing, to perform for the failing selfobject the same functions that he does not receive.

unconsciousness that we term the 'prereflective unconscious' .... It is these unconscious ordering principles crystallized within the matrix of the child–caregiver system, that form the essential building blocks of personality development. (Stolorow and Atwood 1992, p.24)

As far as the therapeutic process is concerned, in the intersubjective perspective a new conception of psychoanalytic change emerges. Instead of being conceived of as a *transformation of representations*, it is conceived as the *formation of alternative organizing principles*:

Successful psychoanalytic treatment, in our view, does not produce therapeutic change by altering or eliminating the patient invariant organizing principles. Rather, through new relational experiences with the analyst in concert with enhancements of the patient's capacity for reflective self-awareness, it facilitates the establishment and consolidation of alternative principles and thereby enlarges the patient's experiential repertoire. More generally, it is the formation of new organizing principles within an intersubjective system that constitutes the essence of developmental change throughout the life cycle. (Stolorow and Atwood 1992, p.25)

We are convinced that the formation of new organizing principles within the group intersubjective system provides two possible pathways of development towards new ordering principles:

1. The repeated interactions, and more precisely the affect states of the interactions, can gradually create some new organizing principles in the individual members. An example of this situation is that of a very shy man who can develop a new organizing principle through the interactions (including the interpretations) in the intersubjective system of the group. In addition to organizing his experience according to the principle, 'Every time I am in a public situation and I feel uneasy, I retreat', he will now also organize his experience by the principle, 'When I am in a public situation and I feel uneasy, I'll try to communicate.' This new organizing principle, even if created in an intersubjective field, may well not be shared by all the other members.

2. When the group-as-a-whole dimension is repeatedly experienced in a very intense, affect-laden way, we can observe the emergence of new organizing principles shared by all the members (organizing principles of the 'group self', paraphrasing Kohut). The formation of these group-organizing principles (very powerfully shared by all members) is in close connection, we surmise, with infant research data, and its application to the adult therapeutic situation (as formulated by Beebe and Lachmann 1994). They aptly describe:

> Interactions are organized through heightened affective moments when the person experiences a powerful state transformation, either positive or negative. (Beebe and Lachmann 1994, p.7)

When the state transformation occurs in a positive way:

> The therapeutic action of heightened affective moments is mediated through state transformation which potentially usher in opportunities for expanded self regulatory range and altered patterns of mutual regulation. (Beebe and Lachmann 1994, p.9)

In addition, the conception of these group-organizing principles gives a much better picture of well known group phenomena (e.g. the idealization of the leader or the lack of accountability in the group) than by those theories based on a traditional, drive model. When the group situation promotes the formation of new and alternative organizing principles, it promotes affect regulation with new creative organizations of experience, giving group members access to one of the most powerful therapeutic factors that group therapy can provide.

Conclusions

The group experience as successful training in empathy

In the original formulation of empathy, given by Kohut, the stress was laid on 'putting oneself in the other person's shoes'. What is added in the intersubjective perspective, which uses the term *sustained empathic inquiry*, is the special attention that has to be devoted to the organizing principles (i.e. the prereflective unconscious) of both analysand *and* analyst, and *the way they interact* in the clinical encounter.

The utility of this vantage point in the group becomes evident when we consider that what is typical of the group experience, as far as empathy is concerned, is the rich opportunity to understand the organizing principles of the individual member in the context of the group. At the same time, there is also the opportunity to discover that the existence and the relevance of the organizing principles of the group-as-a-whole (the experience that one's organizing principles can be understood and shared by a human collective) is in itself an exhilarating self-strengthening event.

From 'transmuting internalization' to the formation of new 'organizing principles'

While we refer to the extended discussion of optimal frustration and transmuting internalization by Stolorow *et al.* (1987, pp.22–24) our view is that Kohut's theory of transmuting internalization is not particularly suitable for conceptualizing the therapeutic change in group. Theoretically speaking, the transmuting internalization seems to be too close to the classical concept of identification with the analyst.[3] Rather, from what we see in the group setting, the creation of new ways of organizing both individual and group experiences is due to an ongoing empathic interaction. Granted, some disruption will occur, and its positive negotiation and working through is of paramount importance, but we do not consider empathic disruption and frustration to be the main factor of the formation of a new organization of experience. The new organization of experience (and thus the therapeutic factors of the group) rests on the *ongoing internalization of positive, consistent, empathic interactions.*

Using the Foulkes (1975) metaphor for the individual 'as a nodal point in a network of relationships', we can see that by his group experience, the individual may become a nodal point in a *new* network of relationships. This may be the main therapeutic factor. At this juncture, we can reconceptualize Foulkes' network of relationships as a *network of organizing principles*, a concept extremely close to what the intersubjective perspective identifies as the *intersubjective field.*

References

Atwood, G.E. and Stolorow, R.D. (1984) *Structures of Subjectivity: Explorations in Psychoanalytic Phenomenology.* Hillsdale, NJ: Analytic Press.

Bacal, H. (1985) 'Optimal responsiveness and the therapeutic process.' In A. Goldberg (ed) *Progress in Self Psychology*, Vol.1. Hillsdale, NJ: Analytic Press.

Beebe, B. and Lachmann, F. (1994) 'Representation and internalization in infancy: Three principles of salience.' *Psychoanalytic Psychology 11*, 127–165.

Foulkes, S.H. (1975) *Group Analytic Psychotherapy: Methods and Principles.* London: Gordon and Breach.

Freud, S. (1921) 'Group psychology and the analysis of the ego.' *Standard Edition 18*, 67–143. London: Hogarth Press, 1955.

Gill, M.M. (1994) *Psychoanalysis in Transition – A Personal View.* Hillsdale, NJ: Analytic Press.

Kohut, H. (1971) *The Analysis of the Self.* London: Hogarth Press.

Kohut, H. (1977) *The Restoration of the Self.* New York: International Universities Press.

Kohut, H. (1984) *How Does Analysis Cure?* Chicago: The University of Chicago Press.

Kohut, H. (1985) *Self Psychology and the Humanities.* New York: W.W. Norton & Company.

Lichtenberg, J. (1989) *Psychoanalysis and Motivation.* Hillsdale, NJ and London: Analytic Press.

Nebbiosi, G. (1995a) 'Modelli d'azione – scene modello.' In A. Correale, C. Neri and S. Contorni (eds) *Quaderni di Koinos, n.2.* Borla, Roma.

Nebbiosi, G. (1995b) 'Assunti di base e scene modello.' *Koinos – Gruppo e Funzione Analitica, Anno XVI N2.*

3   Merton Gill has stressed this theoretical point. He wrote: '… inevitable episodes of failure to empathize correctly to be an essential ingredient of what they call "transmuting internalization", which sound very much like mini-identification with the analyst' (Gill 1994, p.30).

Orange, D. (1995) *Emotional Understanding: Studies in Psychoanalytic Epistemology*. New York: The Guilford Press.

Paparo, F. (1981) 'Self psychology and group analysis.' *Group Analysis 14*, 2.

Paparo, F. (1984) 'Self psychology and the group process.' *Group Analysis 16*, 2.

Paparo, F. (1987) 'Selfobject Theory: How Does Group Analysis Cure?' Presented as keynote address at the 7th European Symposium in Group Analysis. Oxford, England.

Stolorow, R.D. (1986) 'Beyond dogma in psychoanalysis.' In A. Goldberg (ed) *Progress in Self Psychology*, Vol.2. Hillsdale, NJ: Analytic Press.

Stolorow, R.D. and Atwood, G.E. (1992) *Contexts of Being – The Intersubjective Foundations of Psychological Life*. Hillsdale, NJ and London: Analytic Press.

Stolorow, R.D., Brandchaft, B. and Atwood, G.E. (1987) *The Psychoanalytic Treatment – An Intersubjective Approach*. Hillsdale, NJ and London: Analytic Press.

Terman, D.M. (1988) 'Optimum frustration: Structuralization and the therapeutic process.' In A. Goldberg (ed) *Progress in Self Psychology*, Vol.4. Hillsdale, NJ: Analytic Press.

Wolf, E.S. (1988) *Treating the Self: Elements of Clinical Self Psychology*. New York: Guilford Press.

CHAPTER 7

The Group Self, Empathy, Intersubjectivity, and Hermeneutics
A Group Analytic Perspective

Sigmund W. Karterud

In this chapter I point to the neglect in contemporary self psychology of Kohut's concept of 'the group self'. I put forward the hypothesis that this neglect is related to an overemphasis on integrating results from research disciplines outside psychoanalytic psychotherapy. The predominant place to search for the genesis of the self has been the infant–caretaker dyad. However, this directional pursuit has created an imbalance in the theoretical corpus of self psychology. The self concept has an equally important function as a theoretical construct that coheres the entire theory. The self concept is thereby liberated from the location of the individual mind and its selfobjects and lends itself to the analysis of groups. To clarify the meaning of the term group self, I give a short account of the group analytic group self. Then I turn to the issue of empathy and the therapeutic group self and claim that empathy with the group-as-a-whole presupposes a *theoretical understanding of the group self.* This opens up a discussion on the selfobject needs of groups. Finally, some limitations in the current intersubjectivity theory are addressed, since, when it comes to groups, intersubjectivity risks an underestimation of forces embedded in the group self. The thesis of this chapter holds that in order to understand the complexity of the group self, a hermeneutics broader than the theory of intersubjectivity is required.

The group self

Of all of Kohut's contributions to psychoanalysis the most neglected one is the concept of the group self. One reason may be the dominance of individual psychoanalytic psychotherapy in the self psychology movement. With some exceptions (Detrick 1986; Karterud 1990; Pines 1996a; Segalla 1996), even self psychology informed group therapists (Bacal 1985; Baker 1995; Harwood 1992; Maratos 1996; Paparo 1984; Stone 1995; Weinstein 1991) do not use the term. This is all the more surprising since Kohut invested the group self concept with great expectancies (Kohut 1976).

Kohut began to struggle with the understanding of group psychology in the late 1960s. This is evident in manuscripts he wrote at that time, which were published posthumously (Kohut 1985). The term 'group self' probably occurred for the first time in the essay 'On Courage' which was written in the early 1970s. The first published paper introducing the term was 'Creativeness, Charisma, Group Psychology' (Kohut 1976). In this paper he discussed Freud's selfobject functions for the cohesion of the psychoanalytic community. He suggested that a breakthrough of a similar nature to that which followed Freud's self analysis (the theory of dreams) could result from a group that succeeded with a similar analysis of the vicissitudes of its own group self.

Kohut (1976) introduced the concept of the group self as follows:

It will have become obvious to those who are familiar with my recent work that I am suggesting, as a potentially fruitful approach to a complex problem, that we posit the existence of a certain psychological configuration with regard to the group – let us call it the 'group self' – which is analogous to the self of the individual. We are then in a position to observe the group self as it is formed, as it is held together, as it oscillates between fragmentation and reintegration, etc. – all in analogy to phenomena of individual psychology to which we have comparatively easy access in the clinical (psychoanalytic) situation. (p.206)

In the same context Kohut wrote:

And I am now suggesting that these considerations concerning the influence of the basic unconscious configurations in individual existence are valid also with regard to the life of the group, i.e., that the basic patterns of a nuclear group self (the group's central ambitions and ideals) not only account for the continuity and the cohesion of the group, but also determine its most important actions. (p.206)

Therapeutic groups are just one specialized group among a vast number of 'natural' groups. Kohut, though, was not concerned with therapeutic groups; his primary interest was history. Kohut's group self is a transpersonal phenomenon operating within history. Though it exists, it is impossible to define or locate precisely. Is it this implicit transpersonal stamp that has caused the generation after Kohut to avoid the term group self?

The self concept

The above mentioned hypothesis becomes plausible if we scrutinize one of the dominant trends in self psychology after Kohut which is the integration of new empirical findings from child development. The latter was a major topic at the

1980 Third Annual Conference of Self Psychology in Boston and has since then been an important concern at most annual conferences. Some important contributors have been Lichtenberg (1989), Shane and Shane (1989) and Lachmann and Beebe (1993). Their central concern has been comparable to Stern's (1985) tracing the genesis of the infant's sense of self by empirical research based on self psychological clinical knowledge. Although these authors emphasize the relational nature of the self and its capacity to initiate self-nurturing responses from the caregiver(s), this research tradition has been *towards the interior of the (small) individual and its dyadic embeddedness.*

The most elaborately articulated outcome of this focus has been Lichtenberg's theory of motivation. According to Lichtenberg (1989), the self is, from early on, characterized by the following motivational systems:

1. The need for psychic regulation of physiological requirements.

2. The need for attachment–affiliation.

3. The need for exploration and assertion.

4. The need to react aversively through antagonism or withdrawal.

5. The need for sensual enjoyment and sexual excitement.

Kohut's classical selfobject needs are assigned to the attachment motivational system.

This research tradition aims to more precisely conceptualize and describe the self – a conceptualization that is in harmony with and not in discord with knowledge acquired from recent infant research. Kohut was criticized by close collaborators for his reluctance to integrate his theory with infant research. His answer was that this research did not yet rely on the same methodological foundation as self psychology did: empathy and introspection. Thus, one had to be careful in accepting the findings that lacked such a foundation (Kohut 1980).

The efforts on integrating theories and results from infant research, brain research (Basch 1983) and affect research (Monsen 1997), to mention the most influential areas, have run parallel to a decreasing popularity of Kohut's theory of the tripolar self.

Another, and quite minimalistic, route has been advocated by Stolorow and collaborators (Atwood and Stolorow 1984; Stolorow and Atwood 1992; Stolorow, Brandchaft and Atwood 1987). True to their intersubjective paradigm, they doubt if there exists any universal self structures. Since all our selves are formed in the intersubjective matrices with unique others, we all are different and unique beings. We certainly share a series of existential givens, like social embeddedness, linkage to a body, the certainty of death, etc., but our self structures are not necessarily variations of universals like the grandiose self or the idealizing self. Stolorow and collaborators resort to the following definition of the self: it is the sum total of the invariant cognitive–affective schemata that account for the person's organization of his experiences of self.

According to Stolorow and collaborators that is what the self *is*. They propose that our notion (of the self) should correspond to it. In this respect, Stolorow and collaborators share the quest of the child developmentalists – to define and locate the self more precisely than Kohut did.

Defining the self more precisely has been a major concern in the post-Kohutian era. In light of this pursuit, Kohut's concept of the group self must have been highly disturbing. Exploring the group self would have implied a move in the opposite direction, so to speak, from location to dispersion. How could the natural groups which Kohut speaks about, like the national group self, possibly be located in time and space? Where does one encounter the group self, the concerted thoughts and actions (and unconscious activity) that drives millions of people? There is no personal ownership to the group self. Yet it is a reality.

Are they the same, or similar, or comparable selves – the personal and the group self? Do we confuse ourselves by using the same term for highly different, but not comparable entities?

Let us return to epistemology. The search for *correspondence* with research outside psychoanalysis has been a major concern in modern self psychology. I believe it is correct to state that this endeavour has created an imbalance in the theoretical corpus of self psychology. What other eggs are there in the basket? The concept 'self' should correspond to some world realities, no doubt. But the concept should also be helpful in solving practical (therapeutic) problems (*pragmatism*). And above all the concept should have an integrative theoretical function, as *the* most important concept in self psychology. It should serve an anchoring function for all other concepts, thus grounding the theory and uniting it to systematic whole. In this last mentioned sense, the *coherence* theory of truth, it becomes evident that the (self psychological) self is a *theoretical construct*.

In this kind of discourse *we are talking about the same as, but at the same time something more than, the self of everyday language.* We are talking about the same self in a semantic sense, i.e. what we are referring to by the term 'oneself' (Ricoeur 1992). However, what is specific to self psychology is the theory of this self as an unconscious system.

Kohut informs us that we should aim for a construct that is experience-near (corresponds to experience), but which nevertheless is a theoretical construct. Kohut held a Kantian view on the relationship between theory and 'reality'. The thing in itself is unknowable. He resisted giving a concise, textbook-like definition of the self. When challenged by his students and collaborators, he wrote:

> ...I have never undertaken the task of defining my terms in a systematic fashion but have assumed that the actual use of terms should be the defining factor, and

although the passages which I will quote are therefore widely dispersed in my various books and essays, these definitions were not derived in a random fashion. They are united by the fact that I always remained within a specific conceptual framework which determined the form and content of my definitions. (Kohut 1991)

In the above cited essay, Kohut refers to *The Restoration of the Self*:

The self, whether conceived within the framework of the psychology of the self in the narrow sense of the term, as a specific structure in the mental apparatus, or, within the framework of psychology of the self in the broad sense of the term, as the center of the individual's psychological universe, is, like all reality...not knowable in its essence. We cannot, by introspection and empathy, penetrate to the self per se; only its introspectively or empathically perceived manifestations are open to us... Demands for an exact definition of the nature of the self disregard the fact that 'the self' is not the concept of an abstract science, but a generalization derived from empirical data. (Kohut 1977, p.310)

Paul and Anna Ornstein, who are representative spokespersons for mainstream self psychology, are more explicit regarding a coherence grounding of truth:

It is the fitting together of method (empathy), data, and theory that creates the total fabric of psychoanalytic self psychology. Its clinical and theoretical concepts cannot be lifted out of their original context without altering their meaning. Hence, any definition of any of its concepts independently of its original context might easily distort its intended meaning. Whatever self psychology as a psychoanalytic theory encompasses, it does so in its unique matrix, woven together with the threads of method, data, and theory. (Ornstein and Ornstein, unpublished manuscript)

When we thus move from a correspondence to a coherence theory of truth, the concept of group self becomes more acceptable. The self is not any more bound to personal ownership. It refers to a theory and a dynamic network of ambitions, ideals, talents and needs. The personal self and the group self are similar in this respect, yet different. How can we describe more accurately the relationship between them?

The personal and the group self

Group analysis has always maintained that the group (self) is primary and the personal self is secondary. The group exists prior to the individual. The group embodies the cultural traditions in all their complexities, the written as well as the unspoken traditions, which the individual is born into. During its lifetime, the individual will become a member of a multitude of groups which can be characterized as *subgroups* (ethnic, professional, familial groups, etc.) *of the community group self* to which the individual belongs. The community group self predates the individuals and survives them, and makes use of the individual to fulfill its purposes. According to the dynamics and the resources embedded in the community group self, the individual is given certain delineated tasks and roles to perform. The individual has a certain choice in this respect, but the individual will have a hard time if its projects do not resonate with the current dynamics of the group self. Bion (1970) discussed this theme through his reflections on the group and the genius. Kohut (1976) argued that there is a need for a selfobject function from an important other when the individual embarks upon a journey of creativity to explore new intellectual terrain which is at variance with basic convictions of the group self.

The boundaries between the personal self and the group self are vague. One cannot discern where one ends and the other begins. They are intertwined. One is part of the other and they dip far down into each other's unconscious structures. When the group is shattered, so too will the individual be. Bosnia-Herzegovina is the best example in present time. For Kohut it was the rise of Nazism in Germany. He compared Hitler to a 'wild analyst' who offered a false cure to the enfeebled, humiliated, and fragmented German group self.

Several authors, and in particular Pines (1996a; 1996b), have pointed to similarities between Foulkes' concept of the group matrix and the concept of the group as a self. However, it is somewhat unclear what kind of self Pines is talking about. It does not seem to be equivalent to the Kohutian self. It seems less theoretical and more a common sense term. This may be the reason why Pines overlooks the most fundamental element contained in the Kohutian self concept, which is also missing in the more mechanistic (and neurological) concept of the matrix: that is the intentional character of the group self. The self has purposes and needs. The self has a project; it contains ambitions and ideals. It is not merely the historical residue of the communicational network of the group.

In contrast to the intersubjectivist's self, this Kohutian self concept has retained its existential characteristics. This self is not (a sum of) schemata. The Kohutian self is closer to Kierkegaard's self, which was defined as a double relation, i.e., a relation that also relates to itself. This twofold dialectic takes care of both the throwness and the reflective nature of the self. As described by Heidegger (1927), man is fundamentally thrown into the world (Dasein) and thus dependent on the world and its selfobject functions. My reflexive nature, which the reflexive pronoun 'self' reminds us about, is equally unsurpassable and permeates the core of my self: I am, and I have always been, in a constant dialogue with my self.

These characteristics of the personal self have their counterparts for the group self. The group is fundamentally thrown into the world as well. And, if we take the community group self as a example, Kohut (1985) describes how the intelligentsia in a broad sense, e.g. the historians, philosophers, social scientists, artists, etc., perform the self-reflective activity which is paramount for the self-understanding of the group self, and through this very activity transforms the structure of the self in a dialectic manner.

The Kohutian self is thus characterized by these three interrelated processes: the self structure (= organizing principles), throwness (= reliance upon the world), and reflexivity (= the ongoing synthesizing self-reflective activity). This threefold dialectic has implications for psychotherapy since therapy aims at influencing all three processes: the structure of the self, the kind of needs of selfobject functions from the world, and the self-organizing capacity which is related to the reflexive functions of the I.

The group analytic group self

The concept that ambitions and ideals are embedded in the core of the group self may be illustrated through an elaboration of the group analytic group self and eventually brings us to the clinical situation. The group analytic group self was born around 1950 when S.H. Foulkes gathered a group of colleagues who met regularly and who later founded the Group Analytic Society. Foulkes was well equipped for the task which history had designed for him: being a son of a Jewish father who favored modern ideas and action; having a personal analysis in Vienna; firsthand knowledge of gestalt psychology and neurology; collaboration with radical sociologists at the Frankfurter Institute für Socialforschung; having the courage to set up a group practice without any forerunners; and having leadership skills combined with creativity (as displayed through his activity at the Northfield Military Hospital).

Foulkes was certainly not the first to think in terms of group psychotherapy. The western communities were pregnant with these ideas, or to use Bion's phrase: 'the thoughts were floating around, waiting for a thinker.' If a psychoanalytic dialogue could emancipate the neurotic individual, why could not a group dialogue do the same? And why not a hospital if conducted as a group – a therapeutic community? And the radical activist would say, why should these principles be restricted to therapeutics? Why not pedagogic institutions (Jones 1968)? The ambitions and ideals of a healing and self-restorative group/community were widespread.

Although Foulkes was a part of what later has been labeled the first therapeutic community (at Northfield 1943–1945), he restricted himself to the task of cultivating the small therapeutic group. He formulated theoretical concepts of group dynamics, the relationship group – individual, group specific factors, guidelines for composition and boundaries and for the conductors involvement in the group dialogue (Foulkes 1975). He acted on the need for partners (twins), the need for a correspondence and scientific forum (*GAIPAC*, later the journal *Group Analysis*) and the need for a training institution (The Institute of Group Analysis, London). Such are the organized constituents of the group analytic group self, which in concerted action are instrumental in order to set in motion the ambitious essence of the group analytic group self: the ideal of a healing group dialogue.

The history also accounts for the inherent contradictions of the group analytic group self. There is unresolved tension between Foulkes' radical group analytic viewpoints and his ego psychological understanding of individual psychopathology. This tension has hampered the unfolding of the latent potentials of group analysis.

When the individual group analyst fulfills his/her training and becomes a vital part of the group analytic group self, sharing its ambitions and ideals in a personally integrated manner, thereby these become parts of him/herself. S/he simultaneously lets her/himself be used by these ideals. *They work through him/her.* The 'wild' group psychotherapist who practices with a bare minimum of formal training or without any membership in a group psychotherapy association is more prey to the illusion of personal authorship, e.g. that s/he is the personal inventor of a therapeutics and not an integral part of a historical tradition, an individual through which the tradition speaks (Gadamer 1960).

Empathy and the therapeutic group self

How is the therapeutic group self to be understood? The group you and I conduct for therapeutic purposes. This question is not merely theoretical: it has practical consequences; it concerns empathy with the group. What does this mean – empathy with the *group*?

As well as empathy being a necessary precondition for all human encounter, psychoanalytic psychotherapy presupposes a theoretically refined and sustained empathy, a psychoanalytical empathy which is shaped and polished by tradition. Kohut sometimes wrote as if he believed in a faculty of pure empathy, unmediated by tradition, which enabled the analyst immediate access to the inner life of the patient. But if we adopt the Ornsteins' definition of psychoanalytic empathy as empathy with *complex psychological configurations* we realize that such an understanding of the other is inconceivable outside a certain psychological tradition. How could we empathize with the self state subsequent to a subtle failure of mirroring if we did not have a prior understanding of this kind of needs and their vicissitudes? Due to his embeddedness in a male chauvinistic tradition, Freud failed to empathize with Dora when Herr F tried to seduce her by the lake.

In the same manner, empathy with the group presupposes a theoretical understanding of the group self. The therapeutic group self – is that term equal to the group-as-a-whole? No, the terms should not be intermingled. The term group-as-a-whole is used in a rather confusing way in the group literature. One needs to ask, the group (as-a-whole) for whom? Sometimes the term refers to the group as observed by an outside observer, sometimes to the group conductor, and sometimes as the group for one or several group members. The most frequent usage is possibly the group as an object, e.g. the group as a (good or bad) mother, the group as a breast, etc. Bion's understanding of the group follows these lines. According to Bion (1961), the ultimate reason for the basic assumption phenomena is that the group, in the mind of the participants, approximates (as object) too closely very early primal scenes which activate psychotic anxieties. How different is this line of object relational thought from the one emanating from self psychology and the group self.

The therapeutic group self is a *project*. It is the particularization, the enactment of the group analytic group self. It is the ambitions and ideals of a healing community set into action by a particular group analyst and a particular selected brand of patients. The therapeutic group self undergoes the stages of development so well described in the group literature (Gibbard, Hartman and Mann 1974): the early, feeble group self is split between the aspirations in the mind of the therapist and the frightened, confused and yet hopeful yearnings within the mind of the group members. As a means to form an early nucleus of a group self, there is an early stage of defensive idealization which transforms itself through the stages of development and maturation as the group members gradually come to understand what group analysis is all about. Members begin to identify with the same ideals that guide the therapist, progressing to the mature group analytic culture, when the essence of group analysis comes to fruition: a culture for maintenance, repair, and restoration of the self through group dialogue.

Maintenance of the self is an important function that emanates from the regular participation in a vitalizing dialogue. Repair of the self occurs when life events, the more or less everyday setbacks, frustrations, disappointments, and insults, can be talked about, understood, and worked through. Restoration of the self occurs when the thwarted need to grow is set free and activated in the selfobject transferences to the therapist and other significant group members and facilitated by the therapist's interpretations. (For a more detailed account of the moment-to-moment interaction in a group conducted according to self psychological guidelines, I refer to Stone 1996.)

If the group analyst has learned his lesson well, he manages through his directorship, group analytic dramaturgy and interpretations to set in motion healing forces embedded in the western intellectual tradition of self emancipation. He opens a healing text and lets the text play with himself and the group members. Imbedded in the text are stories about what is true and false, about lies and honesty, frankness and hypocrisy, about what is morally right and wrong, about oppression, seduction and evilness, about human rights, belonging and trust, and authentic encounters in contemporary societies. These stories and how the therapist and the other group members have responded to them and co-created them through the life of the group are the historical tissue of the group self. These stories, small narratives of life events in contemporary society, are told, yet all group analysts know that telling a story in a group is also an enactment which make the story come alive in the here and now. The stories assign roles for the group members whereby the life events can be replayed and reinterpreted.

Empathy with the group is empathy with this project, the group qua project.

The moment of the group, the group in session, displays the group's *self state*. The group's self state can be rigid, dull, conventional, in search for a scapegoat, or vital and creative, etc. Group self state interpretations may be needed in order to liberate the group from unproductive blind tracks in favor of more enabling group solutions (Whitaker 1981).

The group's selfobject needs

For the illustration of the selfobject needs of groups, I will use as an example from the day hospital which I am heading for the treatment of patients with personality disorders (Karterud, 1996). The staff group of this unit comprises some 12–14 professionals. The texts and the histories of the great pioneers in this field, e.g. Maxwell Jones, Tome Main, Wilfred Bion, Herluf Thomstad, S.H. Foulkes and Heinz Kohut, as well as the pioneers in hermeneutics such as Hans Georg Gadamer, Jürgen Habermas and Paul Ricoeur, among others, serve *idealized selfobject functions* for this day unit in its ambitious task of treating severely disturbed patients. In the day-to-day work, this idealization is *concretized* to the idealization of the consultant of the unit and myself as the head of the unit. This unit has a certain local fame which results in frequent requests for lectures and opportunities to visit the unit. The resultant praise and admiration serve important *mirroring selfobject functions* for the unit's group self. The unit is not alone and isolated in this world. We have developed a close cooperation with other (pretty much alike) day units in what we call The Norwegian Network of Psychotherapeutic Day Hospitals (Karterud *et al.*, in press). These other units serve important *twinship selfobject functions* for our unit.

Segalla (1996) has recently proposed the term *groupobject needs* to functions which are comparable to what I have outlined above as selfobject needs of the group:

> To summarize, in order to maintain the organization and operation of the group, the group organism must, like the individual self, possess a set of functions, or *groupobject needs*, which, operating on both an individual and group level, serve the needs of the group and ultimately the needs of individual members of that group. (Segalla 1996, p.263)

Apart from the very term groupobject needs which can be misleading and loaded with contradictory meanings, Segalla highlights an important question: how should we conceptualize functions *within* the group that are necessary preconditions for the development and maintenance of the group self?

A preceding paragraph has touched upon the issue about the historical tissue of the group. This discussion can now be taken a bit further. In individual self psychology we do not usually include functions *within* the self, e.g. self-soothing, as selfobject functions. The term selfobject refers to functions 'outside' the person, but which may be taken for granted or *perceived as belonging to the self.* The group self is more complicated in this respect. There is no clear boundary between the individual and the group self, and the vitality of the group self is partly determined by the vitality of the individual selves.

When one group member performs an act of understanding which serves a selfobject function for another, and when this act resonates with the ideals and ambitions which constitute the nuclear group self, one can say that the interchange between these two group members simultaneously confers and strengthens the group self. The act serves both a selfobject function for one individual group member as well as a selfobject function for the group self. Conversely, one might say that this act is also a manifestation of the actual group self. The act occurs in this particular context, and it is determined by the ideals and ambitions embedded in this particular group self. It is a question of *discursive meaning,* which perspective we favor: the act as a manifestation of the group self, as a selfobject function for the individual, or as a selfobject function for the group self.

Thus there is no clear boundary between the group self and intragroup selfobject functions. The self is a dialectical entity in constant flux. Through its very nature of composition and diversity, the group self contains richer self-confirmatory potentials than the individual self. *The group can treat itself in a way which is inconceivable for the individual.* And herein lie its therapeutic potentials. By the ability to partake in self-confirmatory and self-developmental activities of the group self, the individual simultaneously engages in a developmental process of the individual self.

Intersubjectivity and hermeneutics

The conception of group analysis, as outlined above and integrated with Kohut's concept of the group self, differs somewhat from the perspective of intersubjectivity which has become so popular in the United States in recent years. Although appreciating many of the contributions to the self psychology literature by Stolorow and collaborators (Atwood and Stolorow 1984; Stolorow and Atwood 1992; Stolorow *et al.* 1987), there are important aspects of intersubjectivity which are less than optimal when it comes to group analysis.

The two central themes of intersubjectivity, i.e. that the observer influences the observed and the significance of the intersubjective field (Lebenswelt), were articulated by the founder of phenomenology, E. Husserl, sixty years ago (1936). These themes initiated the journey which Stolorow and Atwood set out on in the book *Faces in a Cloud* (1979), where they elaborated in which way (in their opinion) the personality of the theorist (observer) influences his/her theory of personality (of the observed). Later on they elaborated how these principles color theoretical and clinical phenomena like the self, transference, countertransference, and the therapeutic dialogue, etc. Stolorow and collaborators envisage the therapeutic dialogue above all as colored by the protagonist's subjectivity. There is one way of organizing subjective experiences encountering another way of organizing subjective experiences, and the *raison d'être* of the encounter is to bring to awareness the inhibiting invariant organizing principles of the patient and open up for development of other more flexible organizing principles. These transactions take place in the intersubjective field between the interacting subjectivities. The self, which is defined as the sum total of cognitive–affective schemas (organizing principles), is conceived of as repaired when the inhibiting organizing principles are replaced by flexible ones.

What is absent when one reads Stolorow and collaborators' elaborations of the therapeutic encounter is the world at large. The protagonists seem too much locked up in one another's subjective universe. Their conception of therapy differs from group analysis in the following way: in a group indeed there are multiple subjectivities which are partly governed by organizing principles from within and which create an 'intersubjective field' which influences everybody. But Stolorow *et al.*'s intersubjective perspective underestimate how the group self is simultaneously governed by objective realities of the world (therapeutic texts and tradition) and how the participants are engaged in not subjective but actual roles, demanded of them by the necessities inherent in the group self, necessities for the group self in order to fulfill its mission. These roles, such as the gatekeeper, the rulemaker, the rebel, the pet, the scapegoat, etc., carry out functions which the group needs (Beck *et al.* 1986).

When I use the term objective in the preceding paragraph, as opposed to subjective, it is with reference to the concept of organizing principles. In the group situation there are organizing principles in operation above the level of the individual and the subjective. That is what Gadamer talks about when he states that the tradition speaks through the individual. Foulkes (1975) refers to the same when he describes the individual as a node in a communicational network. In Foulkes' words, 'the group passes through the individual.' This perspective is necessary in order to grasp the dialectics. The tradition and the group call upon the participants. But their call for action is not heard by everyone. Certain individuals are more sensitive than others to these calls for action. Foulkes used the term *resonance* for the interplay between the group and the individual.

The historical roots of the contemporary overestimation of intersubjectivity are found in the neglect of hermeneutics within psychoanalytic discourse. Kohut shared this neglect. In their book *Structures of Subjectivity: Explorations in*

Psychoanalytic Phenomenology, Atwood and Stolorow (1984) tried to fill this void by linking developments in psychoanalysis with developments in phenomenology. The main problem is that the authors did not carry the discussion between psychoanalysis, hermeneutics and themselves up to the present. In *Structures of Subjectivity*, Atwood and Stolorow adopted a position similar to that of the German philosopher Dilthey, who declared that the main objective of hermeneutics was the understanding of the intention of the author (the patient) in a historical context and according to the principles of the hermeneutic circle. This position approximates a definition of hermeneutics as *pure psychology*.

Heidegger (1927) challenged this position by his *return to philosophy*. However, Heidegger's work, which is generally regarded as a fundamental contribution to modern philosophy, was devaluated by Atwood and Stolorow (1984) and explicitly read as a psychological account of existential problems, *not as ontology*. They claimed that psychoanalysis did not need to address ontology:

> The question of the meaning of being, as we understand it, does not enter the field of concern of psychoanalysis, *even at the level of pretheoretical assumptions* [italics added]. (Atwood and Stolorow 1984, p.22)

By defining a part of hermeneutics, mainly intersubjectivity, as a kind of metatheory for psychoanalytic psychotherapy, Stolorow and Atwood have not considered fully the developments in modern hermeneutics. They have not taken full advantage of the resources in the debate on ontology (Heidegger 1927), tradition (Gadamer 1960), critique of ideologies (Habermas 1968) and radical text interpretations, narrative structures and the hermeneutics of the self (Ricoeur 1981; 1992). Instead we have witnessed a not so fruitful debate over the claim that intersubjectivity is supraordinate to self psychology (Stolorow 1995).

The above mentioned restrictions become all the more important when we turn from individual psychoanalytical psychotherapy to group analysis. As I have tried to outline in the preceding paragraphs, the move from individual to group analysis amplifies complicated dynamics which are not so easily discernible in the two-person dialogue: the conflicts and mutuality between the personal and the group self; the tradition and texts as important co-determinants for the course of the group; the constraints of the tradition due to old ideologies within the group analytic movement; the internal structural requirements for the unfolding of the group's therapeutic potentials; the enactments of narratives which carry their own functional requirements, etc.

The intersubjectivists' emphasis on the profound influence that persons exert upon each other and the significance of unconscious organizing principles represent valuable perspectives on the above mentioned issues. However, group analysis, with its foundation in a European intellectual tradition, is wise to open itself to a dialogue with modern hermeneutics, of which intersubjectivity is a part.

Theoretical summary

Kohut opened a new way of understanding groups by his concept of the group self. However, he neglected a dialogue with hermeneutics. Stolorow and Atwood discovered this neglect and carried the dialogue to the position of Dilthey. However, they adopted a definition of the self which appears incompatible with Kohut's concept of the group self. In order to unfold the theoretical and therapeutic potentials of the group self concept, I believe the most promising activity would be a dialogue between group analysis, self psychology and modern hermeneutics.

I will end this chapter by referring to Paul Ricoeur, who underlined that the understanding of the other (and the group) cannot be reduced to interpersonal transactions, but takes the detour of the world:

> What would we know of love and hate, of moral feelings and, in general, of all that we call the *self*, if these had not been brought to language and articulated by literature? (Ricoeur 1981, p.143)

References

Atwood, G. and Stolorow, R.D. (1984) *Structures of Subjectivity: Explorations in Psychoanalytic Phenomenlogy.* Hillsdale: Analytic Press.

Bacal, H.A. (1985) 'Object-relations in the group from the perspective of self psychology.' *International Journal of Group Psychotherapy 35*, 483–501.

Baker, M. (1995) 'The complementary function of individual and group psychotherapy in the management and working through of archaic selfobject transference.' In A. Goldberg (ed) *The Impact of New Ideas.* Hillsdale: Analytic Press.

Basch, M. (1983) 'Empathic understanding: A review of the concept and some theoretical considerations.' *Journal of the American psychoanalytic Association 31*, 101–26.

Beck, A.P., Dugo, J.M., Eng, A.M. and Lewis, C.M. (1986) 'The search for phases in group development: Designing process analysis measures of group interaction.' In L.S. Greenberg and W.P. Pinsof (eds) *The Psychotherapeutic Process: A Research Handbook.* New York: The Guilford Press.

Bion, W.R. (1961) *Experiences in Groups.* London: Tavistock Publications.

Bion, W.R. (1970) *Attention and Interpretation.* London: Tavistock Publications.

Detrick, D.W. (1986) 'Alterego phenomena and the alterego transference: Some further considerations.' In A. Goldberg (ed) *Progress in Self Psychology.* New York: The Guilford Press.

Foulkes, S.H. (1975) *Group Analytic Psychotherapy: Methods and Principles.* London: Gordon and Breach.

Gadamer, H.G. (1960) *Truth and Method.* London: Sheed and Ward (1989).

Gibbard, G.S., Hartman, J.J. and Mann, R.D. (1974) 'Group process and development.' In G.S. Gibbard, J.J. Hartman and R.D. Mann (eds) *Analysis of Groups.* London: Jossey-Bass Limited.

Habermas, J. (1968) *Knowledge and Human Interests.* Boston: Beacon Press (1971).

Harwood, I.H. (1992) 'Group psychotherapy and disorders of the self.' *Group Analysis 25*, 19–26.

Heidegger, M. (1927) *Being and Time*. New York: Harper and Row (1962).

Husserl, E. (1936) *The Crisis of European Sciences and Transcendental Phenomenology*. Evanstone: Northwestern University Press (1970).

Jones, M. (1968) *Beyond the Therapeutic Community*. New Haven: Yale University Press.

Karterud, S. (1990) 'Bion or Kohut: Two paradigms of group dynamics?' In B.E. Roth, W.N. Stone and H.D. Kibel (eds) *The Difficult Patient in Group: Group Psychotherapy with Borderline and Narcissistic Disorders*. New York: International Universities Press.

Karterud, S. (1996) 'The hospital as a therapeutic text.' *Therapeutic Communities 17*, 125–129.

Karterud, S., Pederson, G., Friis, S., Urnes, Ɏ., Brabrand, J., Falkum, L.R. and Leirvåg, H. (in press) The Norwegian Network of Psychotherapeutic Day Hospitals. Therapeutic Communities.

Kohut, H. (1976) 'Creativeness, charisma, group psychology.' In J.E. Gedo and G.H. Pollock (eds) *Freud: The Fusion of Science and Humanism*. New York: International Universities Press.

Kohut, H. (1977) *The Restoration of the Self*. New York: International Universities Press.

Kohut, H. (1980) 'Reflections on advances in self psychology.' In A. Goldberg (ed) *Advances in Self Psychology*. New York: International Universities Press.

Kohut, H. (1985) *Self Psychology and the Humanities*. New York: W.W. Norton and Company.

Kohut, H. (1991) 'Four basic concepts in self psychology.' In P.H. Ornstein (ed) *The Search for the Self. Selected Writings of Heinz Kohut: 1978–1981*. Madison: International Universities Press.

Lachmann, F.M. and Beebe, B. (1993) 'Interpretation in a developmental perspective.' In A. Goldberg (ed) *The Widening Scope of Self Psychology*. Hillsdale: Analytic Press.

Lichtenberg, J.D. (1989) *Psychoanalysis and Motivation*. Hillsdale: Analytic Press.

Maratos, J. (1996) 'The emergence of self through the group.' *Group Analysis 29*, 161–168.

Monsen, J. (1997) 'Selvpsykolgi og nyere affektteori.' In S. Karterud and J. Monsen (eds) *Selvpsykolgi. Utviklingen etter Kohut*. Oslo: Ad Notam Gyldendal.

Ornstein, P.H. and Ornstein, A. 'Some distinguishing features of Heinz Kohut's self psychology.' Unpublished manuscript.

Paparo, F. (1984) 'Self psychology and the group process.' *Group Analysis 17*, 108–117.

Pines, M. (1996a) 'Dialogue and selfhood: Discovering connections.' *Group Analysis 29*, 327–341.

Pines, M. (1996b) 'The self as a group: the group as a self.' *Group Analysis 29*, 183–190.

Ricoeur, P. (1981) *Hermeneutics and the Human Sciences*. Cambridge: Cambridge University Press.

Ricoeur, P. (1992) *Oneself as Another*. Chicago: The University of Chicago Press.

Segalla, R.A. (1996) '"The unbearable embeddedness of being": Self psychology, intersubjectivity and large group experiences.' *Group 20*, 257–271.

Shane, E. and Shane M. (1989) 'Child analysis and adult analysis.' In A. Goldberg (ed) *Dimensions of Self Experience*. Hillsdale: Analytic Press.

Stern, D.N. (1985) *The Interpersonal World of the Infant*. New York: Basic Books.

Stolorow, R.D. (1995) 'Introduction: Tensions between loyalism and expansionism in self psychology.' In A. Goldberg (ed) *The Impact of New Ideas*. Hillsdale: Analytic Press.

Stolorow, R.D. and Atwood, G. (1979) *Faces in a Cloud. Subjectivity in Personality Theory*. New York: Jason Arsonson.

Stolorow, R.D. and Atwood, G. (1992) *Contexts of Being*. Hillsdale: Analytic Press.

Stolorow, R.D., Brandchaft, B. and Atwood, G. (1987) *Psychoanalytic Treatment. An Intersubjective Approach*. Hillsdale: Analytic Press.

Stone, W.N. (1995) 'Frustration, anger, and the significance of alter-ego transference in group psychotherapy.' *International Journal of Group Psychotherapy 45*, 287–302.

Stone W.N. (1996) 'Self psychology and the higher mental functioning hypothesis: Complementary theories.' *Group Analysis 29*, 169–181.

Weinstein, D. (1991) 'Exhibitionism in group psychotherapy.' In A. Goldberg (ed) *The Evolution of Self Psychology*. Hillsdale: Analytic Press.

Whitaker, D.S. (1981) 'A nuclear conflict and group focal conflict model for integrating individual and group-level phenomena in psychotherapy groups.' In M. Pines and L. Rafaelsen (eds) *The Individual and the Group: Boundaries and Interrelations in Theory and Practice*. New York: Plenum Press.

CHAPTER 8

Infant Research and Intersubjective Responsiveness in Group Therapy

Joan Schain-West

Little has been written about the impact of infant observational research on intersubjectivity theory applied to treatment in groups, with the exception of Harwood (1983; 1993). These data have been addressed in terms of their relevance in individual psychotherapy by Stolorow, Atwood and Brandchaft (1994). As they report, recent infant researchers find the infant–caregiver dyad to be a psychological unit within which affective exchanges occur for both. These exchanges are influenced by the conscious and unconscious organizing principles of each part of the dyad.

The principles are primarily object-seeking on the part of the infant: they are connecting, nurturing, stimulating and limit setting, but, at times, avoidant and conflictual on the part of the caregiver. Within the interactional field of the dyad, determined as it is by the subjective experience of both parties, infant issues of bonding and attachment, responsiveness, reciprocity, affective attunement and emotional regulation as well as enmeshment, entrapment, intolerance of or need for separateness are played out. While these aspects of the infant–caregiver dyad relate directly to the development of the infant, their gratification or control of them can also be observed to serve resistant or growth promoting functions in psychotherapy with adults. Group therapy, with the therapist as leader and model as well as interpreter and provider broadens the intersubjective field from one dyad to several. In addition, a relationship develops among group members and between group members and the group as a whole. Bacal (1985), Harwood (1983) and Schain (1985) have illustrated self-psychological concepts applicable to group therapy. Intersubjectivity theory and infant observational data further extend the therapist's awareness of treatment considerations. The work of Beebe and Lachmann (1988), Brazelton (1987), Emde (1987), Lichtenberg (1983), and Stern (1985) are consistent with and enhance the clinical application of intersubjectivity theory in group therapy in a variety of ways.

The group experience vividly illustrates the universality of primitive, infant needs which inevitably emerge. These infant and child needs include recognition, validation, acceptance, affirmation, support, stimulation, the need to connect and the need to be separate. In accord with Kohut (1977), such needs are ongoing throughout life and can be met in a variety of relationships. While derailments in these relationships are recapitulated in all modes of therapy, the multiplicity of cohesive and fragmented relationships that arise in a group offer a wide range of opportunities for gratification of needs as well as the working through of defenses against them and the acceptance of ambivalence in relationships.

Current subjective states of mind of the therapist, as well as his[1] genetic history, will affect the character of a group: the degree of encouragement of openness, closeness, spontaneity and interpretations of barriers to intimacy. It is not only the therapist's ability to enjoy life that is significant. It is his access to and comfort with his own organizing principles, and his attitude towards involvement, commitment, joy and love that affect the direction of the group. If the therapist had a caregiver in his history who shamed or deflated him when he was in need of mirroring he may have difficulty feeling his own excitement and be unable to encourage the expression of excitement by others. When excitement is limited by the therapist, verbally or non-verbally, patients can feel ashamed or deflated. Patients' shame is often a result of their feeling that their excitement is exhibitionistic and infantile and is not something to be enjoyed. When such a prohibition results from an unconscious experience related to the therapist's past the intersubjective field of treatment is sharply curtailed.

Beebe and Lachmann (Beebe and Lachmann 1988; Beebe, Jaffey and Lachmann 1992; Lachmann 1986; Lachmann and Beebe 1992) describe derailment and repair in the mother–infant dyad. Likewise, the group therapist needs the ability to maintain and repair connections in the group in spite of differences and following disruptions. He also needs to tolerate the terminations of a group member as a result of growth or separation, without acting out of narcissistic injury. He serves as a model of interaction in ways that are predictably inconsistent or absent from the patient's own experiences. This is true regarding the expression of positive and joyful feelings as well as for the containment of anger, anxiety and depression. As group members become aware of the limits or defects in their experience they can adopt a new style of relating to each other and to themselves. When the therapist can encourage infant yearnings of the group members such needs are demystified and rendered acceptable. In order to do so, the therapist must accept the primitive aspects of his own nature. In an appropriate manner, he acknowledges these to the group and encourages an attitude of appreciation of their positive aspects, such as playfulness and fun.

1   His refers to his or her throughout.

The role of playfulness and teasing in psychic development has been considerably expanded since Winnicott's (1971) landmark book. While the 'gleam in mother's eye' is easily understood as pride and is affirming for the infant, implications of a giggle or the glint preceding a tease are less so.

Playing within the dyad offers both members a sense of adequacy and mastery. One is able to get and keep the other's attention, to elicit a response from the other and to positively affect their mood. Such experiences not only improve the well-being of both, they contribute to the development of a sense of being of value in one's world. When you can make someone laugh you experience a feeling of achievement. That is probably why sensitive spouses know to laugh at their mate's jokes even if they've heard them many times before. They want their partner to feel important, potent and powerful. So it is from the interactions of earliest infancy to the end of life.

A patient, recalling her deathbed conversation with her father, describes her expressions of love for him. The father's reply, 'What's not to like?'

A complex range of emotions is called into play for teasing to be fun-filed and not hurtful. A deep-seated sense of equality is necessary between the participants. When an infant teases his caregiver (as a healthy infant often does) both are on the same emotional level. In addition, a mutual feeling of vitality is enhanced. There are also elements of anticipation, predictability and the fun of teasing. All of these factors contribute to effective development.

In a group treatment situation, laughter brings additional therapeutic benefits. It reduces tension, alleviates anxiety and contributes to the cohesiveness that results from shared experiences. Playfulness can occur in a group between a dyad and spread to the rest of the group or can occur as a total group phenomenon. Teasing is especially effective when it involves the therapist. If the therapist can be teased, in a benevolent way, he is less likely to be either feared or defensively idealized and is experienced as more human and, thereby, more understanding of his patients and compassionate towards them.

Grotjahn (1957; 1977) has described the role of laughter in group therapy. However, infant research highlights the primitive nature of the emotions that are touched in playful interactions. Stern (1985), Trevarthen (1994) and others have noted that it is a securely attached baby that plays and a very secure baby that can tease. The level of comfort and security of the therapist is often reflected in his play, playfulness and fun in the therapy. Thus, the subjectivity of the therapist interacts with the collective subjectivities of the group.

Bonding and attachment

It is the aim of the therapist to form a bond with each group member and to facilitate their attachments to one another. Obstacles to this end are explored and achievements acknowledged. The therapist notes attachments but particularly points out when opportunities for bonding are missed. Data from infant research (Stern 1985) illustrate that the infant bonds because the caregiver attaches. Brazelton (1987) emphasizes the growth potential for the caregiver as well as the infant and thus offers us a fresh view of a system that has frequently been viewed as one-sided. Normally, the therapist is personally gratified as he witnesses group cohesion and bonds forming. In addition to the satisfaction of being 'on target' with an individual patient, he can enjoy contributing to the positive power of the group. Although, if he experienced intense sibling rivalry in his childhood, that experience may lead him to be competitive with such attachments and to keep the group focus upon himself. The group eventually takes off on their own, much like every toddler, to explore the world of relationships. Like the toddler, needs for re-connecting, soothing, comforting and praise will bring the group member back to the group and its leader time and time again. As important as attachment is, the maintenance of a sense of separateness is equally so. They are not mutually exclusive but, in fact, are developmentally related. It is the kind of attachment, with boundaries, without fusion or merger, that promotes growth. Healthy attachment honors the separateness of the infant from the beginning whereas merger states are in the service of the caregiver.

Stern's work graphically describes the infant as 'object-seeking from the start'. But in later infancy there is a need to be separate. Anxiety about closeness and intimacy are frequently related to fear of merger, of feeling 'swallowed up' with resulting anxiety about loss of a sense of self in a relationship. In terms of his own relationship with group members as well as between members, the therapist needs to be alert to the polarity between attachment and autonomy. With many patients, involvement with another seems to them to be inconsistent with preservation of a sense of separateness. The therapist who is comfortable with a sense of self in the context of intimacy can help members of the group respect each other's boundaries enough to be comfortable with closeness and dependency without loss of distinctness.

Extremely subtle defenses against attachment are perhaps less readily recognized in individual therapy than in the group, where some group members may respond intensely to the hostility or avoidance of involvement by others. Pressure towards bonding with peers can be free from certain transferential parental issues such as conflicts about dependency, control, dominance and submission.

A word should be said about temperamental differences that create barriers to bonding. The therapist can help patients understand such differences. The group's culture and attitude of acceptance can contribute to attachments within their emotional limits, both between people in the group and with people in their lives outside of it. Sometimes such attachments free a hidden potential for intimacy which was not suspected at first. For example:

Mr M was referred for a group experience by his individual therapist. She described him as 'lifeless', having a wooden quality, being out of touch with his feelings and emotionally unresponsive to his wife. At first he did indeed fit that description. He told the group that his parents both viewed him as a responsibility to be dealt with in a manner appropriate to their social class and status. He experienced no joy, warmth, closeness or fun even in his earliest memories. He doubted that pleasure existed in his family and felt certain that this atmosphere was not different in his infancy.

The therapist made a mental note not to limit his natural sense of joy in appropriate circumstances related to Mr M. While such circumstances were few and far between, they did occur. Mr M reacted with satisfaction and, later, a modicum of pleasure. He soon sought affirmation from group members when he recounted tales of his successes as a trial attorney. Eventually, he reported examples of increased openness with his wife and, again, met with affirming reactions.

The group enjoys his existence. Mr M can now contemplate that his wife might enjoy his existence as well. In a philosophic mode, he recently told the group that their pleasure in his accomplishments made him feel close to them.

He said that was the most emotional thing he had ever uttered. The goal was attachment; part of the method was tolerance of differences and acceptance of limitations in Mr M's style and character and structure.

Responsiveness and reciprocity

Responsiveness is the essence of the self-affirming experience. Emde (1987) observes that when the caregiver's response on an affective level is greater than the infant's, the infant reciprocates beyond his original starting point and his affective development is enhanced. He further asserts that all affectively responsive experiences facilitate the development of important psychic structures like care of the self, reciprocity, empathy and some aspects of moral internalization such as 'playing by the rules'. Socarides and Stolorow's (1984–1985) landmark paper on affects and selfobjects conceptualized these phenomena.

Another clinical example, from a different group, involves Mr Y, a young man who is somewhat similar to Mr M. He describes himself as 'dead inside', not caring about much of anything one way or another and feeling immobilized in his desire to find a compatible partner. His father had been an extremely driven and financially successful cardiac surgeon who had an emotional breakdown during Mr Y's childhood.

The father is now heavily medicated, sleeps until 2:00 or 3:00 p.m. every day, no longer practices and is emotionally unavailable to himself and his family. In the group, Mr Y was describing his attempts at a new relationship when Miss S asked, 'Do you go to sleep in a relationship like your father does?' Mr Y, startled by the intensity of her response, proceeded to reveal aspects of his family life he 'didn't even know he knew'. He adored his mother's father who was fun-loving, sensitive and playful like his mother was in her youth. Mr Y's father and paternal grandfather were thoroughly contemptuous of the maternal grandfather and squelched attempts by Mr Y to spend time with him. That would lead him to 'a life as a sissy'.

The therapist suggested that Mr. Y might be in a conflict over what kind of man to be – one like his maternal grandfather or like his father. Stolorow (1985), in his paper on conflict, differentiates between the notion of conflict as explained in 'drive' theory and that described in his intersubjectivity theory. In the latter, the essential conflict is between following one's own ambitions and the fear of losing the self object tie. Thus, the conflict is between being true to oneself and 'risking' loss of the bond, or complying, as required, but abandoning the possibility of independent thought and action.

Mr Y acknowledged that he would feel disloyal to disavow himself of his father's commitment to financial success 'at all costs'. Miss S responded, 'Of course you feel stuck. Your life has come to a grinding halt because you don't feel safe to be like the sensitive, playful grandfather you admired and enjoyed.' Miss S's response to Mr Y was a direct reaction to his expression of 'stuckness'. She used his exact words. Her response was filled with caring and she was excited by the prospect of helping him. He drew enthusiasm of his own from her excitement and appeared animated with hope about the prospects for the future.

Affective attunement

According to Stern (1985), unconscious and conscious feelings, via nonverbal cues, are easily sensed by the infant. He defines attunement as 'the performance of behaviors that express the quality of feeling of a shared affect state.' He observes that, from the moment of birth, the infant is a deeply social being who finds and engages in uniquely salient interactions with other humans. The infant's emerging relatedness and social emergence depends upon the caregiver's level of attunement.

This attunement can be experienced by the infant in a variety of ways. Stern discards 'orality' as the single stance for 'taking in the world' and observes the infant as eagerly reactive to visual, auditory and tactile stimuli. No organ or mode seems to have special status with regard to affective attunement. Stern's de-emphasis on the mouth as engaging the world of the infant is welcome. It is applicable in group treatment in underscoring patients' benefit from hearing, learning and looking, as well as talking and being talked to. Trevarthen (1994) further demonstrates the achievement or loss of intersubjective attunement through all of the senses.

Stern's abandonment of the 'so-called' autistic phase re-emphasizes the importance of attunement. When the infant is viewed as separate but not autistic, the infant's needs for the caregiver are seen as changing from moment to moment. The capacity of the caregiver to understand these changes in the infant enhances the infant's sense of self. When we assume that there is no autistic phase, every member of a therapy group can be experiencing attunement with others on some level, be it verbally expressed or not, at different times in their group experience. Stern (1985) suggests that there is not necessarily an undifferentiated developmental phase of symbiosis, as Mahler (1972) sees it. Rather, he states that an 'active process is needed for the infant to acquire the basic sense of connectedness, affiliation, attachment and security.' The implication for group therapy is the increased emphasis on the patient's active search for needed selfobject experiences. While the conflicts, fears and defenses surrounding these needs are to be explained and interpreted, the patient can benefit from encouragement to actively seek fulfillment of the felt need.

Another important function of the group is the containment of painful affects such as anger, anxiety and depression. Patients frequently hide these emotions out of fear, shame or conflict and sometimes are not even aware of what they are feeling. It can take a great deal of attuned awareness to pick up the affect when it is heavily defended. At times the therapist misses the patient's signals and a group member will 'tune in' more accurately if he is sitting close to the anxious or depressed patient or shares the same affect. Group members learn to look for cues from their experience of the therapist doing so. For example:

Mrs S began the group session with complaints about her husband's behavior. In a previous' session Mrs S had described a visit of her fearful mother following the Northridge earthquake. Immediately upon her mother's departure Mrs S became very angry because she 'finally had her mother all to herself' and then the mother decided to leave, planning to rejoin her husband in their damaged home. Mrs S was the eldest of nine siblings born within one to two years of each other, the brother next in line to her being only ten months younger. She clearly recognized a sensitivity to be 'displaced' and a feeling of never getting enough of what she needed. She had often reported intolerance of separation from her husband and a craving for constant connectedness. With this historical information in mind, the therapist attempted to draw links between her anger at her mother and her displeasure with her husband. Interpretations were attempted to help Mrs S see how difficult it was for her husband to satisfy her and how devastated he might feel when he could not. Mrs S appeared to be going along with the direction of the session when Mr L intervened with the comment, 'I don't think Kathleen wants to hear what you have to say; I think she just needs to complain to us and get it all off her chest. After that she might be more receptive to you.' Mrs S responded, 'Thank God someone understands me – I just want to bitch and moan about him and I don't want to think about what he is feeling. I only want to think about what I am feeling.' Needless to say, the session followed the new direction with recognition by the therapist and then by the group of Mr L's attunement and sensitivity towards Mrs S. At the following meeting of the group Mrs S let us know how much better she felt after the previous meeting and that she was now ready to look at how she might help her husband feel better also. This patient seemed to feel she could not be attuned to her husband and preserve an experience of selfhood. She first had to be affirmed; only then could she risk attunement to her husband.

Conclusion

The data from infant observational research places new emphasis upon the therapist's attention to his or her own self-experience and is in support of intersubjectivity theory. Traditional psychotherapy has overemphasized the cognitive factor in treatment; intersubjectivity theory focuses attention on the importance of the affective interaction and on the emotional forces that drive the treatment relationship. Applying intersubjectivity theory to the group modality further extends its usefulness. It stresses the significance of the therapist's own personality structure, focuses upon his use of self-reflection as a tool in therapy and emphasizes his need for containment of painful and aggressive affects.

As with the caregiver–infant dyad, the therapist affects the psychic life of the group in a variety of ways. As leader of the group he sets the tone for acceptance, tolerance, support, encouragement, openness and honesty. As provider, he is attuned to the needs of the others and demonstrates an ability to promote growth, nurture, soothe, comfort, and encourage acceptance and expression of joy, excitement and love. He is ever vigilant of the separate self of his patients and of the boundaries between them. He respects their uniqueness while recognizing their needs.

Most importantly, he is cognizant of his own limitations. To that end, he engages in ongoing self-awareness and personal development because, as with the caregiver and infant, his impact can be profound.

Acknowledgement

The author wishes to express gratitude to Joel Jay West, M.D. for his assistance in the preparation of this chapter.

Bibliography

Atwood, G.E. and Stolorow, R.D. (1979, 1993) *Faces in a Cloud*. New Jersey: Jason Aronson, Inc.

Atwood, G.E. and Stolorow, R.D. (1984) Structures of Subjectivity: Explorations in Psychoanalytic Phenomenology. Hillsdale, NJ: Analytic Press.

Bacal, H.A. (1985) 'Object-relations in the group from the perspective of self psychology.' *International Journal of Group Psychotherapy 35*, 4, 483–501.

Bacal, H.A. and Newman, K.M. (1990) *Theories of Object Relations: Bridge to Self-Psychology.* New York: Columbia University Press.

Beebe, B., Jaffey, J. and Lachmann, F. (1992) 'A dyadic systems view of communication.' In N. Skolnick and S. Warshow (eds) *Relational Perspectives in Psychoanalysis.* Hillsdale, NJ: Analytic Press.

Beebe, B. and Lachmann, F. (1988) 'The contribution of mother-infant mutual influence to the origins of self and object representations.' *Psychoanalytical Psychology 5*, 305–337.

Bion, W.R. (1959) *Experiences in Groups.* New York: Basic Books.

Bowlby, J. (1969, 1973, 1980) *Attachment and Loss* (Vols. 1, 2, 3). New York: Basic Books.

Bowlby, J. (1988) 'Developmental psychiatry comes of age.' *American Journal of Psychiatry 145*, 1, 1–10.

Brazelton, T.B. (1990) *The Earliest Relationship.* Reading, MA: Addison-Wesley Inc.

Chess, S. and Thomas, A. (1986) *Temperament in Clinical Practice.* New York: Guilford Press.

Emde, R.N. (1987), August) The affective core of the self: Motivational structures from infancy. Paper presented at the International Psychoanalytic Congress, Montreal.

Escalona, S. (1963) 'Patterns of infantile experience and the developmental process.' In R. Eissler *et al.* (eds) *The Psychoanalytic Study of the Child,* (Vol. 18). New York: International University Press.

Fraiberg, S.H. (1980) *Clinical Studies in Infant Mental Health: The First Year of Life.* New York: Basic Books.

Grotjahn, M. (1957) *Beyond Laughter.* McGraw, Hill Book Co., Inc., New York.

Grotjahn, M. (1977) *The Art and Technique of Analytic Group on Therapy.* New York: Jason Aronson.

Harwood, I. (1983) 'The application of self psychological concepts to group psychotherapy.' *International Journal of Group Psychotherapy 33*, 469–487.

Harwood, I. (1986) *The Need for Optimal, Available Caretakers: Moving Towards Extended Selfobject Experience. Group Analysis 19*, 291–302.

Harwood, I. (1993) 'Examining early childhood multiple cross-cultural extended selfobject and traumatic experiences and creating optimum treatment environments.' Paper presented at the 16th Annual Conference on the Psychology of the Self. Toronto, Canada.

Kohut, H. (1977) *The Restoration of the Self.* New York: International University Press.

Kohut, H. (1984) *How Does Analysis Cure?* 'Chicago: The University of Chicago Press.

Lachmann, F. (1986) 'Interpretation of psychic conflict and adversarial relationships.' *Psychoanalytic Psychology 3*, 341–355.

Lachmann, F. and Beebe, B. (1992) 'Reformulations of early development and transference.' In J. Barron, M. Eagle and J. Wolitsky (eds) *Interface of Psychoanalysis and Psychology.* Washington, D.C.: American Psychological Association.

Lichtenberg, J. (1983) *Psychoanalysis and Infant Research.* Hillsdale, NJ: Analytic Press.

Mahler, M.S. (1972) 'A study of the separation-individuation process and its possible application to borderline phenomena in the psychoanalytic situation.' *Psychoanalytic Study of the Child 25*, 421–422.

Sanville, J. (1987, March) 'Theories, therapies, therapists: their transformations.' *Smith College Studies in Social Work 57*, 2, 75–92.

Schain, J. (1985) 'Can Klein and Kohut work together in a group?' *Clinical Social Work Journal 13* (4), 293–304.

Socarides, D.D. and Stolorow, R.D. (1984–1985) 'Affects and selfobjects.' *Annual of Psychoanalysis 12*, 105–119.

Spitz, R.A. (1965) *The First Year of Life.* New York: International Universities Press.

Stern, D.N. (1985) *The Interpersonal World of the Infant: A View from Psychoanalysis.* 12–132, 105–119. New York: International University Press.

Stolorow, R.D. (1985) 'Toward a pure psychology of inner conflict.' In A. Goldberg (ed) *Progress in Self Psychology*, Vol.1. New York: Guilford Press.

Stolorow, R.D. and Atwood, G.E. (1992) *Contexts of Being: The Intersubjective Foundations of Psychological Life.* Hillsdale, N.J.: Analytic Press.

Stolorow, R.D., Atwood, G.E. and Brandchaft, B. (eds) (1994) *The Intersubjective Perspective.* New Jersey: Jason Aronson.

Stolorow, R.D., Brandchaft, B. and Atwood, G.E. (1987) *Psychoanalytic Treatment: An Intersubjective Approach.* New Jersey: Analytic Press.

Stolorow, R.D. and Lachmann, F. (1980) *Psychoanalysis of Developmental Arrests: Theory and Treatment.* New York: International Universities Press.

Trevarthen, C. (1994, August) 'Morality without words: moments of self confidence and shame in infants relations with others.' Paper presented for the Psychoanalytic Center of California at UCLA Faculty Center, Los Angeles.

Winnicott, D.W. (1965) *The Maturational Processes and the Facilitating Environment.* New York: International Universities Press.

Winnicott, D.W. (1971) *Playing and Reality.* London: Tavistock Publications.

CHAPTER 9

Examining Early Childhood Multiple Cross-Cultural Extended Selfobject and Traumatic Experiences and Creating Optimum Treatment Environments[1]

Irene N.H. Harwood

Most psychoanalytic literature and research address the person as a product of the Western European, or even more narrowly Anglo-American, nuclear family configuration. The influence of the *extended* family on the developing individual as it operates in the Asian, Black, Eastern European, Middle Eastern, Italian, Spanish, or Latin American cultures, has been virtually ignored. Freud's notation of problematic nannies, Sullivan's credit to the 'significant others', Winnicott's recognition of the 'caretaking environment', and Kohut's focus on 'selfobjects' have been nods in the direction of others in a child's total cultural world.

The developmental contribution or damage that these 'others' make to the psychic structure of the growing child has not been fully appreciated. While diagnosing, understanding the meaning of the transference, analysing and reintegrating fragmentations into a more cohesive psychological structure, it is crucial that we use theoretical paradigms which encompass the *total caretaking and traumatizing environment* with its specific positive or negative contributions in forming cohesive or wobbly psychic structure.

Beatrice Beebe (Beebe and Lachmann 1988a; 1988b; Beebe, Jaffe and Lachmann 1992) in her research and film points to the mother–infant dyad, though she shows us *multiple* caretaking dyads (researchers, research assistants and mothers) interacting with babies (Beebe 1993). The existence of multiple

---

1   Presented at the 16th Annual Conference on the Psychology of the Self, Toronto, Canada, 30 October 1993.

caretaking dyads is, in fact, the operative structure in modern life. Our lives intermix; seldom is the mother alone with her child from sunup to sundown. Others enter the environment, but are often not considered in how they are influencing the child, just as Beebe while commenting on the 'mother–infant mutual influence' fails to discuss the long-term ramifications, for example, of her own significant contribution in a beautifully sensitive and soothing interaction with an infant who would otherwise not receive such attunement if left only to interact in the mother–infant dyad.

In the diverse multiple caretaking environment, the existence and subjective meaning of the *cross-cultural* component (cultural, racial, ethnic, religious, physical or other outstanding characteristics) also needs to be noted and understood for each person. We also need to determine if these components with specific attached affects are being transferred from earlier traumatic and selfobject experiences. This chapter expands the notion of early childhood multiple *cross-cultural extended selfobject and traumatic experiences* to all significant others in the early environment, beyond the selfobject experiences of the extended family I have addressed earlier (Harwood 1986).

Those in related fields of child development, psychology and social research need to understand that both the positive and negative elements of the multiple extended cross-cultural experiences affect the evolving self-structure, as well as the intersubjective context (see Atwood and Stolorow 1984) in which interaction takes place. Such knowledge could prove helpful to a changing society. Kohut (1977) warned that changing social factors influence the parental selfobject matrix and determine the type of prevalent psychopathology that will dominate. He suggested a need for further critical evaluation and work in this area by social scientists who are grounded in psychoanalysis. He also expressed interest and encouragement of written material on group treatment that demonstrates the applicability of self psychology in various areas outside the primary analytic one (Kohut 1980). Today's American society, unlike the one in which psychoanalysis was born or even the one Kohut knew in his lifetime, is struggling to devise effective ways to nurture the young of a large population of single and working mothers and, therefore, the myth of the isolated Madonna and Child needs to be reconsidered in this new context.

In our theories and clinical work we should always be cognizant that a child is not born to a mother alone nor lives in isolation with only one or two caretakers. Even the isolated single mother has friends, significant neighbours and family that can have major impact on the psychological structure of the child. Therefore, these significant others become part of the multiple, cross-cultural extended experiences that from the very beginning an infant can experience as either enhancing or fragmenting his/her virtual/nuclear self that Kohut (1971; 1977) spoke about. Depending on what psychic structure has already been built and how these interactions are experienced by the growing child, further selective internalizations, disappointments or fragmentations occur from the results of significant interactions with the larger world.

Thus, particularly when a person was not brought up in a nuclear family, but had other significant caretakers (grandmothers, older siblings, nannies, etc.), clinicians must ensure that they do not miss the impact and subjective meaning of the early selfobject and traumatizing experiences that are other than with the mother, and recognize how often these preverbal and without conscious memory traumatic experiences are later confused especially with mother.

The first selfobject functions introduced by Kohut – tension regulation and soothing as part of the earlier idealized parent imago, mirroring and twinship (Kohut 1971; 1977; 1984) – and later ones introduced by others, such as integration of affects (through differentiation,. synthesis, modulation, and desomatization) (Socarides and Stolorow 1984–1985), self delineation (Stolorow Atwood and Brandchaft 1992), efficacy and adversarial experiences (Wolf 1988), fantasy (Bacal 1990; 1992) and limit setting (Harwood 1993), all occur within a larger caretaking milieu or what I called the *multiple extended selfobject environment* (Harwood 1986). Optimally, this environment has elements of Wolf's (1980) 'empathic selfobject ambience' and Bacal's (1985; 1990) and Bacal and Newman's (1990) 'optimal responsiveness'. I propose that attuned multiple cross-cultural extended selfobject experiences which include *all kinds of differences* are necessary and optimal for a more healthy, diverse, flexible and creative repertoire of organizing principles to develop as part of the foundation upon which psychological structure begins to build.

In addition, I would like to underline that the existence of multiple cross-cultural extended selfobject experiences buffers the traumatizations and disappointments that a child experiences if he or she only lives within a pathological single or dual parent–caretaking matrix. On the other hand, we must also be alert to the fact that, even with subjectively experienced good-enough mothering and other positive multiple selfobject experiences, other repetitive failures and disorganizing experiences within the multiple extended cross-cultural milieu (any relatives, family acquaintances, friends or childcare persons) can be activated in what Stolorow and Lachmann (1984–1985) called the repetitive, conflictual, resistive dimension of the transference and need to be fully understood and analysed in order to help reintegrate these fragmenting experiences into a more cohesive whole.

Group analytic psychotherapy, in addition to couples and individual treatment, provides a golden opportunity both for activating and observing what Stolorow and Lachmann (1984–1985) called the selfobject dimension of the transference and for the working through of what these authors call the repetitive, conflictual transference. In couples or group treatment, a person's interaction with others will reflect in part transference manifestations of early fragmentation resulting from early traumatizing interactions. But, unlike in individual analysis/treatment, the group analyst/therapist has an advantage in not having her own countertransference or subjectivity *as directly* challenged when the transference manifestations are between others. It should go without saying that awareness is needed in regard to any sibling, partner or other relationship issues with which we may identify. On the other hand, one must be aware that in order to analyse and reintegrate the repetitive, conflictual aspects of displacements/ transferences with others, the transference with the analyst/therapist in individual, couples or group must be experienced by the patient as a holding, containing and idealizing environment which can be dependable, non-retaliatory and trustworthy (Harwood 1992b).

At the Self Psychology Conference in San Francisco, Segalla *et al.* (1989) documented in their presentation cases in which dramatic growth and development of new psychic structure occurred when additional multiple selfobject experiences were provided by adding couples and group treatment. In the.discussion part of the presentation, Morrison (1989) further questioned the accuracy of the notion of a single pivotal transference as the organizer of experience.

Developmental research

Though previous psychoanalytic theorists believed otherwise, current developmental research summarized by Stern (1983; 1985) consistently affirms that the infant is genetically predesigned to discriminate and to form distinct schemas of self and other from the earliest months. Furthermore, s/he does not confuse the functions of caregivers, does not confuse one object with another, and does not exist in an undifferentiated state. Eimas (1971) revealed that infants can sort out speech sounds into appropriate sound units. The work of Meltzoff and Borton (1979) shows that infants demonstrate 'cross-modal equivalence' – e.g. are able to recognize visually what before has only been experienced by touch. The work of Spelke (1976) confirmed the existence of cross-modal integration, verifying infants' ability to recognize appropriately which sound belonged with which object. Spieker's (1982) study presents dramatic evidence that infants know the smiling person remains the same when a frown replaces the smile. In addition, Fagan (1976) finds that the infant distinguishes one facial configuration from another. The above research appears to confirm that the non-traumatized infant can distinguish the face, voice and touch of the mother from those. of the grandmother.

In addition to considering the infant's early ability to differentiate between primary caretakers as well as between caretaker and inanimate object, Lichtenberg (1982) reports on the neonate's biological priming to seek stimuli from its environment. Lichtenberg's finding supports the premise that the infant engages in evocative behaviour to obtain a desired response from his or her total environment. From the very beginning the child whose environment includes community or extended family has a greater probability of getting the responsiveness it needs.

Thus, new infant research allows the conclusion that the non-clinical infant does not confuse one object with another, nor the stimuli or functions that different caregivers provide. That conclusion runs counter to previous psychoanalytic developmental theories, retrospectively based on pathology and fragmentation, which did not appreciate or understand the infant's innate abilities to interact with and integrate the functions of its *total* good-enough environment. Previous formulations (Mahler 1968; Mahler, Pine and Bergman 1975) also confused the infant's need for *at least one* consistent caretaker with *only one* caretaker. Bowlby (1984) confirmed that the infant and mother need not be held in isolation for attachment to occur, but that the contributions of others are welcome as long as they do not become overwhelming.

But, on the other hand, when the environment is overwhelming or traumatizing, the very young child (yet without fully developed cognitive abilities to verbally describe experience) stores in the psyche-soma fragments of these experiences which do confuse the actual traumatizing agent(s) with others. I have found that activating, understanding and sorting out the confusion around these early fragments and compartmentalizations, which may or may not involve the primary caretakers, brings greater cohesion, emotional relief and a sense of integration to our patients.

It is the thesis of this chapter that by adding analytic group treatment, the clinician can observe these old fragmentations through the patient's interaction with others. Thus, by availing him/herself with an expanded clinical arena, the clinician can observe, understand and connect to their genetic roots *at the same time* the multiplicity of transferences that develop with others which have roots in the person's childhood and preverbal/precognitive experience.

New theoretical constructs

New conclusions therefore can be reached about a diverse early selfobject environment in the light of the above research of early infant differentiation of self and other. If 'continuity of environmental provision' (Winnicott 1971, p.141) is taken as a given, and if the functions of the primary caretaker(s) are regarded as contributing 'to the organization of symbolic structure along multiple and yet interrelated developmental pathways' (Petrillo 1984; see also Waddington 1957), it can be surmised that several optimally experienced caretakers would enhance the diversity of the symbolic structure being organized. The above premise is not in total agreement with, but is an extension of, Kohut's (1977) idea that in the matrix of the relation to the second parent (he considered it to be usually the father), compensatory psychic structures can be built to supplement deficiencies in the central psychic structure.

The premise of this chapter would amend Kohut's idea to say that the second parent and others can be *just as* important from the very beginning in contributing toward the organization or disorganization of primary psychic structure. Stolorow and Lachmann (1984–1985) attest that transferences do not evolve in a linear way, but that they exist in a figure–ground relationship among multiple dimensions of the transference. Like them, I also believe that early organizing multiple cross-cultural extended selfobject and traumatizing experiences do not develop linearly, but in an aggregate as well as a figure–ground manner. For each child, the diversity and richness of the environment must be subjectively experienced as optimal and, therefore, not overwhelming. However, if the loss, diversity, or interactional quality of caretakers is traumatically overwhelming or disappointing it can be experienced as fragmenting and, consequently, *the psychological structure will also be weakened, split, fragmented or compartmentalized into many different parts.* When experiences are subjectively felt as overwhelmingly traumatic, the extreme fragmentation, I propose, can result in a multiple personality. It occurs with other traumatizations of self as well, not only in sexual violations.

In emphasizing the need to recognize, analyse and re-integrate early traumatic, disappointing and conflictual experiences, I want to point out that this is sometimes difficult to do when there is an idealizing transference, when the patient experiences a 'real relationship' (Horner 1987), when failures with the analyst/therapist are at a minimum or the patient is not primarily prone to fragmentation. One may continue working for a long time without encountering transferences from the multiple cross-cultural extended traumatic or disappointing experiences.

When we are diagnosing, we are aware of the limitations and results of having a single disturbed or rigid caretaker. Likewise when selecting appropriate treatment modalities, we need to understand the limitations of having (affectively or otherwise) a single analyst/therapist, which can result in a paucity of responsiveness, limited number of transferences, and a less than optimal healing repertoire (Harwood 1986) in the 'selective inclusion and exclusion of psychological structures' (Kohut 1977, p.183). In addition to addressing transference with the analyst/therapist, combining treatment modalities allows a more thorough activation and reworking of early multiple, cross-cultural, extended traumatizing experiences. At the same time, the patient must experience the selfobject bond with the analyst/therapist in place, in order to have less difficulty in examining conflictual aspects of early multiple, cross-cultural, extended disappointing or traumatic experiences when working through transferences with others in couples and. group treatment.

Clinical observations

Clinically, I have been impressed by the diagnostic and functioning differences between patients who apparently had similar primary caretakers. Closer scrutiny revealed that one group of patients were rigid in their responses, and resembled what Winnicott (1960a) described as the 'false self' built on identifications – crude, primitive identifications with a rather disturbed primary caretaker. The other group of patients (even though they, too, had a disturbed primary caretaker) showed less rigid defenses and were more flexible and creative in their 'functioning. They were distinguished from the first group in having had at least one additional significant person in their early caretaking environment.

The first clarification that needs to be made is that how the caretaker experienced his or her own state is not necessarily important to the infant. What is of significance is the subjective experience of *that particular infant* at *that particular time* of *that particular state* of the caretaker. For instance, for an infant who is in a tension-regulated state, a depressed, withdrawn caretaker can be a good-enough or optimal agent of care since at that time it is not impinging and is allowing the infant to experience its own spontaneity along with its own continuity of being. Therefore, that particular depressed, withdrawn caretaker's inability to be available for providing function's is not of any consequence at that time, as it might be at another time when the infant requires those functions. When an infant requires those particular functions and that unavailable caretaker does not provide them, the growing child can fragment or withdraw into whatever resources it has.

Thus, a person who as a baby had numerous selfobject functions to draw from one or more caretakers is not likely to see or experience the world through merely one shade of coloured glasses. That baby, child and adult will also have the hope that there may be a rainbow of colours to experience and choose.

At the beginning of therapy or as a result of a traumatizing experience, a patient may appear to have a depressive or even a schizoid nature, reminiscent of his or her primary caretaker(s). But given an environment (either in individual or in a group analytic matrix) where the patient can establish the needed selfobject bonds and responsiveness from others, it comes as no surprise to me that enfeeblement and agitation quickly disappear and the person appear more cohesive and integrated. Unlike the schizoid person whose rigid self-structure is based on primitive identifications with one primary caretaker who was experienced as overwhelming, the above individual had developed other early dependable bonds and attachments based upon at least one other early significant person. Thus, what makes the difference is the subjective emotional net balance in the person's number of positive and negative experiences with significant others which then allows him or her to recognize and trust a safe environment (as opposed to a potentially traumatizing one) in which growth cam resume. Let me share a clinical example that will illustrate both the multiple dimensions of multiple caretakers as well as the benefits of adding and combining treatment modalities. It will help us understand in which early significant dyads he experienced trauma, disappointment or identification with a feared but idealized other and in which dyads he experienced vitality, twinship or soothing.

Clinical example

When I met Mario, a recently divorced Latin businessman, he appeared quite sad and said he felt very disconnected in Los Angeles. He had not felt understood by the seven therapists he had interviewed. He had started on antidepressants two days before.

We reflected on the losses he must have experienced with his recent move We understood how this move brought up similar feelings of loss when he moved at the age of eight. He told me: 'You get it, unlike the others.' Establishing an idealized transference, he decided to start working with me three times a week, but asked for a lower fee for financial reasons (only later did I learn that Mario earned quite a nice living and he admitted identifying with his manipulative paternal grandfather, whose own father was criminally sociopathic),

At the beginning, he felt I understood his feelings more and more and decided to discontinue medication within a couple of weeks. As treatment proceeded, he continued in a firm idealizing transference with me, though he trivialized his easy-going deceased father and was quite disparaging of his mother, whom he called crazy, smothering, directing, manipulative, abandoning and without boundaries. As he reported his current interactions with his mother, something didn't fit between the picture that emerged and his subjective feelings. I guessed that his feelings were archaic ones directed either to the mother of his early life or maybe someone else. None of these archaic or negative feelings came up in our transference. My ability to stay empathically attuned to him and examine the material with him in an experience-near manner did not bring into the transference the strong negative feelings he was having towards many others in his larger world, I also could not get a full picture of what he did in his interactions with others who, he reported, became infuriated with him. In his eyes, his parents and the outside world were horribly stupid, critical and ungiving while I remained wise, soothing and energetic. Because of such a polarized picture, I decided to add analytic group therapy to see whether these transferences would be stimulated in another clinical environment which I felt would still be optimal, since I composed it, knew all of its members, and the possible selfobject functions and impingements that might be available.

Was I surprised! I met someone very different in group. He first tried to tell another new member in a very condescending way what was wrong with him (as we learned his paternal grandfather did to him). Then, he quickly set up a twinship with a man who, like Mario, would not date women of the same religion or background (crossing over to other cultures to avoid early subjectively experienced impingements with their demanding mothers). He then began to idealize an Asian woman who was very warm, energetic, perceptive, direct and from the same ethnic/racial cultural background as his nanny (the soothing and the later idealizing selfobject function was paired cross-culturally as well).

At that time, he tried to get me to further reduce his fee (he also was beginning to feel a sense of entitlement and no need for reciprocity, as with his nanny who gave unconditionally without asking anything in return while identifying with his paternal grandfather 'who never paid the full asking price'). When I did not further reduce the fee, he accused me of abandoning him as had his 'manipulative mother'. Thus, while he was establishing a firm idealizing transference with the Asian woman in group he started to de-idealize me, assuming that my background was the same as his, thus transferring onto me his culture and pairing with it the subjectively experienced early disappointments, all of which he attributed to his ungiving mother. Later we came to understand that he felt abandoned by his nanny when the family moved and, much later, he courageously admitted attributing to me manipulative aspects of himself.

Feeling deflated and angry by my holding fast to the fee this time, he decreased individual to once a week and then stopped it altogether, saying group was enough. He tried to ally himself with a long-term patient who was working through some adolescent issues with me. She rebuffed him (it reminded him of how often his oldest brother did the same – repeated traumatizations with a sibling). Not quite feeling he was acceptable, he seemed to take on the manner of speaking of the Asian woman he idealized (defensive identification and archaic twinship). She remained accepting of him (maintaining a selfobject bond) which seemed to provide a sense of well-being for him. When she graduated from group, he felt painful longing when he saw Asian women on the street (activating the cross-cultural transference). Sometimes he would follow them, never speaking to them, but feeling that if he only connected, he would feel whole and happy (he was looking for the selfobject bond he lost with his nanny, while pairing it with the cross-cultural characteristics).

He felt somewhat empty and depressed after the object of his idealization left group. Neither his twinship with a male member nor his positive relations with other group members were enough to preclude the longing for the evoked memory of his vital, cohesive and idealized nanny. He gingerly inquired about coming back into individual three to four times a week while remaining in group, but he feared I would retaliate and abandon him. Since I didn't, his depression lifted as he again restored an idealizing transference (now, he considered me to be like his 'solid, wise, limit-setting' and containing maternal grandfather). Within this positive selfobject bond, we both knew we had to dig deeper into the genetic roots and meanings of the multiple cross-cultural extended transferences.

We stumbled upon many new realizations as we worked in group and individual, making genetic connections and utilizing dreams to access some repressed memories (the latter were confirmed by his mother). The journey became developmental. At first, he experienced himself as an empty infant – he would huddle up in a fetal-like position in the mornings. This empty depression we understood to be an archaic merger with his depressed schizophrenic paternal grandmother who, he learned from his parents, had been with him daily for the first eight years of his life, but of whom he had no memory up to this point. He told me that my availability on the phone while I was out of town, along with the consistency of my calmness and vitality, allowed him to trust me enough ad himself to recover both somatic and cognitive painful memories. He also remembered his father's physical violence which preceded his mother's depression during her next pregnancy, and he understood his sense of fear of the former and abandonment with the latter.

One of the recalled traumatic experiences, activated during a move into his new office, was an empty bedroom with only a bed (lack of a caretaking environment which became transferred onto a room). He also remembered trying antisocial behaviour after being rejected by kids in the new neighbourhood (an enfeebled self tries to merge and identify with the ideals of a sociopathic paternal grandfather). As we proceeded with our work both in group and individual (the group interactions providing both positive, mildly disappointing or hurtful experiences which would further stimulate genetic material), joyful happy memories from weekends with his maternal grandparents started emerging which had not come up till then. Understanding the multitude of transferences and making genetic connections to the multiple extended cross-cultural caretaking environment yielded many transmuting internalizations which also allowed integrating, both in group and individual, the positive and negative elements and affects of the original environment into a more cohesive and integrated whole.

A dream condensation described his three stages of treatment so far. In the first stage he was asked by a rigid woman he knows (his early mother) to put a cap on a sewer (medication capsules). He tried, but could not. In the second, he followed bandits (his paternal grandfather and antisocial peers of his adolescence). In the third, he is lying in a bed in a room the size of my office, he says, during a hurricane. A woman friend he knows, likes, trusts, who is a therapist and 'is familiar with the territory' helps him put back into place the windows which have been thrown back and forth by the wind (the rebuilding of psychological structure).

Uncovering early experiences, as well as identifying the displacements and transferences while connecting the diversity of affects to their original emotional and physical environments, allows them to be reintegrated into greater cohesion for Mario. But, it was the adding group to individual that allowed me to activate and vividly start observing *at the same time* multiple transferences and structures of subjectivity (or what in another theoretical language has been called an internal environment). As the multiplicity of transferences were examined along with newly made genetic connections to past disappointing and traumatizing experiences, transmuting internalizations occurred allowing new integration and cohesion. Observing and understanding the multiple transferences that emerged in group allowed me to access them and help re-integrate them more quickly since they were not coming up directly with me in a one-to-one three times a week modality. I ask you to consider what aspects of a patient's early subjective experience you may not be able to observe for a long time, if at all, in individual analysis or therapy, if you do not explore the patient's multiple cross-cultural extended experiences.

Conclusions

It is important to reiterate that clinicians can better determine each person's strengths and prognosis if they make careful assessment of who *all* the important persons were in the person's life and what particular selfobject functions they did and did not provide, instead of narrowing the line of sight to focus on one relationship only – that of mother and child. Sometimes she has received the credit, but most often she has received the blame, for what others did or did not do.

Clinically, for those patients who have been confined or restricted to internalizing the functions, or lack of functions, of one primary caregiver, we should consider complementing the intense one-to-one therapeutic experience with analytic group psychotherapy, where each person has readily available a family of diverse cultural, religious, and ethnic backgrounds and points of view. When there is disappointment with one group member, there can be a transmuting internalization with another, and the possibility of maintaining a responsive connection with yet another. In an analytic group, the role of the therapist is to ensure an optimum environment that is not too traumatic, but where, through the connection or bond with the therapist, other members, or the group as a whole (Durkin 1964; Foulkes 1964; 1975; Pines 1981; Scheidlinger 1974), failures and disappointments can be transmuted bit by bit into self-esteem, cohesiveness, respect and mutuality (Harwood 1983; 1986; 1992a; 1992b).

Last, but no less important, for those clinicians who work with pregnant parents, young parents or families with young children, the concept of multiple cross-cultural extended selfobject bonds may offer a special understanding and allow them to make a special contribution. Not only can the clinician analyse the fragmenting environmental situation but (using the knowledge of how important all caretakers are from conception on) can also suggest additional resources, with the capacity to provide needed selfobject functions, in order to ensure that the children and adults of tomorrow do not develop the borderline and psychotic disorders characteristic of a fragmented culture. More and more, current socioeconomic changes, not just in North America, but in most societies, are taking away both parents from the child, as women take on full-time jobs outside the home. Most of the time the demands of their work leave them too stressed or depleted at the end of the day to take on their second job as parents. Thus, the need for a consistent, good-enough caretaking environment hopefully supplied by daycare workers, nannies, or extended family during the course of the day becomes even more important.

Heinz Kohut was not a linear thinker, nor did he feel obliged to respect the limits and repeat the mistakes of our historical psychoanalytic father of the Oedipal conflict. His own wealth of experience in different cultures and his recognition of the importance of at least one more selfobject experience, the father, led to the integration and birth of the new theory of self psychology. Hopefully, the same kind of recognition can be given to all potentially important others – be they parents, siblings, the extended community family, the cultural family or the larger human family.

References

Atwood, G.E. and Stolorow, R.D. (1984) *Structure of Subjectivity: Explorations in Psychoanalytic Phenomenology.* Hillsdale, New Jersey: Analytic Press.

Bacal, H. (1985) 'Optimal responsiveness and the therapeutic process.' In A. Goldberg (ed) *Progress in Self Psychology 1*, 202–26.

Bacal, H. (1990) 'Does an object relations theory exist in self psychology?' *Psychoanalytic Inquiry 10*, 197–220.

Bacal, H. (1992) Selfobject Relationships Redefined. Presented at the Self Psychology Conference, Los Angeles.

Bacal, H. and Newman, K. (1990) *Theories of Object Relations: Bridges to Self Psychology.* New York: Columbia University Press.

Beebe, B. (1993) 'Contributions from Infant Research.' Film shown at the 16th Annual Conference on the Psychology of the Self. Toronto, Canada, October 1993.

Beebe, B., Jaffe, J. and Lachmann, F. (1992) 'A dyadic systems view of communication.' In N. Skolnick and S. Warshaw (eds) *Relational Perspectives in Psychoanalysis.* Hillsdale, NJ: Analytic Press.

Beebe, B. and Lachmann, F. (1988a) 'The contribution of mother–infant mutual influence to the origins of self and object representations.' *Psychoanalytic Psychology 5*, 305–337.

Beebe, B. and Lachmann, F. (1988b) 'Mother–infant mutual influence and precursors of psychic structure.' In A. Goldberg (ed) *Frontiers in Self Psychology: Progress in Self Psychology 4.* Hillsdale, NJ: Analytic Press.

Bowlby, J. (1984) Personal Communication, London, June 29.

Durkin, H. (1964) *The Group in Depth.* New York: International Universities Press.

Eimas, P.D. (1971) 'Speech perception in infants.' *Science 171,* 303–306.

Fagan, J.F. (1976) 'Infants' recognition of invariant features of faces.' *Child Development 47,* 627–638.

Foulkes, S.H. (1964) *Therapeutic Group Analysis.* London: Heinemann.

Foulkes, S.H. (1975) *Group Analytic Psychotherapy: Methods and Principles.* London: Gordon & Breach.

Harwood, I.N.H. (1983) 'The application of self psychology to group psychotherapy.' *International Journal of Group Psychotherapy 33,* 469–487.

Harwood, I.N.H. (1986) 'The need for optimal, available caretakers: Moving towards extended selfobject experience.' *Group Analysis 19,* 291–302.

Harwood, I.N.H. (1992a) 'Group psychotherapy and disorders of the self.' *Group Analysis 25,* 19–26.

Harwood, I.N.H. (1992b) 'Advances in group psychotherapy and self psychology: An intersubjective approach.' *Group 16,* 220–232.

Harwood, I.N.H. (1993) 'The extended selfobject function of group therapy.' Presented at the American Institute of Medical Education Conference on Creativity and Madness. Santa Fe, New Mexico, August 1993, .

Horner, A. (1987) 'The "real" relationship and analytic neutrality.' In *Primacy of Structure: Psychotherapy of Underlying Character Pathology.* New York: Jason Aronson, 1990.

Klein, M. (1975) *Love, Guilt and Reparation & Other Works.* Delacorte Press/Seymour Lawrence.

Kohut, H. (1971) *The Analysis of the Self.* New York: International Universities Press.

Kohut, H. (1977) *The Restoration of the Self.* New York: International Universities Press.

Kohut, H. (1980) Personal Correspondence.

Kohut, H. (1984) *How Does Analysis Cure?* Chicago: University of Chicago Press.

Lichtenberg, J. (1982) 'Reflections on the first year of life.' *Psychoanalytic Inquiry 1,* 696–729.

Mahler, M. (1968) *On Human Symbiosis and the Vicissitudes of Individuation.* New York: International Universities Press.

Mahler, M., Pine, P. and Bergman, A. (1975) *The Psychological Birth of the Human Infant.* New York: Basic Books.

Meltzoff, A.N. and Borton, W. (1979) 'Intermodal matching by human neonates.' *Nature 282,* 403–404.

Morrison, A. (1989) Discussant of 'Multiple Selfobject Relationships' at the Self Psychology Conference, San Francisco.

Petrillo, L.J. (1984) *Concretization, illusion, and mourning: An examination of the relationship between intersubjective areas of experience, symbolization and mourning.* Unpublished manuscript, Yeshiva University, 1984.

Pines, M. (1981) 'The frame of reference of group psychotherapy.' *International Journal of Group Psychotherapy 31,* 275–285.

Scheidlinger, S. (1974) 'On the concept of the mother-group.' *International Journal of Group Psychotherapy 24,* 417–428.

Segalla, R., Silvers, D., Wine, B. and Pillsbury, G. (1989) 'Multiple Selfobject Relationships.' Presented at the Self Psychology Conference. San Francisco.

Socarides, D.D. and Stolorow, R.D. (1984–1985) 'Affects and selfobjects.' *Annual of Psychoanalysis 12*, 105–119.

Spelke, E. (1976) 'Infants' intermodal perceptions of events.' *Cognitive Psychology, 8*, 533–560.

Spieker, S. (1982) *Infant recognition of invarient categories of faces: Person identity and facial expression.* Doctoral dissertation, Cornell University.

Stern, D.N. (1983) 'The early development of schemas of self, other, and "self with other".' In J. Lichtenberg and S. Kaplan (eds) *Reflections on Self Psychology.* Hillsdale, New Jersey, Analytic Press.

Stern, D.N. (1985) *The Interpersonal World of the Infant A View from Psychoanalysis and Developmental Psychology.* New York: Basic Books.

Stolorow, R.D., Atwood, G.E. and Brandchaft, B. (1992) 'Three realms of the unconscious and their therapeutic transformation.' *Psychoanalytic Review 79*, 25–30.

Stolorow, R.D. and Lachmann, F.M. (1984–1985) 'Transference: The future of an illusion.' *Annual of Psychoanalysis 12*, 19–37.

Waddington, C.H. (1957) In *Structures of Subjectivity: Explorations in Psychoanalytic Phenomenology.* G.E. Atwood and R.D. Stolorow. Hillsdale, New Jersey; Analytic Press.

Winnicott, D.W. (1960) 'Ego distortion in terms of the true and false self.' In *The Maturational Processes and the Facilitating Environment.* New York: International Universities Press, 1965.

Winnicott, D.W. (1971) 'Contemporary concepts of adolescent development and their implications for higher education.' In *Playing and Reality.* London: Tavistock Publications.

Wolf, E.S. (1980) 'On the developmental line of selfobject relations.' In A. Goldberg (ed) *Advances in Self Psychology.* New York: International Universities Press.

Wolf, E.S. (1988) *Treating the Self: Elements of Clinical Psychology.* New York: Guilford Press.

A Multiple Selfobject and Traumatizing Experiences Co-Therapy Model at Work

Damon L. Silvers

Several authors have written about the application of self psychology theory to group therapy (Bacal 1985a; Harwood 1983; 1986; 1992a; 1992b; 1993; 1995; Meyers 1978; Schwartzman 1984; Shapiro 1991; Stone and Whitman 1977; Weinstein 1987), but few (Harwood 1986; 1993; 1995; Segalla *et al.* 1988; 1989) have addressed in depth the impact of treating patients concurrently in self psychological individual and group psychotherapy. Recognizing the clinical value of combining these modalities, I and Segalla, Wine and Pillsbury (1988; 1989) reported effective treatment results with such an approach. A powerful impact on the overall treatment was noted when a group experience, co-led by the patient's individual therapist, was added to an ongoing individual treatment. Articulated as a clinically interactive model whose total impact was greater than the sum of the two modalities utilized, we also observed that members' experiences within the therapeutic group context were often catalytic in activating and deepening aspects of the transference in the individual treatment.

Combining treatment modalities deepens and enriches the overall psychotherapy experience because the addition of a co-therapy group to an ongoing individual treatment dramatically recreates the move from one caretaker to several. Segalla, Wine, Pillsbury and I made this observation in the 1988 paper stating that the individual/group co-therapy paradigm 'dramatically recreates the move from one caretaker to several and so on to such settings as preschool, school and jobs.' We observed that viewing groups as multiple selfobject experiences opened 'to sharper scrutiny relationships with other people such as siblings, hired caretakers, school teachers, grandparents, etc., who in fact may have provided significant experiences for our patients.' Also, in a related but independent contribution, Harwood (1986) made the observation that group therapy was an effective form of treatment to help individual patients internalize a multiplicity of selfobject functions from various constantly available caretakers.

More recently, the individual/group therapy model has been understood to be effective because it expands the therapeutic intersubjective field by exposing patients to a wider range of selfobject and conflictual, repetitive and resistive transference phenomena (Stolorow 1988). Harwood (1993), drawing from this bipolar perspective of transference, states that adding a group experience to an ongoing individual treatment broadens exposure to the total caretaking *and* traumatizing environment. She suggests an individual/group therapy paradigm because it offers increased clinical opportunities for observing, analyzing and working through repetitions of earlier selfobject and traumatizing experiences with multiple caretakers.

While highly compatible with the work of Harwood, the model described in this chapter differs significantly in that it considers selfobject and traumatizing transference phenomena from a co-therapy paradigm, while Harwood utilizes a single therapist model. By adding a second therapist, material emerges that does not emerge in the individual treatment or when there is a single therapist. Early experiences with the co-therapist facilitate the emergence of unconscious organizing principles which have not been activated in the individual treatment. Accordingly, the model has been entitled *a multiple selfobject and traumatizing experiences co-therapy model.*

Clinically, much of the benefit gained from placement in the group context is that patients are provided with new opportunities to explore areas of disturbance which may remain unexamined as part of the individual treatment process. This seems to happen, in part, because early repetitive failures and disorganizing experiences which have not been activated in the individual treatment and, therefore, remain unrecognized to patient and primary therapist, begin to get triggered in the context of the expanded group intersubjective field.

In the multiple selfobject and traumatizing experiences co-therapy paradigm, affectively meaningful experiences are symbolically recreated in the evolving group context. Triggered by both the empathic and unempathic responsiveness of the other group members, as well as the co-leaders, adult patients are able to gain access to early traumatizing experiences which have been denied cognitive articulation. Also, important affect states, which may never have been validated due to the chronic absence of attunement in the child–caregiver system, are differentiated, synthesized, modulated, cognitively articulated and integrated, as Socarides and Stolorow (1984–1985) suggest. From an intersubjective point of view, patients' early developmental traumas may be understood as originating from within a formative intersubjective context. From this theoretical perspective, according to Stolorow and Atwood (1992, p.53), affect becomes traumatic when the requisite attuned or optimal responsiveness that the child needs from the caretaker(s) is absent – leading to the child's loss of affect-regulatory capacity and thereby to an unbearable, overwhelmed, disintegrated, disorganized state.

Considering the potential risks for retraumatization, entering a group may be viewed symbolically as indicative of a deepening level of trust between patient and individual/primary therapist. In deciding to accept the risks, Segalla et al. (1988) suggest that both patient and therapist agree that there are aspects of the work which are best addressed in a setting which more accurately reflects a potential for re-creating previous and present life situations.

Theoretical thinking about the multiple selfobject and traumatizing experiences co-therapy model has had a developmental progression over the years. This progression has been influenced by ongoing advances in self psychology and, more recently, further shaped by the new contributions to intersubjectivity theory by Stolorow, Brandchaft and Atwood (1987–present), and by psychoanalytic researchers in infant development (Beebe and Lachmann 1994; 1992; 1988a; 1988b; Emde 1988; Lichtenberg 1983; Lichtenberg et al. 1992; Stern 1985). These advances have helped in focusing closer attention on the specific affective nuances that take place in the mutually regulated dyadic interactions occurring among members in groups. Also, from their own unique vantage points, the perspectives of infant research, self psychology and intersubjectivity theory have broadened understanding of the selfobject experience. Accordingly, this chapter refocuses attention on the central importance of affects (Socarides and Stolorow 1984–1985), and the selfobject experience, both developmentally and clinically.

Theoretical considerations and developmental research

Theoretically, the multiple selfobject and traumatizing experiences co-therapy model questions the validity of viewing a single, one-at-a-time transference as the sole organizer of self experience. Although it acknowledges the importance of the primary caretaker, symbolically represented in groups by the presence of the patient's individual therapist, this model holds that the contributions of the second parent and the 'others' (siblings, peers, hired caretakers, grandparents, etc.) have been underplayed in classical psychoanalytic theory, and to a lesser degree in early Kohutian thinking. It parallels Segalla et al.'s (1988; 1989) and Harwood's (1986; 1993; 1995) line of thinking that experiences with the second parent, symbolically represented in co-therapy groups in the form of the co-leader, and others (siblings, peers, etc.), symbolically represented in groups by the group members, can be *just as* important in contributing towards the organization of primary psychic structure. It is possible that the enduring preference of treating patients solely from an individual treatment model may be tied in part to classically trained analysts/therapists adhering to rather outdated notions of human development and motivation. This preference may need to be reconsidered in light of more recent psychoanalytic developmental research findings pertaining to the mutuality of influence observed in infant–caregiver interactional systems.

The importance placed on patients' selfobject and traumatizing experiences in groups is consistent with the efforts in contemporary self psychology and intersubjectivity to redefine the term 'selfobject' in light of recent infant development research findings (Beebe and Lachmann 1988b; 1991; 1994; Demos 1988; Emde 1988; Lichtenberg et al. 1992; Stern 1985). According to Lichtenberg (1991), reconsiderations brought about by clinical experience within self psychology and by infant research 'tilt our focus toward intrapsychic affective experiences closely interwoven with relational and intersubjective contexts' (p.455). Contemporary theory shifts the emphasis away from the selfobject as a person and as an internalized function by placing the emphasis on the affective dimension of self experience. From this vantage point, the need for selfobject ties pertains to the need for specific, requisite responsiveness to varying affect states throughout development (Stolorow et al. 1987). Selfobject and/or traumatizing experiences are viewed primarily as affective experiences involving one's sense of self. They are triggered in the context of others' attuned or misattuned responses, leading to experiences of self cohesion or fragmentation. The overwhelming evidence from infant research studies suggests that healthy child–caregiver systems involve mutual attunement, not merger. Thus, there is a theoretical shift 'away from conceptions of archaic merger states, archaic fantasies of omnipotence, and qualities of energy such as narcissistic libido' (Lichtenberg et al. 1992, p.133).

Kohut (1977), as well as Kohut and Wolf (1978), pointed in this direction by suggesting that infants do not begin life with their caretakers in a state of undifferentiation. More recently, theoreticians have found that a vital, self-differentiated person does not develop as a result of optimal frustration due to caretaker(s)' minute, phase appropriate lapses in empathic attunement as Kohut believed. Rather, a cohesive, vital person develops within a context of optimal responsiveness (Bacal 1985b) and mutual regulation (Beebe and Lachmann 1988b), and continues to do so throughout life.

Drawing from extensive empirical research findings, Lichtenberg (1994) stated that 'a sense of self develops as a sometimes independent, sometimes interdependent center of initiation, organization and integration of experience and motivation as needs are met in the intersubjective matrix of infants and caregivers.' Stolorow and Atwood (1992) underscored the notion that the developing organization of the child's experience, both positive and negative, must be seen as a property of the child–caregiver system of mutual regulation. Similarly, Stern (1985) stated that the formation of various senses of self come from the child's interaction with 'self regulating others', while Emde (1988) concluded that personality structures develop from the internalization of infant–caregiver relationship patterns. Additionally, Beebe and Lachmann (1988) concluded that recurrent patterns of mutual influence between mother and infant provide for the development of self and object representation while determining the ways in which expectancies of social interactions are organized. Also, Demos (1988) found support for the notion that affectivity was a property of the child–caregiver system of mutual regulation.

The development of a group ambience which supports optimal responsiveness and mutual regulation in the transferential experiences taking place among members in groups is consistent with the contemporary thinking and research of Demos, Emde, Lichtenberg, Stern, and Beebe and Lachmann. Their findings point out that infants are born uniquely programmed to respond to an empathically sensitive family life that reliably provides vitalizing selfobject experiences. Also, the research strongly confirms that a vital sense of self flourishes within an optimally responsive, mutually regulated intersubjective context. Frequent observations of transformational self experiences taking place for patients within group contexts which support optimal responsiveness and mutual regulation give clinical support for the research findings cited.

By concentrating primarily on the self-organizing and/or disorganizing meanings gained through ongoing exploration of group members' multiple transferences, this model follows two central positions taken by contemporary self psychology and intersubjectivity theory; namely, it emphasizes clinically the central importance of affects (and affective experiences) and it strongly recognizes the intersubjective world in the therapeutic exchange.

Clinical observations

The first glimpse of the impact of the interplay between the individual and group modalities often occurs in individual treatment, where the primary therapist helps to modulate by holding (Winnicott 1960a; b) or containing (Bion 1952) some of the anxiety or fragmentation that patients experience as they enter group. Simultaneously, the therapeutic bond, established through innumerable experiences working with the patient individually from within both the selfobject and conflictual, repetitive and resistive dimensions of the transference, allows the therapist to anticipate, observe and translate the patient's needed selfobject functions as well as impingements and traumas as they arise in group. Thus, the therapist's awareness of the patient's history and the therapist's recognition of how it may interplay in the group process helps the person experience a trusting bond which eventually allows him/her to become an integral part of the group. Segalla *et al.* (1988) and Harwood (1995) describe the above process in placing patients into group.

As the group process unfolds, the individual's feelings about the co-therapist and the other group members begin to emerge. This phase in the developing group process is extremely significant for many patients; for while the therapeutic bond with the primary therapist continues to be strengthened as a result of ongoing contact in the individual and group contexts, it is the initiation and maintenance of ongoing intersubjective experiences with the co-therapist and the other group members that establishes the safety for deeper exploration to take place. In part, these experiences are made possible by the optimally responsive ambience established early by the group co-therapists. This provides an atmosphere of tolerance and empathic relatedness quite early, and helps to build a foundation for group members' interactions in the future.

From the evolving relationship with the co-therapist, the patient comes to recognize patterns inherent in the mobilization of old, constricting organizing principles often developed from within the more pathological child–caregiver matrix, as Segalla *et al.* (1988) suggested. Frequently, the presence of the co-therapist stimulates unconscious material and affect states that may be emerging in treatment for the first time. For some group members, the unfolding of the transferential relationship with the co-therapist is relatively benign, often paralleling the experience with the primary therapist in the individual treatment. For many others, however, a significantly different transferential progression takes place.

In these cases, consistent with the theoretical underpinnings of the co-therapy paradigm, important clinical transference phenomena relating to early traumatizing experiences with the other (second) parent begin to emerge. Transferential feelings evoked by the presence of the co-therapist may be threatening and painful since they are being stimulated within the context of the less ideal caretaking experience. As the group progresses and further disruptions occur facilitating the oscillating bipolar dimensions of the transference with the co-therapist, the emergence of new, alternative organizing principles occurs as a result of working through the connections and disconnections of the selfobject bond with the co-therapist.

Typically, the development of deepening relationships with the co-therapists and other group members happens gradually in that individuals must first experience sufficient empathic attunements to their own subjective experiences. Only then are they able to fulfill reciprocal selfobject needs for others. Initially, while members may have a genuine desire to be empathically attuned to others, many come across as controlling and demanding, or passive and dismissive. It is through the connections, disruptions and restoration of connections taking place among members over the life of the group that bit by bit members develop greater capacities to fulfil selfobject needs for others.

It is difficult to capture the essence of the deepening relationships being established by group members as the group process unfolds. But in considering the developmental progression of the groups, it seems that links between members occur as a result of early negative and positive identifications and internalizations with each other. Early negative intersubjective transactions of limited usefulness are mutually reshaped and interactively integrated into deeper, self-enhancing selfobject experiences over the span of the treatment. Of course, the development of these positive experiences is different for every patient, both in pace and depth.

The depth and richness of members' experiences may be made clearer by imagining the analytic group context at a particular moment in time. From this vantage point, one might observe a disruption being worked through between one patient and the group as a whole, followed by a transforming experience occurring between two other patients or a patient and therapist while the remaining group members participate silently. (See Segalla *et al.* 1988; 1989; Harwood 1992a; 1992b; for further clinical group examples.)

The emotional connections made through the intersubjective processes taking place among group members are of significant therapeutic benefit in their own right, for they offer an alternative to feelings of isolation and despair. Moreover, these connections are the building blocks of group cohesion and coherence (Pines 1981). But it is my conviction that the most important factor about the development of these connections is that they occur in a lived context that recreates the multiple selfobject and traumatizing experiences of childhood. Patients are able to have different experiences within symbolically recreated contexts that often approximate earlier lived experiences with significant others whose positive and negative contributions to the development of psychic structure continue to be instrumental in the organization of their current subjective senses of self.

Let me now share a clinical case example that illustrates a multiple selfobject and traumatizing experiences co-therapy model at work.

Clinical example

The case of Mark illustrates the interplay between the individual and group therapeutic modalities. It underscores how Mark's involvement in his own curative process was enriched by the shifting back and forth between these two modalities, thus enhancing the total impact of his treatment.

Mark, a 38-year-old man, entered individual therapy depressed, disorganized and fragmented after the breakup of a year-long relationship. He was intensely frightened by his depressive affect states which he experienced as signals that he was 'going crazy'. In the early individual treatment, Mark and I came to understand the depth of his depressive episodes as being related to traumatizing experiences of separation and abandonment by his parents. Accessing early disavowed childhood experiences of deprivation and neglect was crucial to understanding his extremely limited capacity to cognitively articulate, differentiate, modulate, and integrate his depressive feelings (Socarides and Stolorow 1984–1985).

Mark experienced his mother as being chaotic, critical and self-absorbed. The extended childhood absences of the father, whose business career kept him away from the family for long periods of time, greatly intensified Mark's relationship with his mother. She seemed to require a sense of oneness (merger) with Mark, more so than with his four younger siblings, to sustain her own sense of self-cohesion.

Throughout his life, Mark felt continuously alienated from his parents, siblings and peers. Life was lacking in any true genuine feeling except pervasive emptiness and hopeless despair. He was the obedient eldest son, but typified what Wolf (1988) has called the 'empty self'. Mark's self-development in the area of self-boundary formation had been obstructed through the enmeshed relationship with mother and the unreliable, angry and unpredictable father. Accordingly, in treatment he was initially compliant with the therapist's interventions continuing the obedient 'good boy' role he had assumed in his family.

Early memories were rare for Mark, consistent with his massive dissociation of affect, a product of chronic lack of attunement to his emotional state by his parents. Because of the pervasive deprivation of self-organizing and self-differentiating selfobject experiences, Mark was left unable to monitor, cognitively articulate and understand his own emotions as indicators of changing self-states (Socarides and Stolorow 1984–1985). This point was dramatically illustrated during an early individual session in which Mark reported that, for extended periods in his adolescent and young adult life, he was so detached from his own internal life experience that he was unable to make the linkage between hunger pangs and eating food as a way of alleviating his stomach pain. Thus, even the most basic of physiological experiences in his body were not labeled and recognized as his own.

In the treatment, Mark maintained an anxious, dependent, somewhat emotionally withdrawn connection with me. His vulnerable sense of self did not allow him to experience the earlier sessions as his own, much as he had been unable to label and experience hunger pangs in his stomach as his own. The selfobject transference which gradually emerged was an idealizing one, although quite unrecognized by me at first, because of his highly detached, compliant style. In his words, he experienced the therapy as 'a series of ongoing plays' in which I was viewed as the director and he had a relatively small part. He would show up religiously one hour before his regular appointment time to sit in the waiting room. He described the time spent in the waiting room before the actual appointment as 'fore play', which naturally then flowed into the main play, or the appointment hour. Gradually, I came to recognize that the time spent in the waiting room before sessions offered a holding environment for Mark and that it symbolized an extension of the early budding selfobject dimension of the transference. In the treatment, it was recognized by both of us as a fairly safe, 'first step' at building a selfobject tie.

Speaking from the perspective of intersubjectivity theory, Stolorow *et al.* (1987) has described the oscillation between the selfobject dimension and the conflictual, repetitive and resistive dimension of the transference in clinical treatment. In the selfobject dimension, the patient longs for the therapist to provide selfobject experiences that were missing or insufficient in the surround of childhood. In Mark's case, the ongoing selfobject experience of having the therapist's empathic attunement, optimal responsiveness and calming strength, coupled with the therapist's efforts to help Mark make affective sense out of his powerful negative emotions (primarily depression), were reflective of the selfobject dimension of the transference. This dimension of the transference was operative in the foreground of the individual treatment almost exclusively in our early intersubjective transactions. I see myself as having been able to establish an effective working alliance with Mark by helping him to understand, label and regulate the extreme tensions brought on by his emerging emotional reactions (Socarides and Stolorow 1984–1985).

As the treatment progressed, inquiries into any personal feelings Mark might have toward me activated the conflictual, resistive and repetitive dimension of the transference. In this dimension, the patient fears the therapist will repeat the traumatic experiences of childhood. Mark's terror would be manifested whenever the notion of a personal relationship with me was addressed. Such disruptions were immediately noticeable because Mark would experience extreme confusion, or 'fogging out' as he called it. He would then flee into a tangential, intellectual discussion.

Through ongoing exploratory work in the selfobject dimension of the transference, it became clearer that our speaking 'too personally' was traumatic for Mark because intimacy unconsciously signaled danger. Questions of a personal nature in his early history had routinely led to his mother's immediate withdrawal or irrational scolding. My misattuned directness in an effort to deepen our budding selfobject connection led to his affective disorganization, for it signalled an unconscious dictate for him to comply reciprocally in a personal manner. Feeling compelled by me to be affectively intimate, he believed the sharing of his personal feelings would precipitate my abandonment and punishment of him, much like it had with his mother.

Moreover, further exploration allowed patient and therapist to see that, in a more general way, Mark had organized his early emotional experiences according to a conviction that affective states of vitality and aliveness needed to be disavowed to insure safety. Positive affective experiences were not only not felt as supportive, they were reorganized defensively as experiences of danger and concern.

Coming to understand this unconscious organizing principle had profound meaning for Mark, which became behaviorally evident in the individual treatment. Mark was able to tolerate disruptions more easily, enabling our interactions to have an incrementally more enlivened, fluid quality. Also, he became somewhat less wary of direct affective expression in his reactions to me, allowing us to draw links between transferential experiences and feedback he had received from the few friends with whom he was able to maintain a semblance of attachment. These friends repeatedly responded to his lack of emotion, and his discomfort at 'being close' with them. Also, it was the reported reason his girlfriend gave for the breakup of the relationship which precipitated his entering therapy.

Accordingly, over the next few months, I was able to use the strengthened selfobject tie which had developed between us as a springboard for a discussion of the possibility of his entering group therapy in conjunction with his ongoing individual work. While he needed the ongoing affirmation and bolstering provided by the idealizing selfobject dimension of the transference, I believed Mark also needed exposure to a broader base of intersubjective experiences. For while Mark was developing a more trusting relationship with me, his emotional connection with peers remained limited. It was my thinking that the group would serve as a catalyst for developing optimal (not too traumatizing) selfobject experiences that could build dimensions of self-complexity and vitality that continued to be lacking in his life, as well as help him to understand more about his impact on others.

Mark's entrance into the group toward the beginning of his third year of treatment was anxiety-provoking, but fairly uneventful for him. Although at times emotionally engaged in the process, Mark generally stayed on the periphery of the group experience. Harwood (1987) suggests that in group the less-than-cohesive individual may present a false self based on identification or compliance with the group's or therapists' norms, typically giving up whatever self-strivings are beginning to emerge. This was certainly true for Mark in the earlier phases of the group, as he chose to expose little of himself, presenting his stylistic false self (Winnicott 1960a) as the dutiful, compliant 'good boy'.

The power of the multiple selfobject and traumatizing experiences model for Mark began to emerge about six months into the group as he found himself disturbed and reacting negatively to the oppositional positions taken by two members of the group. These two male patients were experienced by Mark as critical, emotional and argumentative. One of them was particularly contemptuous of the group in general and, at times, of Mark's politeness and rationality in specific. For Mark, it re-created the incessant emotional struggles between his parents, and while he quietly tolerated it outwardly, he festered inside.

In his individual therapy sessions, Mark moralized about the two male group members, completely unaware of his own contempt and critical judgment of them. By clarifying for him that the intensity of his reactions to these two members might be linked to the reactivation of painful unconscious feelings associated with intense early conflict between his parents, I was able to contain and soothe Mark's agitation to a point where he felt more open to the possibility of sharing his reactions in the group. I noted that together we had worked through significant, anxiety-provoking disruptions in earlier individual sessions, and suggested that a similar possibility existed with these two group members if he would be willing to risk raising the reactions he was having to them in the group. Also, I reminded Mark that I would be present in the group and that, although I believed him to be quite capable of handling his reactions on his own, my presence might benefit him if he became overwhelmingly anxious in the group process.

The important interplay of the sustained calming selfobject experience of my presence both in the group and individual treatment settings allowed Mark to tolerate the chaos he was experiencing in the group without intolerable retraumatization to the newly evolving self-structure. Because Mark's anxiety was modulated by the work done in the individual sessions, he was able to go back to the group and express his reactions, as well as take in feedback from the group.

Reciprocally, the group experience acted as a catalyst for some important individual transference work to take place surrounding Mark's elusive contempt and critical judgment of me. Some of the feedback Mark received from the group when he shared his negative reactions to the two oppositional members centered on his own contemptuous capacity to 'moralize on high' about others. With the feedback Mark received from the group, I was able to build a bridge between group members' reactions to him and the superior, contemptuous position Mark had taken with me in the individual work when he felt misunderstood. Unlike in several previous attempts, he was able to own his contemptuous feelings toward me because my experience in individual treatment echoed similar feedback he received from the group. Equally important, Mark and I, working together from our own subjective experiences in recalling some of our earlier individual sessions involving Mark's contempt, were able to link his dismissive reactions of me with the myriad ways he would dismiss his father's intellectualized lectures 'from on high'. His father's endless speeches would involve moralizing about what was wrong with the world, and how 'stupid' people were, including his children when they did not agree with his (the father's) perceptions.

The selfobject experience of Mark having his anxious affects articulated, legitimized and modulated by me in the individual work, coupled with the group's generally empathic stance, set the stage for Mark and the group to continue working together with an incrementally deeper level of trust. Also, it served as an opportunity to explore new, unrecognized areas of self experience in Mark's individual treatment regarding his inability to experience himself as an effective agent in impacting others. The growing awareness from his group experience that he could be the center of his own initiative and impact others directly was a pivotal point in his treatment, and it became a powerful theme that was repeatedly explored.

Simultaneously, while Mark was establishing closer selfobject ties with the other group members, the unfolding of the bipolar transference with the group co-therapist was taking place. Mark's initial, rather lengthy (approximately six months) avoidance of the co-therapist in the group process was reflective of the conflictual, repetitive and resistive dimension of the transference. From within Mark's transferential perspective, the co-therapist was a female authority whom he expected to engulf and control him. Thus, in the early phases of the group process, Mark avoided eye contact with the co-therapist and never addressed her directly.

Essentially, the development of the idealizing selfobject dimension of transference with the co-therapist followed a similar pattern to the one established with me in the individual treatment. Much like he used the hour in the waiting room before his individual appointment as a less risky, first step toward developing a selfobject connection with me, Mark made his initial attempts at a connection with the co-therapist outside of the group experience. He did this by asking her for names of psychotherapists that she could recommend as referrals for a few of his friends. At first, he would speak to her by telephone; then, gradually, he spoke to her in person after group sessions.

Within the context of the actual (in the room) group process, Mark's resistance to establishing a selfobject connection with the co-therapist was lessened significantly as a result of her taking an affectionate, devil's advocate position with him. The co-therapist was particularly effective in reframing some of the highly intellectualized comments Mark would make about himself and others in the group. Symbolically, Mark came to experience her as a positive alternative to his mother, in that she offered him an ongoing selfobject experience with a calm female authority who could empathically buoy him up even while she was encouraging his needs for active opposition. In a sense, the co-therapist offered the emotional space Mark needed to feel more intimate with her, allowing him to experience her as safe and 'not suffocating'.

Incrementally, over the course of the group treatment, the co-therapist became the person who was most influential in bolstering Mark's sense of personal autonomy and developing assertiveness. Unlike in his relationship with his mother, who demanded a sense of oneness (undifferentiation) with Mark to sustain her own sense of self-cohesion, the co-therapist symbolically represented the opportunity for intimacy without merger or engulfment. After months of not acknowledging the co-therapist's presence in group, Mark was able to address her directly in the group process by telling her that he experienced her as 'calm and strong'. This was a significant accomplishment for Mark, and one that signified another important benchmark in his overall treatment.

Learning from the unfolding of the selfobject dimension of the transference with the co-therapist, Mark was initiating important selfobject experiences with other members of the group. Experiencing greater flexibility and increased interpersonal options developed primarily through his identification with the co-therapist, Mark was able to initiate a selfobject experience for another female member of the group. By taking a position which was similar in manner to the one taken by the co-therapist with him, Mark was highly effective in questioning the woman's positive attachment to her father in light of his (the father's) ongoing lack of receptivity to her. Due to Mark's sustained empathic use of irony, the patient was able to reconsider her emotional attachment to her father, explore its historical antecedents, and put some needed distance between her and her father.

The impact of the group members on effecting Mark's sense of self-efficacy, power and autonomy was evidenced both within the group and in the outside world. In one instance, an articulate but emotionally intense female member of the group reacted with frustration to Mark's relative nonchalance with respect to the ruthless way his boss had not given him a well-deserved job promotion. Having been challenged and supported by this group member, he was able to use this experience to assert himself with the boss.

Mark's growth from his group experience was particularly noticeable in his increased capacity to maintain a supportive, engaged presence in relationships with women outside of the group. This new sense of himself as an effective agent, capable of directing his own life, freed Mark up to a point with women where he felt capable of maintaining his own sense of self autonomy, while at the same time staying connected to them in an enlivened way. Also, in part because of the selfobject experiences with the other group members, Mark grew to become effectively empathic with others at his place of work, and increasingly with his family and friends.

Hopefully, the case of Mark helps to further clarify that the model described is not merely the placement of the patient in individual and group therapy; but, rather, a model by which the individual therapy treatment can be broadened by the group co-therapy experience, and then reciprocally, how the individual's experiences in the group can be catalytic in deepening the analytic transference work with the primary therapist in individual treatment.

Summary

Summarizing the essential aspects of the multiple selfobject and traumatizing experiences co-therapy model from the case material:

1. The bipolar transference with the primary therapist developed over three years and was firmly established prior to Mark's entering group therapy.

2. Mark's selfobject tie with the primary therapist was used to modulate his initial anxiety entering the group, and then to help him tolerate his agitation, without intolerable retraumatization, as difficulties surfaced in the intersubjective experiences with the other group members.

3. The ongoing transference work in the individual treatment was advanced and deepened due to feedback Mark received from others in the group.

4. Early maternal repetitive failures and disorganizing experiences which had not been activated in Mark's individual treatment and, therefore, remained unrecognized to patient and primary therapist, began to get triggered in the developing and deepening bipolar transference with the co-therapist.

5. Consistent with the theoretical underpinnings of the model, important clinical transference phenomena relating to early traumatizing experiences with the second parent (Mark's mother in this case) emerged as a result of utilizing the co-therapy paradigm. Stimulated by the presence of the group co-therapist, Mark transferentially expected her to engulf and control him. Paradoxically, over time, the group co-therapist became a symbolic positive alternative to Mark's mother, offering him an ongoing selfobject experience with a calm female authority that involved intimacy without merger or engulfment.

6. Essential selfobject experiences with the other group members were instrumental in helping Mark gain a sense of self-efficacy, as well as helping him to gain a better understanding of how he impacted and was impacted by others in his life.

Summarizing and identifying four *representative general principles* when working in the multiple selfobject and traumatizing experiences co-therapy model:

1. Adding a group experience to an ongoing individual treatment expands the therapeutic intersubjective field exposing patients to a wider range of selfobject and conflictual, repetitive and resistive transference phenomena. The presence of the second therapist in the co-therapy model stimulates transference material concerning the other (second)

parent which does not emerge in the individual treatment or when there is a single therapist.

2. Individuals placed in an optimally responsive group context can learn to interact in mutually regulating, self vitalizing ways which in turn help them over time to broaden their capacities for self reflection and empathic responsiveness.

3. Disruption–restoration sequences, rather than being viewed as depletive, may be viewed as growth enhancing both in the individual and group contexts. These sequences may serve to strengthen group members' connections with each other, while facilitating growth in the articulation of affects and cognitions, and in the development of enriched self structures.

4. There has been a shift away from theoretical acceptance of merger or symbiosis as an essential developmental phase. Contemporary theory and early development research suggest that person-with-others involves mutual attunement, not merger. Accordingly, intimacy in contrast to merger is viewed as essential, both from a lifelong developmental viewpoint and from the clinical perspective of effecting positive treatment outcomes.

In searching for common threads across these four principles, it can be stated that the multiple selfobject and traumatizing experiences co-therapy model is one that is built on the development of intersubjective experiences among group members and therapists characterized by optimal responsiveness and mutual regulation. Also, it is a model that has, as its overarching, unwavering goal, the development of the patient's increased capacity for selfobject relatedness, greater capacity for tolerance of traumatizing experiences, and deepened self introspection.

References

Bacal, H. (1985a) 'Object relations in the group from the perspective of self-psychology.' *International Journal of Group Psychotherapy 35*, 483–501.

Bacal, H. (1985b) 'Optimal responsiveness and the therapeutic process.' In A. Goldberg (ed) *Progress in Self Psychology*, Vol. 1. New York: Guilford.

Beebe, B. (1993) 'Contributions from Infant Research.' Film shown at the 16th Annual Conference on the Psychology of the Self. Toronto, Canada, October 1993.

Beebe, B. and Lachmann, F. (1988a) 'The contribution of mother–infant mutual influence to the origins of self and object representation.' *Psychoanalytic Psychology 5*, 305–337.

Beebe, B. and Lachmann, F. (1988b) 'Mother–infant mutual precursors of psychic structure.' In A. Goldberg (ed) *Frontiers in Self Psychology: Progress in Self Psychology*, Vol. 4, Hillsdale, NJ: Analytic Press.

Beebe, B. and Lachmann, F. (1994) 'Representation and internalization in infancy: Three principles of salience.' *Psychoanalytic Inquiry 11*, 127–165.

Bion, W.R. (1952) 'Group dynamics – a review.' *International Journal of Psycho-Analysis 33*, 235–47.

Demos, E.V. (1988) 'Affect and the development of the self.' In A. Goldberg (ed) *Frontiers in Self Psychology: Progress in Self Psychology*, Vol. 4, Hillsdale, NJ: Analytic Press.

Emde, R. (1988) 'Development terminable and interminable.' *International Journal of Psychoanalysis 69*, 23–42.

Harwood, I. (1983) 'The application of self psychology concepts to group psychotherapy.' *International Journal of Group Psychotherapy 33*, 469–487.

Harwood, I. (1986) 'The need for optimal, available selfobject caretakers: Moving toward extended selfobject experiences.' *Group Analysis 19*, 291–302.

Harwood, I. (1987) 'The evolution of the self: An integration of Winnicott's and Kohut's concepts.' In T. Honess and K. Yardley (eds) *Self and Individual Change and Development*. London: Routledge & Kegan Paul.

Harwood, I. (1992a) 'Group psychotherapy and disorders of the self.' *Group 25*, 19–26.

Harwood, I. (1992b) 'Advances in group psychotherapy and self psychology: An intersubjective approach.' *Group 16*, 220–232.

Harwood, I. (1993) Examining early childhood multiple cross-cultural extended selfobject and traumatic experiences and creating optimum treatment environments. Presented at the 16th Annual Conference on the Psychology of the Self, Toronto.

Harwood, I. (1995) 'Toward optimum group placement from the perspective of the self or self-experience.' *Group 19*, 140–162.

Kohut, H. (1977) *The Restoration of the Self.* Madison, CT: International Universities Press.

Kohut H. and Wolf, E.S. (1978) 'The disorders of the self and their treatment.' *International Journal of Psychoanalysis 59*, 413–425.

Lichtenberg, J. (1983) *Psychoanalysis and Infant Research*. Hillsdale, NJ: Analytic Press.

Lichtenberg, J. (1991) 'What is a selfobject?' *Psychoanalytic Dialogues 1*, 455–479. NJ: Analytic Press.

Lichtenberg, J. (1994) General principles of self psychology. Presented to the Institute of Contemporary Psychotherapy, Washington, D.C.

Lichtenberg, J., Lachmann, F. and Fosshage, J. (1992) *Self and Motivational Systems: Toward a Theory of Psychoanalytic Technique*. Hillsdale, NJ: Analytic Press.

Meyers, S.J. (1978) 'The disorders of the self: Developmental and clinical considerations.' *Group 2*, 131–140.

Pines, M. (1981) 'The frame of reference of group psychotherapy.' *International Journal of Group Psychotherapy 31*, 275–285.

Schwartzman, G. (1984) 'The use of group as selfobject.' *International Journal of Group Psychotherapy 34*, 229–241.

Segalla, R., Silvers, D., Wine, B. and Pillsbury, S. (1988) Multiple selfobjects: Experiences in group and couples treatment. Presented at the 11th Annual Conference on the Psychology of the Self, Washington, DC.

Segalla, R. Silvers, D., Wine, B. and Pillsbury, S. (1989) Clinical applications of a multiple selfobject perspective in group and couples treatment. Presented at the 12th Annual Conference on the Psychology of the Self, San Francisco, CA.

Shapiro, E. (1991) 'Empathy and safety in group: A self psychology perspective.' *Group 15*, 219–224.

Socarides, D.D. and Stolorow, R.D. (1984–1985) 'Affects and selfobjects.' *Annual of Psychoanalysis 12*, 105–119.

Stern, D. (1985) *The Interpersonal World of the Infant.* New York: Basic Books.

Stolorow, R.D. (1988) 'Transference and the therapeutic process.' *Psychoanalytic Review 75*, 245–254.

Stolorow, R.D. and Atwood, G. (1992) *Contexts of Being: The Intersubjective Foundations of Psychological Life.* Hillsdale, NJ: Analytic Press.

Stolorow, R.D., Brandchaft, B. and Atwood, G. (1987) *Psychoanalytic Treatment: An Intersubjective Approach.* Hillsdale, NJ: Analytic Press.

Stone, W.N. and Whitman, R.M. (1977) 'Contributions of the psychology of self to group process and group therapy.' *International Journal of Group Psychotherapy 27,* 343–359.

Weinstein, D. (1987) 'Self psychology and group psychotherapy.' *Group 11*, 144–154.

Winnicott, D.W. (1960a) 'Ego distortion in terms of the true and false self.' In *Maturational Processes and the Facilitating Environment.* New York: International Universities Press, 1965.

Winnicott, D.W. (1960b) 'The theory of the parent–infant relationship.' In *Maturational Processes and the Facilitating Environment.* New York: International Universities Press, 1965.

Wolf, E. (1988) *Treating the Self: Elements of Clinical Psychology.* New York: Guilford Press.

CHAPTER 11

Motivational Systems and Groupobject Theory
Implications for Group Therapy

Rosemary A. Segalla

Psychoanalytically oriented group therapy has been an integral part of psychoanalysis for many years. An ongoing issue which has been problematic for group therapy has been an effort to find a unified theoretical approach most likely to prove beneficial for the group patient. While finding a coherent theory of group treatment may be laudable, it seems, in this time of energetic theory development, that this is a goal no more likely to be achieved than it was in the early history of group therapy.

Following the tradition of many practitioners (Bion 1969; Ezriel 1973; Foulkes 1973; Whitaker and Lieberman 1964; Yalom 1985), I will attempt to consider how theories which have evolved out of the dyadic clinical environment can usefully inform a psychoanalytically oriented group treatment. Specifically, I will explore an expansion of Kohut's selfobject concepts (1971; 1976; 1984) to include groupobjects (Segalla 1996) and Lichtenberg's motivational systems (Lichtenberg 1989).

Kohut and selfobject theory

Because Kohut developed his theory from his clinical experiences with psychoanalytic patients, he did not expand it beyond a dyadic model of treatment. His paper, 'Creativeness, Charisma, Group Psychology' (Kohut 1976), however, captures his awareness and sensitivity to group issues. He suggested that just as there is an individual 'self', there is a 'group self'. He viewed the study of group phenomena as essential, recognizing that all aspects of group, from its formation through its '...oscillations between group fragmentation and reintegration', were significant (p.376). As relevant as the issues of group were to Kohut, he did not have the opportunity or therapeutic group experience needed to expand his ideas to include a coherent group theory. That task has been undertaken by many group therapists. The contributions made by group therapists to selfobject theory is unique in that it addresses what is essentially an intrapsychic experience within a group setting. In moving from a dyadic experience, in which selfobject theory was created, to group necessitates some changes in perspective. The task becomes one of determining which aspects of a theory can be usefully applied to group treatment and raises the question of what parts of the theory need revision in order to advance group treatment.

Groupobjects: an expansion of selfobject theory

Understanding selfobject needs within a group setting has been well explored by other group therapists (Harwood 1986; 1993). The emphasis on the functioning of the individual in the group is, however, only part of the picture. The missing element in this exploration occurs because, in considering selfobject needs, more emphasis is placed on the individual group members. What remains significant, however, is the differences in experience created by being in group therapy. In an effort to consider this different level of engagement, I suggested an expansion of the selfobject, calling this the groupobject. This attempt to expand a concept seen as an intrapsychic experience of an individual to an intrapsychic experience within a group was an effort to account for particular group phenomena unavailable in the milieu of individual therapy. I have suggested that, just as selfobject experiences occur in an intersubjective context, 'groupobject experiences' arise in a group context (Segalla 1996), and suggested that selfobject experiences vitalized the self of the individual, while groupobject experiences filled in missing aspects of the group self. This concept was based on the postulate: 'that we are hard-wired, not only for reciprocal mutual responsiveness on the dyadic level...we are also social animals who are hard-wired to be part of groups. Thus, just as we come to dyadic relationships innately prepared to engage with the other, we come to group experiences similarly prepared' (Segalla 1995, p.8).

In that paper, I postulated that: 'Although dyadic relationships are our earliest mode of engagement, we also quickly move beyond a dyad to increasingly large and more complex systems' (Segalla 1995, p.8). In suggesting groupobject experiences, an assumption is made about an inherent design in which there is a need to be able to function effectively in groups, beyond self or dyadic experiencing.

With the existence of groupobject experiences, one can start speculating on the success or failure an individual will have in having groupobject experiences. Since there are significant developmental events which determine the relative success an individual will have in groups, I would like to suggest a relationship between selfobject and groupobject experiences. If an individual has had selfobject experiences which have served to support and enhance the self, chances are that that individual will be prepared for groupobject experiences. That is, the individual will come to feel a part of groups and will feel his/her self enhanced by successfully engaging in groups. Furthermore, the individual will maintain throughout life the need for engagement with groups, be this as a member of a family, religion, work, or political or social group. The individual who has not been successful in filling selfobject needs will probably be faced with difficulty in groups.

Factors preventing activation of groupobject needs

If an individual has been historically unable to activate groupobject needs, there are reasons to explain why this occurs. There is an ongoing fear of the loss of self. First, the person may feel threatened by engaging at the group level and allowing the emergence of groupobject experiences, fearing that it will result in the loss of self. This kind of person is often seen in group as someone unable to take from other group members. This person persists in this position, despite efforts by group members to engage them. The inability to feel safe enough in group is often reflective of failed efforts at connecting in the original family group. Further exploration can lead the person to re-engage with groupobject yearnings and mourn the lost opportunities in the family.

A second fear is possibly losing the group self. That is, the patient fears that, unless they accommodate to the group norm, they will be attacked or rejected. This type of patient harbors intense wishes to be part of the group, no matter what the cost, often replicating family requirements – that to be part of the group requires relinquishment of individual needs.

Both loss of the individual self and the group self can lead to feelings of alienation. Also, losses at the group self level can lead to feelings of fragmentation at the individual level and vice versa. As I suggest: 'there is an intersubjective tension between an individual's selfobject needs and their groupobject needs. This tension can be creatively transformed into a process which enhances the growth of both the individual self and the group self' (Segalla 1996, p.262).

The group self on the group level

Kohut was mindful of the power of the group and its potential for destructiveness, and spoke of caution in group encounters. The potential of dangerous impacts on the individual has been present alongside the view that groups can be extremely therapeutic. Rutan and Stone (1993), in reviewing the history of small group theory, cite LeBon who viewed groups resulting in diminishing the individual. Rutan and Stone state: '...LeBon identified three factors: First, he believed individuals in groups experience a sense of *increased strength*, even invincibility, by virtue of their group membership. Second, he spoke of the *contagion* that occurs in groups, describing it as akin to a hypnotic state induced by the group on its members. Finally, he felt *suggestibility* (for LeBon, the most important factor) was generally increased in groups' (Rutan and Stone 1993, p.10). In discussing the groupself, I suggested that groupobject needs for solidification and potency are part of the group. I further suggested that: 'Solidification refers to the need for experiences in which the group operates as a whole, cohesive, bonded and unbreakable unit…' (Segalla 1996, p.265), suggesting that 'groupobject failures result in real or perceived fragmentation of the group.' The groupobject experience of potency references the group's experience of its robustness.

Clinical example

Sandy added group therapy after three years of individual treatment. Group was suggested because, despite progress in individual therapy, he remained isolated, without any friendships. His connection to his family was, at best, guarded. He frequently experienced 'them' as critical and evaluative of his isolation and lack of an intimate partner.

When Sandy entered group, he was full of fear and anxiety, fantasizing about being viewed as 'strange', inadequate or hopeless. His first two years in group were torture for him. He maintained almost complete silence. When he occasionally spoke, it was to comment about another person. He did not self-reveal. As this became a topic of discussion in group, Sandy offered small tidbits of himself, hoping to ward off further inquiry. After such a session, he would be in intense emotional turmoil for days. I began to question my judgment, fearing that I had not been careful enough to consider his capacity for group.

As he found his voice, a striking capacity to understand the experiences of other group members emerged. His observations were astonishingly astute for someone who maintained an isolated existence. He was an expert at sensing the needed selfobject experiences and would unconsciously supply them. What became clear was that one way in which he survived in his nuclear family was in being carefully attentive to others' needs, particularly those of his parents.

Sandy's mode of operation in group appeared to be replicating a childhood pattern. There was no evidence of a positive gain. He was no less isolated and no more interested in self-revelation in the group. After three years in group, there was a gradual shift in Sandy. He began feeling deeply connected to several group members, speaking with deep emotion in his individual work about 'the group'. I was pleased to see this level of engagement, and observed that, as Sandy progressed in his individual treatment, having positive selfobject experiences with me and with the woman he would ultimately marry, he began to feel a deep sense of connection with the 'idea' of being part of the group. In turn, the group members came to feel a special fondness for him. They began to look to him for his clarity. Gail, for example, would turn to him when she wanted an idea explicated. Jeff admired his phrasing and vocabulary, forming a twinship bond around the creative use of language. Mara felt that he understood her as a woman in a way she had rarely encountered. The activation of groupobject experiences was a turning point in Sandy's work and in the group's work. He not only felt more connected to the members, but he began to form bonds with others outside group, even having a party for fifty people. Additionally, he reconnected with his family of origin, sustaining his connections with them despite some disappointments.

I would like to suggest that as Sandy's capacity to allow groupobject experiences grew, there was a distinct shift in his affiliative capacity. However, the selfobject experiences of his group therapy and with his girlfriend set the stage. He felt more like the others, gradually giving up the notion of his strangeness. The activation of groupobject experiences was a crucial part of Sandy's growth. I doubt that he would have been able to make the transition to positive affiliative experiences without group therapy.

Motivational systems

Lichtenberg, in his ground-breaking book, *Psychoanalysis and Motivation*, states that: 'psychoanalytic theory at its core is a theory of structural motivation...' (Lichtenberg 1989, p.1). He sees motivation as a 'series of systems designed to promote the fulfillment and regulation of basic needs... Each motivational system is a psychological entity', neurobiologically based, in which fundamental needs are expressed in clearly observable behaviors. These motivations, which exist throughout life, are 'based on behaviors clearly observable, beginning in the neonatal period' (p.1). Most importantly, from the perspective of group therapy, Lichtenberg states that: '...motivations arise solely from *shared experience*' (p.2). Lichtenberg suggests five motivational systems inherent in the individual which are operative to regulate and fill basic needs. These are:

> (1) The need for psychic regulation of physiological requirements, (2) the need for attachment and, later, affiliation, (3) the need for exploration and assertion, (4) the need to react aversively through antagonism or withdrawal (or both), and (5) the need for sensual engagement and sexual excitement. (Lichtenberg 1989, p.1)

Lichtenberg suggests that the 'needs, wishes, desires, aims and goals that derive from those needs in each motivational system may be rearranged in different hierarchies indicated by different conscious and unconscious preferences, choices, and proclivities' (Lichtenberg 1989, p.1).

In group, the motivational systems most likely to be activated would be the need for attachment/affiliation, exploration/assertion and aversiveness. Though there may be an engagement of the other two motivational systems, they are less likely to be in the foreground of a group. Any one of these motivational systems can dominate for different group members at the same time, while the group as a whole can be dominated by only one of these systems. It is the exploration of these systems which provides the fine-tuning necessary for group cohesion.

But the motivational system which will ultimately supply the cohesion for the group to be an effective treatment modality is that of affiliation. While the other systems may assume dominance at various moments in the life of the group, the affiliative system is necessary for the maintenance of the group because of the inevitable affective fluctuations in the group.

Lichtenberg, in discussing affiliation, which is part of the attachment motivational system, offers some insights into group life. He maintains that a person: '…begins to be motivated to develop affiliations with groups with a shared relational bond, goal, belief or ideal' (Lichtenberg 1989, p.116). Although he is not able to document these affiliative needs, he believes that there '…may be an innate, preprogrammed pattern to affiliate that begins with a young child's regarding his or her parents and siblings, not only as individuals, but as a unit – the family' (p.116). He states: 'My main assertion is that, at a fork in development, a person not only continues to be strongly motivated to adhere to old attachments and to form new ones, but also begins to be motivated to develop affiliations with groups with a shared relational bond, goal, belief, or ideal' (p.116). Lichtenberg believes there is a preprogrammed pattern to affiliate. This phenomenon in both the individual's and group's needs for a groupobject have also been observed while working with therapy and large groups. Lichtenberg suggests that if affiliative needs are present, the child 'can gain pleasure in intimacy and the sense of belonging, not only…from caregivers, but also from the family group' (p.116).

Lichtenberg makes an important point when he suggests that psychoanalysis has often emphasized the negative aspects of affiliation and has not valued the need for affiliation as integral to development. It is the feared loss of individuality and the following of the group that leads to destructive behaviors, as Freud has suggested. Lichtenberg states that the 'motivation for affiliation is as integral to development and as universal in its occurrence as that of attachment' (p.117). This view aligns with the experience of group therapists. It is the basis of our belief that group therapy is a significant treatment model because of the need for successful affiliative experiences. Lichtenberg goes on to state that pleasure in attachment, the experience of pleasure in intimacy, can evolve to experiencing pleasure within the family and a sense of intimacy with the group. As he says: 'The difference between attachment and affiliation is in the composition of the unit – not in the affect sought. And the affective experience sought is the positive sense of sharing and gaining and growing' (p.118). Lichtenberg goes on to describe potential differences in attachment and affiliative needs which I believe are basic to why group psychotherapy is effective. His clinical example captures this well. A man describes his Passover Seder experience in which he felt ambivalent about his grandparents – attachment – but unambivalent about the importance of the family and religious group in building a cohesive self – affiliative motivation (p.119).

Often, we see the pattern Lichtenberg described above in group, where the affiliative needs serve as a container which allows the therapeutic work to unfold. Within this containing affiliative environment, attachment, as well as exploratory, and assertive, aversive, sensual/sexual and physiological motivations may arise. It is the fluctuation among these motivational systems that becomes the focus of therapy. In exploring the psychological organization of the various group members and how they impact on each other, one gets a hint of the complexity of group life. Each member's engagement in the group will be dominated by a particular motivational system and how that person's system impacts the functioning of other members' systems. In addition, there will be a dominant system operating in the group as a whole.

The motivational systems of individuals or the whole group can be observed as a continuum. For a group therapist, where to attend can be informed by observing which motivational system is at play. In a stable group whose members are actively engaged with a particular issue (either from within the group or something reported by a particular group member), the exploratory motivational system can be observed. In a group as it bids farewell to a member, we can see the affiliative needs emerge. In a group where there is an active struggle between members, we can see the aversive system in operation as members engage in fight and/or flight behavior. With two therapists present, there is considerable flexibility with the two therapists alternating their focus between the whole group motivational system and the dominant motivational system of a particular member or a particular dyad. These experiences are used to create model scenes which inform the action of the group. Lichtenberg, Lachmann and Fosshage (1996) describe model scenes as follows:

> Analyst and patient construct model scenes to organize the narratives and associations of the patient, to capture important transference configurations and role enactments, and to focus further explorations of the patient's experience and motivations. (p.99)

An example of such an engagement occurred when Mary was discussing her marriage and moving to another state. One therapist was working actively with her around her anxiety that she would be unable to adjust to this new and temporary location, and that her difficulties would have a negative impact on her relationship. As the male therapist empathically engaged with her, asking questions and creating a clearer picture of her discomfort, I observed the other members whom she experienced as becoming progressively more withdrawn.

Mary suggested that there was something that people were feeling, but were not expressing. Members responded to Mary's observation and began to speak, stating that they felt that despite their interest and engagement earlier in the session, Mary was not engaged with them. They did not feel listened to and felt that they were of no help. The group, which had begun in an affiliative engagement with Mary, had moved to an aversive position characterized by withdrawal. There were several comments which suggested that Mary was whining. The group had moved to an aversive position and, in an effort not to respond negatively, had used flight into silence, failing to see that their reactions would in fact be useful information for Mary. The co-therapist began to explore with Mary what the impact of the withdrawal had been. This led to a model scene: Mary did not expect any comfort, had in fact expected to be rejected by the group because of her departure. This had, in fact, occurred when she graduated from college and returned home. She found that her large family had essentially written her off. She was not accepted back into the home, and moved out within two months. This move occurred with little reaction from the family. This explained why the group's earlier efforts to contain and support Mary could not be taken in because: 'I know that as soon as I'm gone I'll be forgotten, and when I come back in six months, it will be too late and I'll never fit back in.' The creation of this model scene, a model of an earlier and current experience, proved to be a very useful metaphor for Mary, as well as for the rest of the group. Members found that her resistance to being helped had in fact threatened their own sense of their ability to be useful to each other, an aversive experience which threatened their well intentioned exploratory activity.

Affect and the use of the model scene in group therapy

Motivational dominance, as well as shifts in motivation, are informed by affective reactions. Within each motivational system, model scenes can emerge to inform us both about which motivational system is dominant and what selfobject experience is occurring. Model scenes, described by Lichtenberg *et al.* (1992), bring together two powerful trends:

> They draw on the fundamental inclination of analyst and analysand to organize experience in terms of events or episodes. Because of the clinical purpose they serve, the events selected are those amplified by an affective response triggered when the needs of a motivational system are met or, more likely for the analysis, unmet. (p.25)

The authors state:

...we believe that the concept of a model scene integrates knowledge of both content and process. Contents are contained in the idea of 'scene', with its analogy to the theater and its unities of time, place, and characters. The process aspect...enters into model scene construction in that the work (1) focuses on an empathic entry into analysand's state of mind... (2) involves the intersubjective influence of empathic ambience, shared exploratory motivation, and the recognition and struggle with aversive motives as they affect the imaginative nature of the associative flow; and, (3) requires a constant sensitivity to state in the constructions of the sources of disruptions that occur during the analysis... (p.77)

Attention to model scenes within a group setting enriches the group by providing a particular kind of continuity that is cohesion-producing on both the individual and group level. An example of a model scene's emergence into the group can be seen when there is a disruption which, when explored with the individual, dyad and/or whole group, provides a depth of understanding that becomes a part of the group culture. The work is further deepened as the exploration continues in the interplay between the individual and group therapy.

Clinical example of the use of a model scene

By employing a model scene perspective in the group, the therapists attempt to understand the experience both of individual members and of the group as a whole. An example of the construction and use of a model scene occurred when Ruth complained that she was experiencing the group as a dangerous place to bring personal material. Her exclamation came during a group session which had in fact been quite fruitful in its exploration of a difficult problem of another member. The group reacted with surprise to Ruth's experience and wanted to know more about it. Ruth, in turn, was stunned when she realized that her experience of the session was so different from that of the other members and the two therapists. She stated that it was her experience that everyone was feeling unsafe. A careful exploration of Ruth's feeling uncovered a transference issue familiar to the group – that is, that Ruth was often scapegoated in her family for saying what was obvious to all but never acknowledged by a family member. Her willingness, in her language, to call 'a spade a spade' endlessly got her in trouble – not just in the family, but everywhere. The model scene which emerged after considerable effort by all the members was that for Ruth there was one reality and it was her painful task in life to define and name the reality that others avoided. The group encounter allowed her to expand her own awareness of her early experience and how that had shaped her current reality – one which, in fact, left little room for the realities of others. The model scene of having to be the one who speaks and sees the truth became an enduring one for the group and was often called upon. The scene which emerged was co-created not only by Ruth and her individual therapist, but also by the other group members, who shared their own experiences of Ruth with her. The scene was, in fact, particularly significant in that Ruth's experiences within her own family group were the basis of her reactiveness in the group. The advantages of a combined treatment model are evident, since the model scene had initially been constructed in the individual therapy, but its re-emergence in the group caused a powerful affective experience which could be addressed intersubjectively and thus be further modified. Having a reality different from the rest of the family for which Ruth was punished was instead met in the safety of the group with considerable interest and curiosity by both therapists and the rest of the group.

Model scenes beget model scenes

There are many other possibilities for model scenes presented by group treatment other than one member working with the whole group. For example, a model scene can emerge in work between one of the therapists and a group member or between two group members and the group as a whole or between the therapist who is not the individual treatment therapist and the patient. This can reflect historical experiences of members or it can reflect the history within the group. The model scene work can be particularly powerful when it occurs between a patient and the 'other' therapist. This occurred in a group in which Mark, an individual patient seen by me, constructed a model scene with my co-therapist which helped us understand his relationship with a withdrawn and disinterested father. During one session, the therapist spontaneously asked Mark about his efforts at job hunting, expressing considerable interest in the possibilities which Mark outlined. Mark suddenly began to cry. As a result of this affective reaction, the two of them began to explore Mark's strong emotional response. What became clear was that the co-therapist's interest in Mark activated by contrast a memory of Mark's father's disinterest in his undertakings and Mark's efforts to spark his interest as the father persisted in reading the newspaper. As a result of this rather intensive work with Mark, other group members gained access to related material, including their experiences within the group – some feeling that the leaders or some members were not engaged with them. Mindy felt moved by Mark's encounter with the male therapist, gaining access in the hour to similar feelings with her mother who was not able to mirror Mindy's successes in her musical performance with pride or pleasure. Robert experienced a similar affective moment, remembering that he had, in effect, been pushed out of the family because of his interest in sporting events. These experiences were constructed into model scenes by both the therapist and the patient(s), as well as by other group members. In the group, one can see that model scenes beget model scenes, leading the group members to deeper work with each other and the co-therapists.

Selfobjects

Stolorow, Brandchaft and Atwood (1987) and Lichtenberg *et al.* (1992) posit a reconceptualization of the selfobject, viewing it in terms of experience rather than function. Lichtenberg *et al.*'s position is carefully delineated in terms of the motivational systems. They conceptualize selfobject experiences occurring within each of the five motivational systems, thus considerably expanding what can be defined as a selfobject experience. They move away from the conceptualization of selfobject function, stating that the attribution of this function to a person has created considerable confusion and a sloppy use of the term, redefining selfobject experiences as affective experiences. In their focus on selfobject experiences rather than function, they emphasize what is happening in the clinical or interpersonal exchange. Selfobject experiences are viewed as restoring cohesion and vitality to the self, and are the result of empathic engagement of either the caregiver, speaking developmentally, or the therapist. They state that in normal development: 'The self is strengthened or vitalized by experiences of appropriate responses to the needs in any motivational system and any motivation may dominate the foreground of an analytic exchange' (Lichtenberg *et al.* 1992, p.129). Their description of what happens when the caregiver fails to provide necessary empathic responsiveness is a clinically relevant perspective in the therapeutic encounter. They suggest that when there is failure of empathy, what evolves is an 'expectation of non-responsivity that leads to aversion to attachment. Such aversiveness is the consequence of interferences in vitalizing selfobject experiences sought from ordinary sources in all five motivational systems' (p.141). They state that, as a result of this depletion: 'one may seek vitality and cohesion from maladaptive, perverse or pathogenic sources' (p.141). In the clinical setting the patient will demonstrate both efforts to have vitalizing selfobject experiences as well as a repetition of trying to create selfobject experiences from more maladaptive approaches.

This redefinition of the selfobject concept is particularly useful for understanding the action of the group in which members are constantly alternating between trying to have vitalizing experiences and rejecting these efforts, and demanding answers, rebelling, and submitting. An example of this occurred in a long-term group when the leaders announced that there would be two new members entering the group in four weeks. The group fell silent; both therapists waited to hear members' reactions. Sally, who consistently tried to please the leaders, stated that she thought it would be good to have a few new stories. Jamie sneered at Sally, stating that she thought it was a lousy idea, that she didn't want to have to deal with anyone else, and in fact might leave. Mark grew anxious at the conflict, and tried to soothe by reassuring Jamie that it would be all right: 'After all, we've taken in Peter and Pam and that worked.' Chuck suggested that it wasn't worth talking about because the therapists would do whatever they wanted anyway. This was reinforced by Jamie who said, 'Just look at it this way...it's more money in their pocket. Why would they turn that down?' Peter said that he was interested in having new members, adding, 'I think we're getting too comfortable, too nice; this will shake things up a bit. I like that.'

The unfolding of this particular scenario took place over the next three groups, with the result that the new members were ultimately welcomed and the group felt free to continue the discussion of their reactions with the new members. A good deal of the time was spent on the disappointment and anger with the therapists, who were viewed as threatening the cohesion of the group. As the therapists were able to respond to the members, they provided a new selfobject experience for several of the members because they met the reactions with interest and curiosity, exploring at length and in depth the various feelings of the members. This reinforced an atmosphere in the group which allowed for diversity of reactions which led to further cohesion of the group in that everyone survived the disruption, the therapists included; no one was silenced or dismissed. Or, as Lichtenberg et al. (1992) state:

> Some of the most intensive experiences involving one's sense of self are triggered in the context of empathic responsiveness of others. When empathic responsiveness ensures an experience of cohesion and vitality of the self, we designate it as a selfobject experience. (p.132)

They go on to state that 'the self is strengthened or vitalized by experiences of appropriate responses to the needs in any motivational system...' (p.129)

Discussion

It was noted that many theoretical advances in psychoanalytically oriented group therapy have emerged from theories which originated in the treatment of the individual. These concepts can be more or less successfully applied to the group. Kohut's selfobject concept, considered by many to be his most outstanding contribution, has been a useful addition to group treatment, giving rise to the multiple selfobject and the multiple, cross-cultural extended selfobject and traumatic experiences in group (Harwood 1986; 1993). The addition of these expanded ideas of selfobject experiences were then further expanded to include groupobject needs of the individual and the group, a concept which is based on the built-in need to affiliate which is present in all. Lichtenberg's motivational systems theory (Lichtenberg 1989) has been another significant contribution to understanding the action in group therapy. Access to motivations of individual and the group as a whole occurs within the containing of the affiliative motivational system, allowing the needs of the other systems to dominate for a particular group member or the group as a whole. Using model scenes to understand both the action of the group as well as content has been a significant contribution. This, along with an expansion of the selfobject concept, is part of a continuing effort to propose a psychoanalytically oriented theory which can account for both the individual in the group and the group as a whole.

References

Bion, W.R. (1969) *Experiences in Groups.* New York: Basic Books.

Ezriel, H. (1973) 'Psychoanalytic group therapy.' In L. Wolberg and E. Schwartz (eds) *Group Therapy* (1973, pp. 183–210). New York: Stratton Intercontinental Medical Book.

Foulkes, S.H. (1973) 'The group as the matrix of the individual's mental health.' In L. Wolberg and E. Schwartz (eds) *Group Therapy.* (pp. 183–210). New York: Stratton Intercontinental Medical Book.

Harwood, I. (1986) 'The need for optimal, available selfobject caretakers: Moving toward extended selfobject experiences.' *Group Analysis 19*, 291–302.

Harwood, I. (1993) Examining early childhood multiple cross-cultural extended selfobject and traumatic experiences and creating optimum treatment environments. Presented at the 16th Annual Conference on the Psychology of the Self, Toronto.

Kohut, H. (1971) *The Analysis of the Self.* New York: International Universities Press.

Kohut, H. (1976) 'Creativeness, charisma, group psychology.' In P. Ornstein (ed) *The Search for the Self: Selected Writings of Heinz Kohut, 1950–1978*, Vol. 2. New York: International Universities Press, pp. 793–843.

Kohut, H. (1984) *How Does Analysis Cure?*, In A. Goldberg and P. Stephansky (eds). Chicago: University of Chicago Press.

Lichtenberg, J.D. (1989) *Psychoanalysis and Motivation.* Hillsdale, NJ: Analytic Press.

Lichtenberg, J., Lachmann, F. and Fosshage, J. (1992) *Self and Motivational Systems.* Hillsdale, NJ: Analytic Press.

Lichtenberg, J., Lachmann, F. and Fosshage, J. (1996) *The Clinical Exchange.* Hillsdale, NJ: Analytic Press.

Rutan, J.S. and Stone, W.N. (1993) *Psychodynamic Group Psychotherapy.* New York: Guilford Press.

Segalla, R. (1995) 'The evolution of the self psychological perspective of group psychotherapy.' Presented at the National Group Psychotherapy Training Institute of the Washington School of Psychiatry, Washington, D.C.

Segalla, R. (1996) '"The unbearable embeddedness of being": self psychology, intersubjectivity and large group experiences.' *Group 20*, 4, 257–271.

Stolorow, R., Brandchaft, B. and Atwood, G. (1987) *Psychoanalytic Treatment: An Intersubjective Approach.* Hillsdale, NJ: Analytic Press.

Whitaker, D.S. and Lieberman, M.A. (1964) *Psychotherapy Through the Group Process.* New York: Atherton Press.

Yalom, I.D. (1985) *The Theory and Practice of Group Psychotherapy* (3rd ed.). New York: Basic Books.

CHAPTER 12

Can Group Analysis/Psychotherapy Provide a Wide Angle Lens for Self Psychology?[1]

Irene N.H. Harwood

At the 18th Self Psychology Conference, Susan Sands' (1995) paper: 'Countertransference: What the Self Psychological Lens Obscures' challenged me to think further whether the dyadic one-to-one self psychological analytic lens could also obscure through a 'theoretically caused countertransference'. I started wondering whether self psychology could not also utilize a wide angle lens which could focus on a wider panoramic view of the person within the larger environment. Heinz Kohut did not perceive his to be a complete theory. He warned (Kohut 1977) that changing social factors influence the parental selfobject matrix and determine the type of prevalent psychopathology that will dominate. He suggested a need for further critical evaluation and work in this area by social scientists who are grounded in psychoanalysis. Thus, both Kohut and Sands provoked me to ask not only what can group psychotherapy continue to learn from self psychology, but what can self psychology learn from group analytic theory?

To date, self psychology has made a significant contribution to help group therapists understand the needs of some of our more vulnerable group patients and how to address their developmental deficits within the group context. These applications have been addressed through the numerous contributions of: Arensberg (1990), Ashbach and Schermer (1992), Bacal (1985b; 1991; 1992), Harwood (1983; 1986; 1987; 1992a; 1992b; 1993; 1995a; 1995b), Kriegman and Solomon (1985), Meyers (1978), Morrison (1989a), Paparo (1984), Schain

1   Presented at the 19th Annual Conference on the Psychology of the Self, Washington, DC, October 1996.

(1985; 1989), Schermer (1988), Schwartzman (1984), Segalla (1995), Segalla *et al.* (1989), E. Shapiro (1991), Silvers (in press), Stone (1992), Stone and Gustafson (1982), Stone and Whitman (1977; 1980), Weinstein (1987; 1991), Wilson (1982) and Wong (1979).

I will not review the above mentioned contributions, but will focus on the latest advances in self psychology and intersubjectivity highlighted in the last Self Psychology Conference. For the self psychological/intersubjective group therapist, these advances bring up further questions when they are examined both from an analytic dyadic system perspective, as well as from analytic multiple dyadic systems perspective.

Developing theoretical paradigms: dyadic systems

At the 1995 Self Psychology Conference, in addressing the new developments, Frank Lachmann pointed out that there is a new focus on learning from cognitive researchers about systems. He said that new attention is being given to systems: the mother–child system, the father–child system, and the patient–analyst system. This general formulation of dyadic systems includes Stolorow, Atwood and Brandchaft's intersubjective system (Stolorow, Brandchaft and Atwood 1987; Stolorow and Atwood 1992; 1994). In their system, each person experiences a given situation according to his/her organizational principles, the latter being a product of a multiplicity of causes including genetic history and current psychic organization. Stolorow (1995) saw the 'intersubjective systems' as a specific class of dyadic systems with a dyadic interaction between two subjective worlds.

Utilizing the work of Thelen and Smith (1994) and his work with Beebe and Jaffe (Beebe, Jaffe and Lachmann 1992), Lachmann emphasized paying special attention to how the above mentioned dyadic systems mutually influence each other's subjectivities. Other possible systems which were *not* mentioned are the person or self-as-a-group system, the sibling–person system, the total family of origin–person system, the significant other–person system, the extended family–person system, the work-group–person system, the social or political group–person system, the community–person system, and the larger world community–person system. These other systems impact the child developmentally at different times. These important 'group systems' should not be neglected or alluded to only symbolically – for example as the Kleinians use the breast to symbolize the 'total caretaking environment'. Often the breast and the mother become concretized while the larger caregiving environment is forgotten. An example of this is the anger of the National Alliance of Mental Health with clinicians for making mothers solely responsible for causing schizophrenia in their children.

Though Lachmann underlined the importance of looking at the context and that the observed is never independent of the observer, most psychoanalysts do not mention, (except for Oedipal configurations), that the very dyadic systems that they study and analyze also can include organizing systems which stem not only from singular and dyadic experiences, but also from *three or more persons* interactions. The interaction between systems can either be dyadic or group interactive with the individual, and their impact can be singular or multifaceted.

Example: Andrew

An example of such an interaction between systems would be an analyst who is working in the selfobject dimension of the transference. With his patient, Andrew, he recognizes how the mutuality of their respect and admiration for one another has helped his patient be a more effective and respected manager at work. At the same time what may be neglected, since it did not come up in the transference, is a very difficult and hurtful relationship with a brother, who let him know how Andrew was left out from the uncle's family dinner party due to his political party affiliation. More about Andrew later.

Good and bad selfobjects

Bacal (1995), in response to criticisms from the greater world of psychoanalysis, has balanced Kohut's concept of *selfobject* with *bad selfobject(s)*. He described a bad selfobject as analogous to the term hostile introject in object relations theory or the internalized bad object. He clarified that a selfobject connotes a good experience and is experienced as relatively good and that the term bad selfobject denotes that the selfobject is experienced as relatively bad. If we re-examine these terms in relation to Foulkes' (1973) concept of the mind consisting of interacting processes between a number of closely linked persons, commonly called a group, one might translate to say that *the individual consists of interacting processes between a number of closely linked selectively internalized (persons or) experiences that could add up to a group experience.*

Reconceptualizing Wolf's (1980) need for an 'empathic selfobject ambience', Bacal has added the concept of 'optimal responsiveness', not only to individual psychoanalysis (Bacal 1985a), but also to group (Bacal 1985b; 1991; 1992). He warned about needing to maintain a balance between 'reactiveness and responsiveness in the group process'. If reactiveness is too strong, I believe the group therapist has to separate what is too reactive for the person-system, as opposed to what is too reactive for the entire group-system. After summarizing what has been ruptured in the different subjective systems, the group therapist would *first* address who appears to be the most vulnerable – one or more individual(s) or the entire group. Later the group conductor would address and understand the meaning of the 'reactivity' for the other dyadic or multiple systems.

Reflecting on how to maintain a balance between responsiveness and reactiveness in the group process, Harwood (1995a; 1996) suggested that this balance can only be accomplished with first understanding what contributes to 'optimal (or good-enough) group placement'. I strongly emphasized that without preliminary sessions it is difficult to accomplish a good-enough group placement or create an optimum group environment. The preliminary sessions help the group composer to understand the prospective member's historical and current subjective experiences, to become aware of what kinds of functions may be needed and what kind of impingements may need to be kept in check in order to ebb and flow between a group ambience of optimum responsiveness and reactiveness, as well as to get a sense of emerging intersubjectivities between therapist and the prospective group member. The affective quality of the interviewing experience between therapist and patient needs to be comfortable-enough in order to continue exploring group placement with that therapist. A good-enough selfobject bond or attachment must be strong-enough in order for the group therapist to become dependable-enough to be relied upon for understanding and clarification when intersubjectivities emerge to be worked through with the other group members.

Attachment as a life-span issue

Stern (1985) asserted that the essential state of human existence is togetherness rather than aloneness, with a most basic sense of connectedness, affiliation, attachment and security as givens (p.240). He further recognized that, for infants, the 'quality of relatedness' – that is, attachment – extends beyond the initial mother–infant bond and develops throughout childhood, applying to peers as well as to mother. In fact, it is a life-span issue (pp.186–187). Stern also clarified how attachment and security are affectively intertwined. He cited how in examples of 'social referencing', one-year-old infants who first approach with uncertainty a visual cliff will crawl across it in response to an encouraging smiling face of a significant other. On the other hand, the strength of the bond shows its force if the person the infant is attached to shows fear; the child then retreats.

Innate pattern to affiliate develops as a variant of attachment

Among self psychological theorists and psychoanalysts who practice only in the individual mode, Lichtenberg (1989) is a pioneer in his advancement that: 'there may be an innate, preprogrammed pattern to affiliate that begins with a young child's regarding his or her parents and siblings not only as individuals but as a unit – the family' (p.116). He has suggested that the small child can gain pleasure in intimacy and the sense of belonging not only from the ministrations of each caregiver but also from the family group. In the family group he included positive attachments to regular baby sitters and even dolls and pets, who the child experiences as part of the family unit. He has suggested that: 'a basic need for affiliation exists as a normal adaptive motivation, the central goal of which is to experience pleasure in intimacy.' For him: 'affiliative motives develop imperceptibly as a variant of attachment motives' and that 'at times attachment experiences with individuals and affiliative experiences with groups serve similar functions.'

Aversive affiliation and anxiety

Conversely, Lichtenberg has cited research by Schacter (1959) which concluded that: 'under conditions of anxiety, the affiliative tendency is highly directional.' Lichtenberg has built on Stern's (1985) contributions and cited other research in which it becomes clear that when a mother signaled negative affect toward an object which a child initially favored, the child started treating it as aversive. Such repetition of affective, social referencing events can help us understand the difference between affiliative systems based on displays of intimacy, connection and pleasure and the affiliative systems based on aversion. The latter may lay the groundwork for bedrocks of splitting, prejudice and externalization of unwanted parts of oneself into another person or group(s).

Let us continue with our example: Andrew, as a little boy, had a non-conflictual attachment to his mother. She could still delight in the way he found new creative ways to play with an old toy, even though he left unexamined the new one she had just brought. On the other hand, Andrew's paternal uncle, would insist that Andrew start playing with the birthday present he brought him right away and throw away the old, broken one. The old toy did not become aversive to Andrew, since Andrew had a stronger attachment bond with his mother which was based on pleasure, rather than on fear and compliance. Needing to repair his narcissistic injury, Andrew's uncle drew Andrew's younger brother aside and told him that he would get him a bigger present if he minded him, unlike Andrew.

Affiliation involves differential bonding

Lichtenberg (1989) reached to Freud (1918) to spell out this important concept: 'It is precisely the minor differences in people who are otherwise alike that form the basis of feelings of strangeness and hostility between them.' In the example that is being interwoven throughout this paper, one could say that Andrew's uncle's initial bonding, security, and affiliation was based on aversion to following one's own inclinations. When the uncle failed to get Andrew to affiliate with him on the same basis, he seduced Andrew's brother with bigger toys.

Lichtenberg (1989) added: 'Affiliation … involves differential bonding. This means that the negatively bonded may be treated as friendly or unfriendly rival, as respected or despised antagonist, or constructive critic or the source of unforgivable narcissistic injury. The ascending order of aversiveness with which negatively affiliated others are experienced means that signals of aversion … can progress to angry mobilization of our powers to the point of persistent grudge holding and narcissistic rage' (p.118). In 1930 Freud added: 'It is always possible to bind together a considerable number of people in love, so long as there are other people left over to receive the manifestations of their aggressiveness …' Lichtenberg replaced Freud's usage of aggression with 'aversive affiliation'.

We could safely surmise that Andrew's brother was acting as an ambivalent rival. He formed a strong affiliative aversive bond with the uncle, particularly since he now holds a high position in the uncle's firm. As long as he does not follow inclinations which differentiate him from his uncle, or proclaims that Andrew is entitled to his own political points of view, the affiliative aversive attachment will remain.

The self as a group: the group as a self
Group analysis: a culture of inquiry

Pines (1996a; b), who practices both individual and group analysis and who integrates self psychological concepts, sees 'the self as a group: the group as a self'. He has underlined that there is an essential element of 'group' in the individual. In congruence with group analysis he asserted that: 'the individual is conceived of as being born into and constituted out of a network of other persons and who gains a sense of personal identity from the possibilities that are offered by the nature of their network.' To this he added that: 'therefore notions of culture, politics, religion, economical and historical circumstances have to be considered as constituents of the individual self.' He proposed that the group analytic situation offers a 'culture of inquiry' in which group members have the opportunity to self-reflect on the nature of one's own self and to ponder on the nature of their group neighbors' selves. Whether we treat people in individual, couples, family, group or combination of modalities, it is essential that we keep in mind the multifaceted dimensions that come to form the individual, in our attempts to both understand and work through the myriad of transferential intersubjectivities that arise in the 'group self'.

Now, let us go back to Andrew's treatment. If the individual psychoanalyst or therapist ventured out of the room to include the multiplicity of systems affecting Andrew's life, in addition to the transference, there should be no problem in the treatment. But, if the only dyads that are explored are the analyst/

therapist–patient dyad, the mother–patient dyad and the father–patient dyad, an investigation of a major part of the patient's life is missing. If as individual analyst/therapist one stays only in the selfobject dimension of the transference and examines only the positive mutually influencing dynamics between patient and healer, we may either never get to the repetitive, resistive, conflictual transferences (Stolorow, Brandchaft and Atwood 1987), or not for a very long time, particularly if little or no attention is paid to other important dyads or systems in the person's life.

Contributions from self psychological multiple systems models

The multiple selfobject model

In the context of group theory, Segalla *et al.* (1989) argued the theoretical and clinical importance of *the multiple selfobject model*. To individual treatment, they added couples and/or group treatment, utilizing a team of co-therapists, including one from the original individual treatment dyad. They stated that the opportunity for multiple selfobject experiences has the potential to activate different kinds of earlier selfobject experiences and the working through of transferences along with empathic ruptures.

Multiple cross-cultural extended selfobject and traumatic experiences

In 1993, I separated the *positive* from the *negative* effects of what I first called the multiple or extended selfobject experiences (Harwood 1986) and called them the multiple *cross-cultural* extended selfobject and *traumatic* experiences. The addition of cross-cultural experiences was to include the diversity of ethnic, racial, religious and *all other kinds of differences* that can both enrich a person's psychological repertoire of organizing principles as well as generate other traumatic experiences. Who the person becomes is, in addition to his/her inborn talents and predispositions, a combination of subjective experiences with significant others from his/her caretaking and larger interactive matrix.

Example: A young woman from Yugoslavia

The impact of the larger interactive matrix on the individual presented itself as I went to buy a raincoat. I asked the young woman who helped me from where was her lovely accent. She answered: 'Yugoslavia. I am a product of a mixed marriage. My father is Serb, my mother is Croat. I could not be myself there.' A vast panorama of images and feelings came up for me. This woman's cross-cultural traumatic experiences may never be addressed either in individual or group through transference alone or just by looking at the affective experiences between her primary caretakers and herself, especially if these were good-enough.

I start thinking of what would be required of a human being who loved both parents. In the fragmented Yugoslavia, now she would probably have to denounce one religious ethnic identity to remain in a given polarized area (or hide an aspect of her authentic self in a neighboring area). Most likely she would be ostracized by both ethnic/religious groups for possessing a persecuted, rejected part of their own psyches. Beyond her attachment to her parents, there would be little possibility to be part of an affiliative group, when communities are organized based on similarity and not on diversity containing human universal affective similarities. White Anglo-American/European therapists should not lose sight of the freedom we experience for the most part in being able to ignore the diversity of our own cultural backgrounds. We should take special care to understand the internal pulls and *multiple fields of reciprocal conflictual influences* of our patients from different and mixed national, racial, ethnic and religious backgrounds.

Though somewhat similar to Bacal's (1995) conceptual contribution of the 'bad selfobject', Harwood's (1993) emphasis is on a developing person's *impingements* or *traumatic experiences* and not on a selfobject, though these experiences may have occurred in conjunction with actions by another person who was experienced as traumatizing. My shift in emphasis is consistent with Stolorow and Atwood (1992; 1994) who tried to point out that it is not the object, nor the other's functions, actions or subjective motivations that are taken in, but the person's unique subjective experience of those functions, actions or motivations that become the organizing principles of a person's world. However, the term *internalized bad object* or *single limiting caretaking experience* may be needed to more precisely describe a person who lacked in the first three to five years the richness of a multiplicity of important others in the environment. Instead, there may be a crude, primitive identification with a primary or disturbed single caretaker (Harwood 1986; 1987), a person whom Winnicott (1960) called a 'false self' built on identification. This type of person seems to possess more rigid defenses and is less flexible than a person who had at least one additional significant early consistent caretaker who added to the intersubjective repertoire.

The need for a groupobject

Some group therapists still forget the individual in the group-as-a-whole interpretations. Many psychoanalysts working in the context of observing dyadic intersubjective systems do not yet recognize the conceptual need for both dyadic and multiple fields of reciprocal mutual influence. On the other hand, Segalla (1996) in a thoughtful paper integrated contributions from infant research and proposed that infants are not only hard-wired for reciprocal mutual responsiveness on the dyadic level as Beebe and Lachmann (1988a; 1988b) suggested, *but are hard-wired to be part of groups as well*. This human need she called the need for a 'groupobject' or what can also be called groupobject experiences.

Returning to Andrew: he also needs a 'groupobject experience' where he could be accepted for being himself. Though Andrew's attachments and intersubjective affiliative dynamics can be explored in individual treatment, adding psychoanalytically based group treatment from a self psychological/ intersubjective perspective would allow transference observations with other group members. These are difficult, if not sometimes impossible, to observe in one at a time single transference in individual treatment. A combination of individual and group can provide a more effective working through of the hurts and rejections that Andrew, in our example, experiences with his brother, uncle and possibly with other persons in his extended family. The diversity of people, styles and intrapsychic issues in the group provide an ample arena for possible re-enactment of the family dynamics, rebonding with supportive others who may also hold self-delineation as an important value. The group setting also allows the working through of differential bonding which encompasses different degrees of attachment, affiliation and meaning.

Group dynamics enable connectedness, affiliation, attachment and security on one end of the spectrum ('a groupobject experience') with a contamination of affects, archaic identifications, and the acting out of destructive rage on the other, which becomes 'a group traumatic experience' both for the participants and their targets. We have observed these in our own communities, in the Los Angeles riots for example and in our world communities – Chechnya, the Middle East, and the destruction of the individual self in the group self of cults. On the other hand, effective group ambience can be created by problem solving, understanding of the transference, separating out the past from the present, processing separate subjectivities, breaking and restoring the selfobject bond, and understanding the universality of human affects within all cultural diversity. Keeping reactiveness at an optimal level (Bacal 1991), while balancing it with a responsive atmosphere towards those who may be significantly or moderately different from others, is an essential skill required of the group conductor.

The colleagual/professional work-group–person system

Group analytic understanding and further developing of positive affiliative systems may be a beginning towards helping solve an existing conundrum in psychoanalysis. Kohut experienced hundreds of analytic backs turning when he dared to self-delineate from classical psychoanalysis, while Bion had to find a new analytic society in another country for daring to think that he had more to contribute to the theories of his Oedipal mother, Melanie Klein. Sensitized by the aversive affiliation of his own larger psychoanalytic group system, Kohut warned against the power of the group and the potential for diminishing individual strivings and urged a courageous self-scrutiny in the psychoanalytic community. Could there be attachments and identifications with the founders of different theoretical schools by psychoanalysts who are experiencing demand for compliance within their own psychoanalytic societies and institutes? Is the growing 'theoretical tower of Babel' a result of analytic institutions not having a built-in multifaceted system which would allow inquiry and self-reflection of their group-self dynamics when individuals try to self-delineate, question or add to the contributions of their self psychological, Kleinian or Oedipal parents?

Provisions for good-enough group selfobject environments

What can group therapists/analysts who have experienced good-enough healing environments in their own groups contribute to those psychoanalysts who work in dyadic systems and are unfamiliar in exploring the repetitive, resistive and conflictual aspects, not in the one-to-one dyadic systems but in the institute and psychoanalytic societies' group-systems to which they belong? Is it a coincidence that the City of Los Angeles has at least seven analytic institutes and societies with at least seven different theoretical points of view? Is it so hard to understand, translate and integrate the different theoretical languages along with the many affective experiences they evoke? Could we first try to listen and acknowledge the subjectivities of others and then proceed to share our own as well? Is this much easier said than done? Right now, obviously the answer is yes.

I have been very impressed by The Washington School of Psychiatry which brings together individuals from different parts of the country and the world, representing diverse theoretical schools, in an attempt to learn, self-examine, integrate, and experience small and large group affiliation at work. It is a model that other analytic societies and institutes could consider, both for training as well as for self-reflection. Can all of us as clinicians and human beings risk exposing and examining our own shame and vulnerability (both difficult affects that Morrison (1989b) and Lansky (1994) have particularly brought to our attention) rather than projecting our own discomfort onto our neighbor? Can we admit what makes us full of rage, confusion and discomfort with our own selves, and, consequently, not require another close to us to contain and hold our most negative aspects?

The larger world community person system

Last holiday season I received a card and a note which moved me deeply. At the last year's International Group Psychotherapy conference in Argentina I was very fortunate to have an analyst from Croatia on the panel: 'Facilitating Empathy and Human Understanding through Diversity in the Group Process'. She told me that she put together a group of Muslim women all of whom have been raped. It seemed that the affiliation would be strong and aversive against their common enemy. But none would bring up in the group the fact that they were raped. She explained that a woman as a rule would be humiliated, blamed and discarded by her own family if the members found out about the rape. Even though this group of Muslim women was set up as a homogeneous support group, there was no trust, no support, and no healing, while rage and fragmentation did continue. It is not so much the traumatic experience that damages the person, but *the non-empathic traumatic reaction/action of significant others*. I pondered with my colleague if the failure in this group process began with the group composition. Discovering that she also worked with groups of Catholic women, we came up with another group composition – to integrate two Muslim women at a time into each different group.

The holiday note affirmed the beginning of success of the plan. Two Muslim women could establish a twinship experience at first, not feeling alone amidst those religiously and culturally different. In different groups, they first joined the Catholic women in aversive affiliation against the Serbs. At the same time, they heard the Catholic women discuss similar violations without shame, while receiving empathy and sympathy from the others. The Catholic women, as a group, did not fear rejection or ostracism from their own families. Little by little the Muslim women started to grieve openly in the group their own violations and their inability to discuss their pain with their own families and community. With the empathic understanding from the Catholic women, the healing had begun. Both my Croatian colleague and I share hopes for new attachments based on understanding of diversity, within which there is recognition of the universality of human affects, rather than just continued affiliation and attachments to those with similar labels.

The political/therapeutic person systems

At the International Group Conference in Buenos Aires, those from abroad asked the Argentinian group therapists whether the issues of the Desaparecidos were being dealt with in therapy. The question seemed to throw out of denial most of the therapists to whom it was addressed. With further exploration it became clear that these group therapists were not dealing with this issue in either individual or group, nor did they bring it up in their own treatments. In fact, there were hardly any heterogeneous groups left in Argentina, only groups for individual families or one-issue homogeneous support groups. Part of the psychotherapeutic community still remains in fear in dealing with past events and actions openly. The Desaparecidos did not represent particular cultural, ethnic or religious groups. Many of those never to be seen again were not involved in any political groups; their sole crime was to not totally comply and cower into isolation out of fear, but to attempt to live their lives by continuing to affiliate with those who they considered friends, with whom they shared common human values, rather than political schisms. Analysing mutual reciprocal influences in dyadic intersubjectivities in empathically attuned individual treatment is not enough!

These Argentinian psychoanalysts and group therapists need to re-establish enough trust in both their dyadic and group therapeutic systems to examine both the multiplicity of group traumatic experiences to individuals, families and the larger groups.

Group therapists in the United States and elsewhere may also want to re-examine the potential dangers in today's popular homogenous groups. What material becomes 'tutti non grata', not evident, or not admissible for discussion in groups that are all alcoholic, all gay, all straight, all black, all white, all immigrants, all wealthy or all disadvantaged? What do we as American or other nationality therapists not see about ourselves or are afraid to admit? How are we starting to endanger the confidentiality of our patients by letting into our offices an intrusive third party – the managed care insurance system which manages without care? What alternatives can we come up with, when we affiliate in an attempt to problem solve?

Managing with care individual and group interactions: listening perspectives

Once optimum group placement is accomplished with reasonable success, we need to listen carefully in many different ways to group interactions to make sure that we understand, help interpret and facilitate the working-through process as intersubjective systems emerge between therapist and patient, therapist and group, two members, one and several members, and one member and the entire group. The individual psychoanalyst or therapist also needs to pay attention to how these dyadic or multi-dyadic systems arise in a person's life, not only when they come up in one-to-one dyadic transferences. These may not come up for a long time if the analyst/therapist is in the selfobject dimension of the transference. Ignoring reciprocal fields of influence in a patient's outside-of-the-therapy-room-life can sometimes expose the person to dangerous consequences. Remember when Kohut spontaneously and caringly called his patient an 'idiot' for exposing himself to danger! He was not analyzing the present transference alone, but he was also aware of how the patient acted outside of the session and provided the necessary functions of setting limits (Harwood 1993; 1995a; 1995b) and reacted out of personal involvement and passion. Needed functions cannot be handed out in a role-like automatic manner – they may be experienced as a deficit and ring with the same hollowness of a previous caretaker's gestures.

Group therapists can listen, analyze, and respond to group interaction by utilizing listening perspectives from group psychotherapy, as well as the newly emerging ones in self psychology. Rutan and Stone (1993) and Yalom (1985) before them pointed to the importance of paying attention to the affect–cognition continuum. They felt that a combination and integration of both are needed for effective therapy to take place. So Shapiro (1995) recommended paying attention to both the degree and quality of affect and the *direction of content* in the interaction between psychoanalyst and patient. His listening stance can be easily translated to group. If an interaction between a group member(s) and therapist, or member and group, or between members brings up more flow in the communication, not to worry. If the interaction is staying in the selfobject dimension of the transference, if it brings up new memories or content, if it brings up more affect that further opens the communication, not to worry again. But, we do need to pay attention if the interaction and total group ambience shifts from Bacal's (1991) 'optimum responsiveness' to 'reactiveness' and if the interaction closes down any other members into silence or compliance. An exception to staying in the selfobject dimension of the transference is a group configuration where all members are stagnating – that is, when members do not emerge with their own authenticity and self-delineation, fearing the loss of a somewhat secure attachment or the loss of the affiliative bond. The therapist should ask if there is a need for an adversarial selfobject function. To determine this, the therapist may need to use more than Kohut's empathic mode of listening – immersing oneself into that patient's particular affective point of view.

Fosshage's (1993) other-centered mode of listening, involving two separate subjectivities, is very similar to Schermer's (1988) view advocating an empathic and objective observational point of view. Schermer has given a very effective visual metaphor in describing the therapist as being both a 'mirror' and a 'window' on the patient's and group's unconscious, providing a binocular perspective which gives a richer picture. Self psychologists would only disagree with the idea that anyone's point of view (including the therapist's) is objective. Fosshage's listening mode includes the empathic mode of listening from the patient's perspective and the other-centred mode of listening from the therapist's perspective. His perspectives can be translated to the multiple system model and to group, thus also expanding the mutual reciprocal fields of influences, not only for the individual, but the group as well.

In group, the therapist listens in *the empathic mode* from: (1) a group member's subjective perspective, (2) each group member's subjective perspective vs. another group member's subjective perspective, and (3) a member's perspective vs. the total group's perspective. From *the other-centered mode*, he/she listens from: (1) the conductor's perspective vs. another group member's subjective perspective, (2) the conductor's perspective vs. several other group members' perspectives, and (3) the conductor's perspective vs. the total group's perspective.

As a group therapist, one addresses the greatest tension or need first and tries to avoid any casualties, including the possible destruction of the group. The whole group should not be sacrificed for one person, no matter what early trauma-based need they may have. The group conductor needs to closely check his/her perspective against the perspectives of group members to determine whether his/her perspective indeed adds a panoramic view to the picture, or whether it presents a countertransference issue from his/her own past.

The group therapist needs to look for differences in both the (a) subjective affective experiences, and in the (b) subjective content of cognitive/intellectual perspectives, both his/her own and the group's. Before responding to a group interaction: (1) the conductor first needs to understand the intersubjective field of all the group members, and (2) the conductor also silently needs to deal with one's own intersubjectivity and what it brings up from his/her own internal good and bad selfobjects or experiences. Then and only then can (3) the conductor bring to the group his or her affective and cognitive/intellectual resonance.

Whenever any member seems to become closed down, quieter or compliant, rather than authentically responsive, group therapists need to understand and bring out the intersubjective component in operation, and interpret or intervene, if nobody else does. If the whole group closes down or reacts defensively, the therapist needs to recognize that there may be a threat to every member and/or the entire group. For example, to ask: 'Is this a sibling–person system transference in operation or some other type of transference?'

Clinical group example

After the graduation of two members, an outpatient analytic group needed a rebalancing between expression of spontaneous affect and cognition. After evaluating the various functions and potential impingements that this group could provide for Flores and experiencing her directness and affective spontaneity, the group conductor decided that there was a potential good match. Flores sat quietly at first, trying to determine if the interactions in the group were safe-enough or if a certain kind of compliance was required as in her family.

After several initial quiet sessions Flores brought her 'true self' out of hiding and talked about problems with her boyfriend, who appeared manipulative and even sociopathic from her description. She was wondering whether she was the selfish one. In the next session, she again questioned herself about a different situation which appeared crazy-making. The group as a whole, with the exception of Zelia (who after making a couple of comments kept looking at her watch), was working in the selfobject dimension. Thus, the group was working in a supportive, inquiring manner, validating whatever pieces of Flores' reality she was able to accept and pointing out how she allowed others to take advantage of her. They also seemed to enjoy her enthusiasm and how appreciatively she considered their offerings. Flores was able to engage the group in interactions of positive mutual reciprocal influence – one building on another.

Flores had to leave early. Zelia brought up how nobody should be allowed to speak for that long (although she has often spoken for very long periods of time when she was needy). Group members confronted her strongly about her pattern with women newcomers and asked her to examine whether she was showing the group how she was treated by her older sister (the group has heard many stories of how Zelia's sister taunted her for years and tried to grab all verbal and literal space for herself – the person–sibling system). In the past, Zelia could not consider exploring how she may be replaying these early experiences in the group. Then, Zelia still experienced shame about an identification with the aggressor (or what Bacal would call the bad selfobject). Also there was an unconscious hope of finding someone else to contain the intimidation and fear of her early experiences, which understandably as a preverbal child she could not differentiate, synthesize, modulate, cognitively articulate or integrate (Socarides and Stolorow 1984–1985) without someone's help in an emotionally unresponsive family system. Attempts were made to find affiliative aversive attachments to help regulate the unconscious early painful ones. This time strong spontaneous affect flowed with Zelia's comments. The group's reactivity became modulated and did not appear traumatic for Zelia. She was able to stop, self-reflect, and to say that she realized that having Flores in group, someone who exhibited strong emotion and received the attention she wanted, did remind her of herself and made her uncomfortable. With affective self-reflective process moving the group forward, there was no need for comment on the process from the therapist. On the other hand, I felt that it was important for Zelia to know that I saw new courage and ability to self-reflect in her and to consider the other's perspective as well as her own feelings.

After a little silence, the next session started with Victor talking about his sister not speaking to their mother directly about their inheritance after the mother remarries. It made Victor feel crazed and he was not sure he could speak to their mother. No connection was made to how a sibling in this group was not bringing up directly Zelia's feelings about no longer inheriting the right to a certain amount of time and attention with another female entering the group family. Instead, the group responded cognitively to Victor's manifest content about differentiating from his older sister, and suggested that Victor speak directly to his mother. After this easy solution the group grew quiet. The intellectual solution did not liberate affect or new associations. Paying attention to the group's somewhat restrictive solution and to S. Shapiro's (1995) warning about investigating a patient's closing down of affect and content applied here. The silence and *constriction of affect* pointed to the group being uncomfortable with having a secret. While different members looked toward Zelia, she just looked away (as her parents apparently did when she looked towards them for help). Flores looked puzzled. I asked if there was something here in the group that the group was not sure it could speak of directly. Nobody responded. Some members looked toward Zelia – nothing. Tony started speaking about his frustration with his new work assignment and how he did not like doing other people's work. He went on about his own work for a while – others continued to look uncomfortable and did not respond to him.

At first, I chose to respond to Tony from an empathic listening mode, saying work did appear to be frustrating for him (addressing manifest content). Then I addressed him and the group, from a therapist's listening perspective, saying that neither he nor the group wanted to do someone else's work in the group nor share their own feelings directly about the uncomfortable silence. Flores asked what was going on. Lou broke through saying he was uncomfortable and frustrated with the secret, and asked Zelia to share with Flores what had happened after she had left the group the previous week (affect increases, I stay out). Zelia said she did not feel like it right then (self-delineation). She looked toward Tony (looking for twinship or affiliative aversive bonding), who decided to continue talking about his work. Tony felt safer in ignoring me and Lou, from whom he does not fear retaliation and with whom he experiences secure predictable affiliative bonds. Zelia, he still sometimes experiences and fears as his older, angry traumatizing brother.

Victor, building on the previous encouragement he got about clarifying the inheritance issue directly with his mother, angrily said he had had enough of maintaining the secret in the group. He would bring up the end of last week's session, if Zelia did not. She invited him to go ahead (she apparently needed someone in this family group to act as a fair validator or reflective mirror of last week's experience, something neither of her parents did). Victor succinctly described the end of last week's session. Flores asked Zelia if she was creating a problem by speaking too long. Zelia told her how she realized that she perceived her own need for time and attention in Flores, and how difficult it was seeing herself acting-out jealously like her sister had done with her. She hoped she could share better than her sister did without forgetting what she needed. There is a renegotiation for Zelia in affiliating with Flores in an ascending order of friendliness, rather than aversiveness. This new modulation – from the extreme of resentment and total compliance as a victim or from the extreme of identifying with the 'bad selfobject' or traumatizing person of her childhood – could not have happened for Zelia without the group accepting her needs over many sessions and listening empathically to how she felt alone and unprotected in her own family. Zelia looked warmly and acceptingly at Flores. The group showed feelings of relief and accomplishment through the opening up of flowing affect and warm smiles.

As an analytically informed group therapist, I listen and do not offer anything when I feel that each individual is heard and interacted with empathically and that other members are also able to bring up their own points of view as well. When there is open, affective interchange in the intersubjective group dynamics, there is no need for the group conductor to intervene. The group orchestra does not need to express itself in unison. On the other hand, if any individual voice becomes overwhelmed and goes into hiding and the group does not address this, it is the role of the group conductor to help the group bring this up for inquiry. When nobody in the group is presenting a perspective that the therapist has (after examining it for self-serving or countertransferential components), the group conductor can offer it for consideration. The group's opening up of further affective content will determine the usefulness of the group conductor's other-centered mode of listening. Tony, for example, carried into the next session his fear and shame in bringing up his negative feelings in the group, in his family, and in his work.

I hope that the ideas in this chapter do not cause further divisions or theoretical misunderstandings and, where there are differences, I hope we can effectively and affectively utilize the transitional space to be playful and build further bonds of clarification, theoretical translation, and mutual understanding.

References

Arensberg, F. (1990) 'Self psychology groups.' In I.L. Kutash and A. Wolf (eds) *Group Psychotherapist's Handbook: Contemporary Theory and Technique*. New York: Columbia University Press.

Ashbach, C. and Schermer, V. (1992) 'The role of the therapist from a self psychology perspective.' In R.M. Klein, M.S. Bernard, D.L. Singer and C.T. Madison (eds) *Handbook of Contemporary Group Psychotherapy*. New York: International Universities Press.

Bacal, H. (1985a) 'Optimal responsiveness and the therapeutic process.' In A. Goldberg (ed) *Progress in Self Psychology 5*. Hillsdale NJ: Analytic Press.

Bacal, H. (1985b) 'Object relations in the group from the perspective of self psychology.' *International Journal of Group Psychotherapy 35*, 483–501.

Bacal, H. (1991) 'Reactiveness and responsiveness in the group therapeutic process.' In S. Tuttman and C.T. Madison (eds) *Psychoanalytic Group Theory and Therapy: Essays in Honor of Saul Scheidlinger*. New York: International Universities Press.

Bacal, H. (1992) 'Contributions from self psychological theory.' In R.M. Klein, M.S. Bernard, D.L. Singer and C.T. Madison (eds) *Handbook of Contemporary Group Psychotherapy*. New York: International Universities Press.

Bacal, H. (1995) 'The essence of Kohut's work and the progress of self psychology.' *Psychoanalytic Dialogues 5*, 3, 353–366.

Beebe, B. and Lachmann, F. (1988a) 'Mother–infant mutual influences and precursors of psychic structure.' In A. Goldberg (ed) *Frontiers in Self Psychology: Progress in Self Psychology 3*. Hillsdale NJ: Analytic Press.

Beebe, B. and Lachmann, F. (1988b) 'The contribution of mother–infant mutual influences to the origins of self- and object representations.' *Psychoanalytic Psychology 5*, 305–357.

Beebe, B., Jaffe, J. and Lachmann, F. (1992) 'A dyadic systems view of communication.' In N. Skolnick and S. Warshaw (eds) *Relational Perspectives in Psychoanalysis*. Hillsdale, NJ: Analytic Press.

Fosshage, J. (1993) 'Countertransference: The Analyst's Experience of the Analysand.' Presented at the 16th Annual Conference on the Psychology of the Self. Toronto, Canada.

Freud, S. (1918) 'The taboo of virginity.' *Standard Edition 11*. London: Hogarth Press, 1957.

Freud, S. (1930) 'Civilization and its discontents.' *Standard Edition 21*. London: Hogarth Press, 1961.

Foulkes, S.H. (1973) 'The group as matrix of the individual's mental life.' In L.R. Wolberg and E.K. Schwartz (eds) *Group Therapy*. New York: Stratton Intercontinental Medical Books.

Harwood, I. (1983) 'The application of self psychology concepts to group psychotherapy.' *International Journal of Group Psychotherapy 33*, 469–487.

Harwood, I. (1986) 'The need for optimal, available selfobject caretakers: Moving toward extended selfobject experiences.' *Group Analysis 19*, 291–302.

Harwood, I. (1987) 'The evolution of the self: An integration of Winnicott's and Kohut's concepts.' In T. Honess and K. Yardley (eds) *Self and Identity: Individual Change and Development*. London: Routledge & Kegan Paul.

Harwood, I. (1992a) 'Group psychotherapy and disorders of the self.' *Group Analysis 25*, 19–26.

Harwood, I. (1992b) 'Advances in group psychotherapy and self psychology.' *Group 16*, 4, 220–232.

Harwood, I. (1993) 'Examining Early Childhood Multiple Cross-Cultural Extended Selfobject and Traumatic Experiences and Creating Optimum Treatment Environments.' Presented at the 16th Annual Conference on the Psychology of the Self. Toronto, Canada.

Harwood, I. (1995a) 'Towards optimum group placement from the perspective of the self or self-experience.' *Group 19*, 3, 140–162.

Harwood, I. (1995b) 'Examen de las experiencias del objeto/sí-mismo extenso múltiple transcultural en la infancia temprana y también de las experiencias traumáticas, para crear ambientes óptimos de tratamiento.' *Revista Argentina de Clínica Psicológica 4*, 3, 221–235.

Harwood, I. (1996) 'Towards optimum group placement from the perspective of self and group experience.' *Group Analysis 29*, 2, 199–218.

Kohut, H. (1977) *The Restoration of the Self*. New York: International Universities Press.

Kriegman, D. and Solomon, L. (1985) 'Cult groups and the narcissistic personality: The offer to heal defects in the self.' *International Journal of Group Psychotherapy 35*, 239–361.

Lachmann, F. (1995) 'Advances in Self Psychology.' Advanced course presented at the 18th Annual Self Psychology Conference. San Francisco.

Lansky, M. (1994). 'Shame and Suicide in Sophocles' Ajax.' Presented to the Los Angeles Society for the Self. Psychoanalytic Quarterly, 1996, 65: 761–786.

Lichtenberg, J. (1989) *Psychoanalysis and Motivation*. Hillsdale, NJ: Analytic Press.

Meyers, S.H. (1978) 'The disorders of the self: Developmental and clinical considerations.' *Group 2*, 131–140.

Morrison, A. (1989a). Discussant of 'Multiple Selfobject Relationships' at the Self Psychology Conference, San Francisco.

Morrison, A. (1989b) *Shame: The Underside of Narcissism*. Hillsdale, NJ: Analytic Press.

Paparo, F. (1983) 'Self Psychology and the Group Process.' Presented at the 6th Annual Self Psychology Conference, Los Angeles.

Pines, M. (1995) (a) 'The Self as a Group: the Group as a Self.' Presented to the Los Angeles Society for the Study of the Self. January 6, 1995. (b) *Group Analysis* (1996) *29, 2.*

Rutan, J.S. and Stone, W.N. (1993) *Psychodynamic Group Psychotherapy,* 2nd Edition. New York: Guilford Press.

Sands, S. (1995) 'Countertransference: what the self psychological lens obscures.' Presented at the 18th Annual Conference on the Psychology of the Self, San Francisco, CA.

Schacter, S. (1959) *The Psychology of Affiliation.* Stanford, CA: Stanford University Press.

Schain, J. (1985) 'Can Klein and Kohut work together in a group?' *Clinical Social Work Journal 13,* 4.

Schain, J. (1989) 'The new infant research: some implications for group therapy.' *Group 13,* 2.

Schermer, V. (1988) 'The Mirror and the Window: A Self Psychology and Object Relations Paradigm for Psychotherapy.' Presented to Jefferson Medical College. Department of Psychiatry.

Schwartzman, G. (1984) 'The use of group as selfobject.' *International Journal of Group Psychotherapy 34,* 229–241.

Segalla, R. (1995) 'The Unbearable Embeddedness of Being: Self Psychology, Intersubjectivity, and the Larger Group Experiences.' Presented to the Washington School of Psychiatry.

Segalla, F., Silvers, D., Wine, B. and Pillsbury, G. (1989) 'Multiple Selfobject Model: Patients in Individual and Group or Couples Therapy.' Presented at the Twelfth Annual Conference on the Psychology of the Self. San Francisco.

Shapiro, E. (1991) 'Empathy and safety in group: a self psychology perspective.' *Group 15,* 219–224.

Shapiro, S. (1995) *Talking with Patients: A Self Psychological View.* NJ: Aronson.

Socarides, D. and Stolorow, R. (1984–1985) 'Affects and selfobjects.' *The Annual of Psychoanalysis, 12/13,* 105–119. Madison, CT: International Universities Press.

Stern, D.N. (1985) *The Interpersonal World of the Infant: A View from Psychoanalysis and Developmental Psychology.* New York: Basic Books.

Stolorow, R.D. and Atwood, G.E. (1992) *Contexts of Being: The Intersubjective Foundations of Psychological Life.* Hillsdale, NJ: Analytic Press.

Stolorow, R.D. and Atwood, G.E. (1994) 'Toward a science of human experience.' In R.D. Stolorow, G.E. Atwood and B. Brandchaft (eds) *The Intersubjective Perspective.* NJ: Aronson.

Stolorow, R.D., Brandchaft, B. and Atwood, G.E. (1987) *Psychoanalytic Treatment: An Intersubjective Approach.* Hillsdale, NJ: Analytic Press.

Stone, W.N. (1992) 'The clinical application of self psychology theory.' In R.M. Klein, M.S. Bernard, D.L. Singer and C.T. Madison (eds) *Handbook of Contemporary Group Psychotherapy.* New York: International Universities Press.

Stone, W.N. and Gustafson, J.P. (1982) 'Technique in group psychotherapy of narcissistic and borderline patients.' *International Journal of Group Psychotherapy 32,* 29–47.

Stone, W.N. and Whitman, R.M. (1977) 'Contributions of the psychology of the self to group process and group therapy.' *International Journal of Group Psychotherapy 27*, 343–359.

Stone, W.N. and Whitman, R.M. (1980) 'Observations on empathy in group psychotherapy.' In R. Wolberg and M.L. Aronson (eds) *Group and Family Therapy*. New York: Brunner/Mazel.

Thelen, E. and Smith, L. (1994) *Dynamic Systems Approach to the Development of Cognition and Action*. New York: Bradford Books.

Weinstein, D. (1987) 'Self psychology and group psychotherapy.' *Group 11*, 144–154.

Weinstein, D. (1991) 'Exhibitionism in group psychotherapy.' In A. Goldberg (ed) *The Evolution of Self Psychology: Progress in Self Psychology* (Vol. 7). Hillsdale, NJ: Analytic Press.

Wilson, A. (1982) 'Treatment of the narcissistic character disorder in group psychotherapy in the light of self psychology.' *Group 6*, 6–10.

Winnicott, D. (1960) 'Ego distortion in terms of the true and false self.' In D.W. Winnicott (ed) *The Maturational Processes and the Facilitating Environment*. New York: International Universities Press, 1965.

Wolf, E. (1980) 'On the developmental line of selfobject relations.' In A. Goldberg (ed) *Advances in Self Psychology*. New York: International Universities Press.

Wong, N. (1979) 'Clinical considerations in group treatment of narcissistic disorders.' *International Journal of Group Psychotherapy 29*, 325–345.

Yalom, I. (1985) *The Theory and Practice of Group Psychotherapy*. New York: Basic Books.

CHAPTER 13

Notes on Optimal Responsiveness in the Group Process

Howard A. Bacal

In a previous article (Bacal 1985), I conceptualized the job of the individual therapist as *optimal responsiveness* (see also Bacal, in press). This chapter is a companion piece to that work insofar at it draws attention to certain modes of relating in the group that can centrally affect the members' therapeutic experience. Thus, it expands my ideas on *reactiveness* and *responsiveness* in the group therapeutic process (Bacal 1991), the balanced promotion of which by the group leader constitutes a major aspect of his optimal responsiveness to the therapeutic needs of the members.

For the patient in the two-person psychotherapy setting, the therapist will at times represent the *group*. However, the therapist does not obviously intrude with his 'group' expectations and is expected to intrude minimally with his personal requirements. The setting is therefore conducive to exploring and working through the patient's selfobject needs in relation to a therapist who is experienced by the patient as representing both his family group as well as one or another of its members. In this setting, the introduction of the therapist's own needs and standards is usually regarded as 'countertransference'. Therefore, in the setting of individual psychotherapy, the individual may, paradoxically, experience more of the 'group's' optimal responsiveness to the expression of his selfobject needs than in group psychotherapy. In the group therapy setting, the individual will face other members who will naturally and 'legitimately' tend to react spontaneously to him, often without consideration of his feelings, thoughts and needs.

Psychological disturbance in the individual can be conceived of as the result of problems he encounters in life due both to the group's reaction to him for not fitting in with their expectations and to his experience of inadequate response from the group to his particular needs. Clearly it is important to deal with both of these in therapy. The group is pre-eminently able to do this if the therapist enables the group members to interact in ways that address these problems effectively.

When a group meets for the purpose of therapy, the members, on balance, are more likely to *react* to their experiences of others who frustrate their psychological needs, rather than to *respond* with any consistent consideration of the psychological needs of individuals who disturb or deprive them. Put in another way, interactions between members of the group, whatever their content and however defended and disguised they may be, are expressed in two modes: 'reactiveness' and 'responsiveness'. In the group, reactiveness tends to be the more prevalent mode.

Reactiveness and responsiveness reflect different modes of listening and experiencing others.[1] Reactiveness is a way of communicating and relating that is relatively experience-distant, and responsiveness is a way of communicating that is relatively experience-near. When reactiveness predominates, the experience of others is registered in terms of a sense of how the experience affects one's self. The Tavistock groups, for example, which were conducted by Bion and Ezriel and their colleagues, exemplify, par excellence, this mode of relating, since the leader's communications to the group consistently reflect an understanding of the group process primarily as it affects him. In effect, many other group therapy leaders wittingly or unwittingly tend to foster the use of reactiveness as the predominant communicative mode in the group, even though they may not relate to the group as remotely as the 'classical' Tavistock consultant does.

Reactiveness as a way of communicating makes sense in its correspondence to the legitimate expectations that the family group has of the child; that is, it is based on widely accepted norms within the subculture as to how people should behave. The messages conveyed, whether from the therapist or other members of the group, are going to inevitably imply, and sometimes accurately specify, psychopathology, distortion of reality, and an expectation of change. Little or no empathy is required; it is *behavior* – verbal or non-verbal – that is at issue, and the use of experience-distant reactiveness as a communicative mode is therefore both expected and appropriate. In a particular situation, though, it may or may not constitute the optimal response.

Reactiveness, as a mode of communication, tends to mediate the requirements of the group in relation to the individual, and *responsiveness* respects the importance of personal discovery of one's self in relation to the group. Optimal responsiveness to the therapeutic needs of the members of the group requires that the therapist *cultivate a group ethos*, or *ambience*, that recognizes the value of both. In such an ambience, the group will be variously experienced as selfobject for the individual,

---

1   Fosshage (in press) has described a similar perspective in his identification of two modes of analytic listening/experiencing – subject-centered and other-centered – that reflect the emphasis of self psychology, and of object relations and interpersonal approaches, respectively.

and the individual will be variously experienced as selfobject for the group – that is, his compliance with the reactive expectations of the group will contribute to the group's cohesion.[2]

We would certainly not wish to deprive our patients of the experience of the spontaneous expression of their feelings toward each other which, in addition to providing grist for the mill of understanding, may constitute, at times, what is optimally responsive for the individual. Yet, it is important, in my view, that members of the group be prepared to respond also on the basis of their empathically informed perceptions of others' needs for selfobject responsivity. We must, however, recognize that problems in mutual understanding that occur at the intersection of the subjectivities of participants in a therapy group are the order of the day, and that experiences of selfobject disruption, which are frustrating and, at times, enraging, are frequently experienced at these interfaces. The repair of these disruptions, when possible, and their thoroughgoing understanding when harmomy cannot be restored, will also constitute significant therapeutic experiences for the members of the group.

The group therapeutic process entails a paradoxical truism. Our patients will mature and grow stronger both from recognizing that others with whom they are closely involved, have problems with certain of their needs, attitudes and behavior, and as a result of feeling entitled to expect everyone in the group to recognize and value their own unique needs and experiences. Reactiveness is the natural expression of the one, and an ambience of empathically-informed responsiveness in the group is required for the other. It is the group leader's task to ensure that the group does not lose sight of the value of either. Perhaps psychoanalytic institutes might even have evolved differently if Freud and his small group of pioneering colleagues had been able to manage a more harmonious balance between the two.

In this regard, it is instructive to study Kanzer's (1971) account about what happened in the remarkable group that met weekly, as Kanzer puts it, to discuss psychoanalysis with the professor. In that group, unresolved tensions prevailed that led to recurrent revolts and breakdowns of the operation, and to a number of dropouts, the most famous of which was Alfred Adler. Despite the stimulating discussions that Freud promoted, he apparently conducted a leader-centered group, with a certain quality of remoteness, and the superiority of his views ultimately carried the day. Thus, the creative uniqueness of the members of the group was inadequately recognized (mirrored). The sense of their personal value that they derived from their association with Freud as an idealized figure did not quite make up for this lack of mirroring. In addition, not only did Freud not allow

---

2   An example of this would be when the caucus of a political party requires its members to vote uniformly on a motion, even if they disagree with it.

anyone to seriously challenge his views, he would seem to have sanctioned, or even to have fostered, a somewhat opposite ambience in the group – one of ongoing challenge and confrontation between the members. None of this was worked through. To my knowledge, no processing of their experience occurred in the group, although the members apparently made interpretations to each other in an unrestrained and sometimes wild manner. They were all excited about the beginnings of instinct theory and they were interpreting each other's sexual and aggressive impulses, their dreams, and so on. But this was not therapy. In fact, this group (after it went through a more or less effective theoretical 'cleansing') eventually became the Vienna Psychoanalytic Society.[3]

Thus, not only therapy groups, but also groups of psychoanalysts – as well as many other groups – have floundered, fragmented, or split because of the lack of adequate leadership in either promoting an optimal balance between reactiveness and responsiveness, or in working through the disruptions in the group that result in an imbalance in favor of the former. On the other hand, we all know some groups that become strikingly and colorlessly cohesive, not through a process of working through disruptive reactiveness, but through collusive avoidance of its spontaneous expression.

The question we may now usefully ask is, how can the group and its individuals survive and perhaps even thrive when they comprehend their experience differently? Or, to put the question somewhat differently, what are the problems encountered in establishing an ambience of optimal responsiveness, not only in psychoanalytic therapy groups, but in groups of psychoanalysts – as well as in other groups? Another reason for focusing on this area from a broader perspective is because of the disruptive schisms that recurrently threaten the cohesiveness of our scholarly groups. Although ideological differences are apparently their *raison d'être*, in my view the more powerful fuel for these schisms is not basically ideological, but rather psychological, that is to say, psychological tensions that centrally arise from unaddressed disruptions in the relationship between the individual and the group.

Wilfred Bion's odyssey is illustrative. Bion left London for Los Angeles shortly after his term ended as President of the British Psychoanalytic Society. He was, in some ways, a controversial figure in London. In my view, he must have constituted something of a dilemma for the Kleinian group, of which he was a highly respected, senior member. In effect, I think it indisputable that Bion was the de facto heir to the leadership of the Kleinian group in the British Psychoanalytic Society, a throne that had been left vacant by the death of Melanie Klein in 1960, but which was never officially filled. There were a few other rivals for that position, such as Hannah Segal and Herbert Rosenfeld, but Bion was undeniably

3   That is when the minutes started.

the brightest – and the most original – thinker in the Kleinian group. And that was the problem. While ostensibly devoted to the tenets of Mrs Klein, Bion very much had his own ideas. The last paper he presented to the British Psychoanalytic Society prior to leaving for Los Angeles was entitled, 'On Catastrophic Change'. Its major theme was the resistance of the group to accepting the messiah, as such acceptance could be expected to cause upheaval and transformation of the group. Bion was, I suspect, painfully aware that the reception accorded a messiah by the group might not be optimally responsive. Bion could not have expected much responsiveness from his group if he were to stay and become more openly himself within the Kleinian group. In effect, he could not have expected anything much less than catastrophic reactiveness from this group to his views – another of which he expressed in a brilliantly telling paper in 1967 called 'Notes On Memory and Desire'. In that paper, he recommended that one should, as one listens to the patient, expunge totally from one's awareness any prior knowledge – any memory and desire, as he put it. This was not a view that a group with highly organized ideas could welcome with a viable balance of reactiveness and responsiveness. Bion left London for a place that he hoped would be receptive to fresh ideas.

In an attempt to apprehend comparable problems that arise within the group that threaten its cohesion, Heinz Kohut propounded a point of view which, interestingly, has some points of contact with those of Bion. It was Kohut who pointed out that the idealized parental imago functioned not only to maintain the integrity of the self of the individual but also that of the group. When that idealized imago is threatened, as it may be by the introduction of new ideas by an important group member, especially by a creative/charismatic member of the group who has significantly shifted his theoretical position or who claims to have done so, the group self may feel threatened, as this member may be perceived as attempting to assume leadership of the group. Such a member threatens both the integrity of the existing group and the self-cohesiveness of certain members of the group that have been significantly maintained by idealizing transferences to the prevailing conceptualizations and their originators. The new member is, in effect, treated as a messiah – a false one, of course. What follows regularly is the defensive denigration and isolation of the new ideas and its propounder, and a reactive assertion by the latter that no one need concern themselves any longer with the existing ideology of the group.

As long as there is no awareness that the insistence on maintaining the validity of the one position to the total exclusion of the other derives not only and not even mainly from ideological differences, but rather from the injury that is experienced at the devaluing hands of the other, then neither can even hear, nor acknowledge, the other's subjectivity when they speak, let alone expect an optimal response. Neither subgroup can hear whether the other views emerging from within the group are significantly divergent or not; they simply know that they have to defend themselves against the other's position which threatens their self-cohesion and, in effect, their self-esteem.

Kohut was, in fact, reacted to by his classical psychoanalytic colleagues in the same way, I suspect, that Bion feared that his British confrères would react to him. For many years, Kohut was known and admired as 'Mr Classical Psychoanalysis'. He told me, one day in the late 1970s, that, from the time he began elaborating his self-psychological ideas, some of his most intimate colleagues – which included such luminaries as Anna Freud, Heinz Hartmann, and the Eisslers – turned away from him, literally[4] as well as figuratively. He was deeply hurt by this. The way he put it was, 'I just cannot understand why they would do that!' Of course, he, of all people, pre-eminently understood this. What he meant, I believe, was that he could not bear to think that those whose scholarliness he deeply respected would *react* so to his ideas, without also *responding* with empathically-motivated interest.

References

Bacal, H.A. (1985) 'Optimal responsiveness and the therapeutic process.' In A. Goldberg (ed) *Progress in Self Psychology*. New York: Guilford Press.

Bacal, H.A. (1991) 'Reactiveness and responsiveness in the group therapeutic process.' In S. Tuttman (ed) *Psychoanalytic Group Theory and Therapy*. New York: International University Press.

Bacal, H.A. (1998) *Optimal Responsiveness: How Therapists Heal Their Patients*. Hillsdale, NJ: Jason Aronson.

Bion, W.R. (1967) 'Notes on memory and desire.' In *Psychoanalytic Forum*. Ed. J. Lindon. New York: Basic Books.

Fosshage, J. (1998) 'Optimal responsiveness and listening/experiencing perspectives.' In H.A. Bacal (ed) *Optimal Responsiveness: How Therapists Heal Their Patients*. Hillsdale, NJ: Jason Aronson.

Kanzer, M. (1971) 'Freud: the first psychoanalytic group leader.' In H. Kaplan and B. Sadock (eds) *Comprehensive Group Psychotherapy*. Baltimore: Williams and Wilkins.

4   They would actually turn their backs on him when he entered a room in which they were present!

The Contributors

Frederic Arensberg is a faculty member, Senior Supervisor and Training Analyst in the Group Department at the Postgraduate Center for Mental Health, New York. He has also held a full-time private practice in New York City since 1964. He is also a Senior Supervisor, Training Analyst and member of the Senior Faculty at the Training Institute for Mental Health, New York.

Howard A. Bacal is Training and Supervising Analyst at the Institute of Contemporary Psychoanalysis and at the Southern California Psychoanalytic Institute, both in Los Angeles. He is Supervising Analyst at the Institute for the Psychoanalytic Study of Subjectivity in New York, and has a private practice in Los Angeles.

Irene N.H. Harwood is the co-founder of the Society for the Study of the Self and holds a joint assistant clinical professorship at the University of California, Los Angeles, and at the Veterans Administration in the Department of Psychiatry. In addition, she is on the Los Angeles Group Psychotherapy Board representing public education; she teaches Group at the Extension Division of the Southern California Psychoanalytical Institute; and she consults in and practises analytic cross-cultural psychotherapy.

Sigmund W. Karterud is Professor of Psychiatry at the University of Oslo and Medical Director of the Department for Psychiatric Day Care Treatment and Outpatient Services, Ulleval University Hospital. He is founding President of the Norwegian Group Psychotherapy Association and a training group analyst at the Institute of Group Analysis in Oslo.

Martin S. Livingston is on the Faculty of the New York Institute for Psychoanalytic Self Psychology, the Training and Research Institute for Self Psychology, and the Group Therapy Department of the Postgraduate Center for Mental Health. He is the editor of *Issues: the Journal of the Alumni Association of the Group Department of Postgraduate Center for Mental Health*, the co-chair of the Association for Psychoanalytic Self Psychology, and the author of *Near and Far: Closeness and Distance in Psychotherapy*.

Gianni Nebbiosi is the Vice President of the Società Italiano di Psicologia del Sé, [Italian Self Psychology Society]. He is a co-founder, faculty member and Training and Supervising Analyst at the Instituto per lo Studio Psicoanalitico della Soggettività [Institute for the Psychanalytic Study of Subjectivity, Rome]. He is also the co-founder and a member of the core faculty of ARSPI [Association for the Research and Development of Psychoanalytic Psychotherapy in the Public Service]. He is a corresponding member of the Institute for Contemporary Psychoanalysis in Los Angeles.

Franco Paparo is Emeritus Senior Consultant Psychiatrist at the Psychiatric Public Hospital in Rome. He is a member of the International Council for Psychoanalytic Self Psychology. He is also a full member of the Group Psychoanalytic Society in London. In addition, he is President of the Società Italiana di Psicologia del Sé, [Italian Self Psychology Society] and co-founder, faculty member, and Training and Supervising Analyst at the Instituto per lo Studio Psicoanalitico della Soggettivà [Institute for the Psychoanalytic Study of Subjectivity, Rome]. He is an associated member of the International Psychoanalytic Association.

Malcolm Pines is a psychiatrist, psychoanalyst and group therapist and is based at the Group-Analytic Practice in London. He is past President of the International Association of Group Psychotherapy and former Consultant at the Tavistock Clinic. He is the editor of the *International Library of Group Analysis* series and author of *Circular Reflections: Selected Papers on Group Analysis and Psychoanalysis*.

Joan Schain-West is a member of the Clinical Consulting Faculty at the California Institute for Clinical Social Work and has a private practice in West Los Angeles.

Rosemary A. Segalla is a founding member of and a Coordinator at the Institute of Contemporary Psychotherapy in Washington D.C. She is also in the faculty of the Group Training Program of the Washington School of Psychiatry, and co-director of the Self Psychology Group Conference. She is past President and currently a faculty member of the Washington Society of Psychoanalytic Psychology.

Emanuel Shapiro is a faculty member, Senior Supervisor and Training Analyst in the Group Department at the Postgraduate Center for Mental Health in New York City. He is Supervisor of the National Institute for the Psychotherapies there and is on the editorial board of the journal *Group* of the Eastern Group Psychotherapy Society.

Damon L. Silvers is the Program Coordinator and a founding member of the Institute of Contemporary Psychotherapy in Washington D.C. He is a member of the adjunct faculty of the Department of Counselling Psychology at the

University of Maryland, College Park. He was formerly President and is now a faculty member of the Washington Society of Psychoanalytic Psychology.

Robert D. Stolorow is a faculty member, and Training and Supervising Analyst at the Institute of Contemporary Psychoanalysis in Los Angeles. He is a faculty member of the Institute for the Psychoanalytical Study of Subjectivity, New York City. He is also Clinical Professor of Psychiatry at the UCLA School of Medicine.

Ernest Wolf is a member of the faculty and a Training and Supervising Analyst at the Chicago Institute for Psychoanalysis and Assistant Professor of Psychiatry at the Northwestern University Medical School in Chicago.

Subject Index

Author Index